David Stern
Editor

Digital Libraries: Philosophies, Technical Design Considerations, and Example Scenarios

Digital Libraries: Philosophies, Technical Design Considerations, and Example Scenarios has been co-published simultaneously as *Science & Technology Libraries*, Volume 17, Numbers 3/4 1999.

Pre-publication
REVIEWS,
COMMENTARIES,
EVALUATIONS . . .

Digital Libraries: Philosophies, Technical Design Considerations, and Example Scenarios

Digital Libraries: Philosophies, Technical Design Considerations, and Example Scenarios has been co-published simultaneously as *Science & Technology Libraries*, Volume 17, Numbers 3/4 1999.

The *Science & Technology Libraries* Monographic "Separates"

Below is a list of "separates," which in serials librarianship means a special issue simultaneously published as a special journal issue or double-issue and as a "separate" hardbound monograph. (This is a format which we also call a "DocuSerial.")

"Separates" are published because specialized libraries or professionals may wish to purchase a specific thematic issue by itself in a format which can be separately cataloged and shelved, as opposed to purchasing the journal on an on-going basis. Faculty members may also more easily consider a "separate" for classroom adoption.

"Separates" are carefully classified separately with the major book jobbers so that the journal tie-in can be noted on new book order slips to avoid duplicate purchasing.

You may wish to visit Haworth's website at . . .

http://www.haworthpressinc.com

. . . to search our online catalog for complete tables of contents of these separates and related publications.

You may also call 1-800-HAWORTH (outside US/Canada: 607-722-5857), or Fax 1-800-895-0582 (outside US/Canada: 607-771-0012), or e-mail at:

getinfo@haworthpressinc.com

Sci/Tech Librarianship: Education and Training, edited by Julie Hallmark, PhD, and Ruth K. Seidman, MSLS (Vol. 17, No. 2, 1998). *"Insightful, informative, and right-on-the-mark. . . . This collection provides a much-needed view of the education of sci/tech librarians." (Michael R. Leach, AB, Director, Physics Research Library, Harvard University)*

Chemical Librarianship: Challenges and Opportunities, edited by Arleen N. Somerville (Vol. 16, No. 3/4, 1997). *"Presents a most satisfying collection of articles that will be of interest, first and foremost, to chemistry librarians, but also to science librarians working in other science disciplines within academic settings." (Barbara List, Director, Science and Engineering Libraries, Columbia University, New York, New York)*

History of Science and Technology: A Sampler of Centers and Collections of Distinction, edited by Cynthia Steinke, MS (Vol. 14, No. 4, 1995). *"A 'grand tour' of history of science and technology collections that is of great interest to scholars, students, and librarians." (Jay K. Lucker, AB, MSLS, Director of Libraries, Massachusetts Institute of Technology; Lecturer in Science and Technology, Simmons College, Graduate School of Library and Information Science)*

Instruction for Information Access in Sci-Tech Libraries, edited by Cynthia Steinke, MS (Vol. 14, No. 2, 1994). *"A refreshing mix of user education programs and contain[s] many examples of good practice." (Library Review and Reference Reviews)*

Scientific and Clinical Literature for the Decade of the Brain, edited by Tony Stankus, MLS (Vol. 13, No. 3/4, 1993). *"This format combined with selected book and journal title lists is very convenient for life science, social science, or general reference librarians/bibliographers who wish to review the area or get up to speed quickly." (Ruth Lewis, MLS, Biology Librarian, Washington University, St. Louis, Missouri)*

Sci-Tech Libraries of the Future, edited by Cynthia Steinke, MS (Vol. 12, No. 4 and 13(1), 1993). *"Very timely. . . . Will be of interest to all libraries confronted with changes in technology, information formats, and user expectations." (LA Record)*

Science Librarianship at America's Liberal Arts Colleges, Working Librarians Tell Their Stories, edited by Tony Stankus, MLS (Vol. 12, No. 3, 1992). *"For those teetering on the tightrope between the needs and desires of science faculty and liberal arts librarianship, this book brings a sense of balance." (Teresa R. Faust, MLS, Science Reference Librarian, Wake Forest University)*

Biographies of Scientists for Sci-Tech Libraries: Adding Faces to the Facts, edited by Tony Stankus, MLS (Vol. 11, No. 4, 1992). *"A guide to biographies of scientists from a wide variety of scientific fields, identifying titles that reveal the personality of the biographee as well as contributions to his/her field." (Sci Tech Book News)*

Information Seeking and Communicating Behavior of Scientists and Engineers, edited by Cynthia Steinke, MS (Vol. 11, No. 3, 1991). *"Unequivocally recommended. . . . The subject is one of importance to most university libraries, which are actively engaged in addressing user needs as a framework for library services." (New Library World)*

Technology Transfer: The Role of the Sci-Tech Librarian, edited by Cynthia Steinke, MS (Vol. 11, No. 2, 1991). *"Educates the reader about the role of information professionals in the multifaceted technology transfer process." (Journal of Chemical Information and Computer Sciences)*

Electronic Information Systems in Sci-Tech Libraries, edited by Cynthia Steinke, MS (Vol. 11, No. 1, 1990). *"Serves to illustrate the possibilities for effective networking from any library/information facility to any other geographical point." (Library Journal)*

The Role of Trade Literature in Sci-Tech Libraries, edited by Ellis Mount, DLS (Vol. 10, No. 4, 1990). *"A highly useful resource to identify and discuss the subject of manufacturers' catalogs and their historical as well as practical value to the profession of librarianship. Dr. Mount has made an outstanding contribution." (Academic Library Book Review)*

Role of Standards in Sci-Tech Libraries, edited by Ellis Mount, DLS (Vol. 10, No. 3, 1990). *Required reading for any librarian who has been asked to identify standards and specifications.*

Relation of Sci-Tech Information to Environmental Studies, edited by Ellis Mount, DLS (Vol. 10, No. 2, 1990). *"A timely and important book that illustrates the nature and use of sci-tech information in relation to the environment." (The Bulletin of Science, Technology & Society)*

End-User Training for Sci-Tech Databases, edited by Ellis Mount, DLS (Vol. 10, No. 1, 1990). *"This is a timely publication for those of us involved in conducting online searches in special libraries where our users have a detailed knowledge of their subject areas." (Australian Library Review)*

Sci-Tech Archives and Manuscript Collections, edited by Ellis Mount, DLS (Vol. 9, No. 4, 1989). *Gain valuable information on the ways in which sci-tech archival material is being handled and preserved in various institutions and organizations.*

Collection Management in Sci-Tech Libraries, edited by Ellis Mount, DLS (Vol. 9, No. 3, 1989). *"An interesting and timely survey of current issues in collection management as they pertain to science and technology libraries." (Barbara A. List, AMLS, Coordinator of Collection Development, Science & Technology Research Center, and Editor, New Technical Books, The Research Libraries, New York Public Library)*

The Role of Conference Literature in Sci-Tech Libraries, edited by Ellis Mount, DLS (Vol. 9, No. 2, 1989). *"The volume constitutes a valuable overview of the issues posed for librarians and users by one of the most frustrating and yet important sources of scientific and technical information." (Australian Library Review)*

Adaptation of Turnkey Computer Systems in Sci-Tech Libraries, edited by Ellis Mount, DLS (Vol. 9, No. 1, 1989). *"Interesting and useful. . . .The book addresses the problems and benefits associated with the installation of a turnkey or ready-made computer system in a scientific or technical library." (Information Retrieval & Library Automation)*

Sci-Tech Libraries Serving Zoological Gardens, edited by Ellis Mount, DLS (Vol. 8, No. 4, 1989). *"Reviews the history and development of six major zoological garden libraries in the U.S." (Australian Library Review)*

Libraries Serving Science-Oriented and Vocational High Schools, edited by Ellis Mount, DLS (Vol. 8, No. 3, 1989). *A wealth of information on the special collections of science-oriented and vocational high schools, with a look at their services, students, activities, and problems.*

Sci-Tech Library Networks Within Organizations, edited by Ellis Mount, DLS (Vol. 8, No. 2, 1988). *Offers thorough descriptions of sci-tech library networks in which their members have a common sponsorship or ownership.*

One Hundred Years of Sci-Tech Libraries, A Brief History, edited by Ellis Mount, DLS (Vol. 8, No. 1, 1988). *"Should be read by all those considering, or who are already involved in, information retrieval, whether in Sci-tech libraries or others." (Library Resources & Technical Services)*

Alternative Careers in Sci-Tech Information Service, edited by Ellis Mount, DLS (Vol. 7, No. 4, 1987). *Here is an eye-opening look at alternative careers for professionals with a sci-tech background, including librarians, scientists, and engineers.*

Preservation and Conservation of Sci-Tech Materials, edited by Ellis Mount, DLS (Vol. 7, No. 3, 1987). *"This cleverly coordinated work is essential reading for library school students and practicing librarians. . . . Recommended reading." (Science Books and Films)*

Sci-Tech Libraries Serving Societies and Institutions, edited by Ellis Mount, DLS (Vol. 7, No. 2, 1987). *"Of most interest to special librarians, providing them with some insight into sci-tech libraries and their activities as well as a means of identifying specialized services and collections which may be of use to them." (Sci-Tech Libraries)*

Innovations in Planning Facilities for Sci-Tech Libraries, edited by Ellis Mount, DLS (Vol. 7, No. 1, 1986). *"Will prove invaluable to any librarian establishing a new library or contemplating expansion." (Australasian College Libraries)*

Role of Computers in Sci-Tech Libraries, edited by Ellis Mount, DLS (Vol. 6, No. 4, 1986). *"A very readable text. . . . I am including a number of the articles in the student reading list." (C. Bull, Kingstec Community College, Kentville, Nova Scotia, Canada)*

Weeding of Collections in Sci-Tech Libraries, edited by Ellis Mount, DLS (Vol. 6, No. 3, 1986). *"A useful publication. . . . Should be in every science and technology library." (Rivernia Library Review)*

Sci-Tech Libraries in Museums and Aquariums, edited by Ellis Mount, DLS (Vol. 6, No. 1/2, 1985). *"Useful to libraries in museums and aquariums for its descriptive and practical information." (The Association for Information Management)*

Data Manipulation in Sci-Tech Libraries, edited by Ellis Mount, DLS (Vol. 5, No. 4, 1985). *"Papers in this volume present evidence of the growing sophistication in the manipulation of data by information personnel." (Sci-Tech Book News)*

Role of Maps in Sci-Tech Libraries, edited by Ellis Mount, DLS (Vol. 5, No. 3, 1985). *Learn all about the acquisition of maps and the special problems of their storage and preservation in this insightful book.*

Fee-Based Services in Sci-Tech Libraries, edited by Ellis Mount, DLS (Vol. 5, No. 2, 1985). *"Highly recommended. Any librarian will find something of interest in this volume." (Australasian College Libraries)*

Serving End-Users in Sci-Tech Libraries, edited by Ellis Mount, DLS (Vol. 5, No. 1, 1984). *"Welcome and indeed interesting reading. . . . a useful acquisition for anyone starting out in one or more of the areas covered." (Australasian College Libraries)*

Management of Sci-Tech Libraries, edited by Ellis Mount, DLS (Vol. 4, No. 3/4, 1984). *Become better equipped to tackle difficult staffing, budgeting, and personnel challenges with this essential volume on managing different types of sci-tech libraries.*

Collection Development in Sci-Tech Libraries, edited by Ellis Mount, DLS (Vol. 4, No. 2, 1984). *"Well-written by authors who work in the field they are discussing. Should be of value to librarians whose collections cover a wide range of scientific and technical fields." (Library Acquisitions: Practice and Theory)*

Role of Serials in Sci-Tech Libraries, edited by Ellis Mount, DLS (Vol. 4, No. 1, 1983). *"Some interesting nuggets to offer dedicated serials librarians and users of scientific journal literature. . . . Outlines the direction of some major changes already occurring in scientific journal publishing and serials management." (Serials Review)*

Planning Facilities for Sci-Tech Libraries, edited by Ellis Mount, DLS (Vol. 3, No. 4, 1983). *"Will be of interest to special librarians who are contemplating the building of new facilities or the renovating and adaptation of existing facilities in the near future. . . . A useful manual based on actual experiences."* (Sci-Tech News)

Monographs in Sci-Tech Libraries, edited by Ellis Mount, DLS (Vol. 3, No. 3, 1983). *This insightful book addresses the present contributions monographs are making in sci-tech libraries as well as their probable role in the future.*

Role of Translations in Sci-Tech Libraries, edited by Ellis Mount, DLS (Vol. 3, No. 2, 1983). *"Good required reading in a course on special libraries in library school. It would also be useful to any librarian who handles the ordering of translations." (Sci-Tech News)*

Online Versus Manual Searching in Sci-Tech Libraries, edited by Ellis Mount, DLS (Vol. 3, No. 1, 1982). *An authoritative volume that examines the role that manual searches play in academic, public, corporate, and hospital libraries.*

Document Delivery for Sci-Tech Libraries, edited by Ellis Mount, DLS (Vol. 2, No. 4, 1982). *Touches on important aspects of document delivery and the place each aspect holds in the overall scheme of things.*

Cataloging and Indexing for Sci-Tech Libraries, edited by Ellis Mount, DLS (Vol. 2, No. 3, 1982). *Diverse and authoritative views on the problems of cataloging and indexing in sci-tech libraries.*

Role of Patents in Sci-Tech Libraries, edited by Ellis Mount, DLS (Vol. 2, No. 2, 1982). *A fascinating look at the nature of patents and the complicated, ever-changing set of indexes and computerized database devoted to facilitating the identification and retrieval of patents.*

Current Awareness Services in Sci-Tech Libraries, edited by Ellis Mount, DLS (Vol. 2, No. 1, 1982). *An interesting and comprehensive look at the many forms of current awareness services that sci-tech libraries offer.*

Role of Technical Reports in Sci-Tech Libraries, edited by Ellis Mount, DLS (Vol. 1, No. 4, 1982). *Recommended reading not only for science and technology librarians, this unique volume is specifically devoted to the analysis of problems, innovative practices, and advances relating to the control and servicing of technical reports.*

Training of Sci-Tech Librarians and Library Users, edited by Ellis Mount, DLS (Vol. 1, No. 3, 1981). *Here is a crucial overview of the current and future issues in the training of science and engineering librarians as well as instruction for users of these libraries.*

Networking in Sci-Tech Libraries and Information Centers, edited by Ellis Mount, DLS (Vol. 1, No. 2, 1981). *Here is an entire volume devoted to the topic of cooperative projects and library networks among sci-tech libraries.*

Planning for Online Search Service in Sci-Tech Librares, edited by Ellis Mount, DLS (Vol. 1, No. 1, 1981). *Covers the most important issues to consider when planning for online search services.*

Digital Libraries: Philosophies, Technical Design Considerations, and Example Scenarios has been co-published simultaneously as *Science & Technology Libraries,* Volume 17, Numbers 3/4 1999.

The development, preparation, and publication of this work has been undertaken with great care. However, the publisher, employees, editors, and agents of The Haworth Press and all imprints of The Haworth Press, Inc., including The Haworth Medical Press® and Pharmaceutical Products Press®, are not responsible for any errors contained herein or for consequences that may ensue from use of materials or information contained in this work. Opinions expressed by the author(s) are not necessarily those of The Haworth Press, Inc.

The Haworth Press, Inc., 10 Alice Street, Binghamton, NY 13904-1580, USA

Cover design by Thomas J. Mayshock Jr.

Library of Congress Cataloging-in-Publication Data

Digital libraries: philosophies, technical design considerations, and example scenarios/David Stern, editor.
     p. cm.
     "Has been co-published simultaneously as Science & technology libraries, volume 17, numbers 3/4 1999."
     Includes bibliographical references and index.
     ISBN 0-7890-0769-X (alk. paper)
     1. Digital libraries–United States. 2. Libraries–United States–Special collections–Electronic information resources. I. Stern, David, 1956 Dec. 30 II. Science & technology libraries.
ZA4082.U6D54 1999
025'.00285–dc21
                                                                                        99-25629
                                                                                              CIP

Digital Libraries: Philosophies, Technical Design Considerations, and Example Scenarios

David Stern
Editor

Digital Libraries: Philosophies, Technical Design Considerations, and Example Scenarios has been co-published simultaneously as *Science & Technology Libraries*, Volume 17, Numbers 3/4 1999.

The Haworth Press, Inc.,
New York • London • Oxford

INDEXING & ABSTRACTING

Contributions to this publication are selectively indexed or abstracted in print, electronic, online, or CD-ROM version(s) of the reference tools and information services listed below. This list is current as of the copyright date of this publication. See the end of this section for additional notes.

- *AGRICOLA Database*

- *Biosciences Information Service of Biological Abstracts (BIOSIS)*

- *BUBL Information Service, and Internet-based Information Service for the UK higher education community*

- *Cambridge Scientific Abstracts*

- *Chemical Abstracts*

- *CNPIEC Reference Guide: Chinese National Directory of Foreign Periodicals*

- *Current Awareness Abstracts of Library & Information Management Literature, ASLIB(UK)*

- *Current Index to Journals in Education*

- *Educational Administration Abstracts (EAA)*

- *Engineering Information (PAGE ONE)*

- *Environment Abstracts*

- *IBZ International Bibliography of Periodical Literature*

- *Index to Periodical Articles Related to Law*

- *Information Science Abstracts*

- *Informed Librarian, The*

- *INSPEC*

(continued)

- *Konyvtari Figyelo-Library Review*

- *Library & Information Science Abstracts (LISA)*

- *Library and Information Science Annual (LISCA)*

- *Library Literature*

- *Medicinal & Aromatic Plants Abstracts (MAPA)*

- *Newsletter of Library and Information Services*

- *PAIS (Public Affairs Information Service) NYC*

- *PASCAL Institute de L'information Scientifique et Technique*

- *Referativnyi Zhurnal (Abstracts Journal of the All-Russian Institute of Scientific Information and Technical Information)*

Special Bibliographic Notes related to special journal issues (separates) and indexing/abstracting:

- indexing/abstracting services in this list will also cover material in any "separate" that is co-published simultaneously with Haworth's special thematic journal issue or DocuSerial. Indexing/abstracting usually covers material at the article/chapter level.
- monographic co-editions are intended for either non-subscribers or libraries which intend to purchase a second copy for their circulating collections.
- monographic co-editions are reported to all jobbers/wholesalers/approval plans. The source journal is listed as the "series" to assist the prevention of duplicate purchasing in the same manner utilized for books-in-series.
- to facilitate user/access services all indexing/abstracting services are encouraged to utilize the co-indexing entry note indicated at the bottom of the first page of each article/chapter/contribution.
- this is intended to assist a library user of any reference tool (whether print, electronic, online, or CD-ROM) to locate the monographic version if the library has purchased this version but not a subscription to the source journal.
- individual articles/chapters in any Haworth publication are also available through the Haworth Document Delivery Service (HDDS).

Digital Libraries: Philosophies, Technical Design Considerations, and Example Scenarios

CONTENTS

ABOUT THE EDITOR

Arleen N. Somerville is Head of the Science and Engineering Libraries and Chemistry Librarian at the University of Rochester in Rochester, New York. She holds a bachelor's and master's degree from the University of Wisconsin, Madison. From 1972 to 1973, she served as President of the Special Libraries Association Upstate New York State Chapter and as Chairman of the Chemistry Division from 1975 to 1976. In addition, she was the Liaison Representative between the SLA Chemistry Division and the American Chemical Society Division of Chemical Information for eight years. She was Chairman of the American Chemical Society's Division of Chemical Information in 1988 and has been Chairman or Member of its Education Committee since 1983. She currently serves on three American Chemical Society committees: Chemical Abstracts Service, Copyright, and Publications. In 1983, she received the Special Libraries Association John Cotton Dana Award for exceptional service to special librarianship. She is also a member of the American Library Association and the Association of College and Research Libraries. She edits "The Chemical Information Instructor" column in the *Journal of Chemical Education*. She is the author of numerous articles about chemical information, as well as on other aspects of scientific resources and information services to scientific clientele. She has given presentations on chemical information at meetings of the American Chemical Society. Special Libraries Association, and the Association of College and Research Libraries, as well as at the Institute of Photographic Chemistry (Bejing), the Academy of Sciences (Moscow), and St. Petersburg State University (St. Petersburg, Russia).

Introduction

As the virtual library becomes a reality it is apparent that the "Digital Library" is a very complex and dynamic entity. The Association of Research Libraries' October 23, 1995 "Definition and Purposes of a Digital Library" definition at http://sunsite.berkeley.edu/ARL/definition.html is:

> There are many definitions of a "digital library." Terms such as "electronic library" and "virtual library" are often used synonymously. The elements that have been identified as common to these definitions[1] are:
>
> - The digital library is not a single entity;
> - The digital library requires technology to link the resources of many;
> - The linkages between the many digital libraries and information services are transparent to the end users;
> - Universal access to digital libraries and information services is a goal;
> - Digital library collections are not limited to document surrogates: they extend to digital artifacts that cannot be represented or distributed in printed formats.

This volume intends to serve as an overview of selected directions, trends, possibilities, limitations, enhancements, design principles and ongoing projects for integrated library and information systems.

There are many excellent works on Digital Libraries available as paper and electronic publications (see Selected Recommended Readings for URLs and titles for follow-up and current awareness). This volume will not address the migration of library material to an online environment using the same paper distribution paradigm (a simple technical feasibility issue), but instead will look for areas in which we can highlight possible improvements and

[Haworth co-indexing entry note]: "Introduction." Stern, David. Co-published simultaneously in *Science & Technology Libraries* (The Haworth Press, Inc.) Vol. 17, No. 3/4, 1999, pp. 1-8; and: *Digital Libraries: Philosophies, Technical Design Considerations, and Example Scenarios* (ed: David Stern) The Haworth Press, Inc., 1999, pp. 1-8. Single or multiple copies of this article are available for a fee from The Haworth Document Delivery Service [1-800-342-9678, 9:00 a.m. - 5:00 p.m. (EST). E-mail address: getinfo@haworthpressinc.com].

trends for "beyond paper" scenarios–moving toward a new means of electronic scholarly communication. Of course we understand that the digitization of paper (and the continued use of paper tools) will still remain very important and must be integrated into all resulting user interfaces.

There is no one simple solution to digitizing and distributing online library material–satisfactory approaches should be based upon niche situations. Considerations should include any previous search and subject knowledge expected of the user, the scope and level of material desired, any subject-specific vocabulary or interface needs (i.e., chemical structure searching), special user needs (i.e., tools for the visually impaired), institutional support/funding and technical resources. The advances in computer technology are occurring so quickly that it is often impossible to predict what or when new tools might arise. It is our hope that careful analysis and collaboration between library and computer personnel will identify the most appropriate techniques required to solve library-specific problems and will guide the development of future technologies.

In attempting to prepare this volume it was determined that while archiving issues are very important to the future of digital libraries, it is still too early in the development of archiving solutions to have a well thought out presentation that could add significantly to the already available literature. The field is too dynamic and embryonic, still needing group collaboration for the development of shared vision, standards, and shared solutions as compared to the current compartmentalization/competition and duplication/diversion that exists among the commercial players.

Topics covered in this volume are (1) the organization of digital libraries, (2) collection assessments, (3) enduser assessments, (4) network infrastructure considerations for the successful federation of independent databases, (5) XML and related metadata enhancements, (6) interface design considerations, (7) an object-oriented interface system, and (8) GIS and Patent discipline overviews.

This volume is divided into three related sections: Philosophies, Technical Design Considerations, and Example Scenarios.

Philosophies includes four articles. The first article, by Michael E. Lesk, Director of Information and Intelligent Systems for the National Science Foundation, addresses the administration of these newly forming digital libraries. Topics include current library organization and possible changes in staffing, budgeting, and structure; the supplementation of traditional collection building through additional emphasis on providing advice, evaluation, and selection of remote access gateways; the implications of the inevitable technology changes in libraries; legal issues; economic considerations; and cooperative ventures among libraries.

The second article, by Daniel Jones, Assistant Library Director for Collection Development at the University of Texas Health Science Center, discusses many complexities and considerations in this new collection development scenario. Some areas addressed include the many new media options and interfaces available, changing responsibilities and support tasks, licensing issues, validation [and identification] of users, equipment compatibility, local loading versus remote access options, client software support, training, migration and conversion of data over time, and user evaluation.

The third article, by Barbara Buttenfield, Associate Professor of Geography at the University of Colorado, and leader of the user evaluation effort for the Alexandria Digital Library Project, addresses the important but rarely documented area of evaluation of these developing systems. She identifies and explores the relevancy of traditional usability evaluation methods for these new dynamic and interactive library systems, suggests that "convergent methods" offers higher reliability, and provides lessons learned through a case study of evaluation from the Alexandria Digital Library Project. She also discusses the delicate timing and tension involved in constructive usability evaluation analysis leading to system revision along the stages of system design, development, and deployment.

The fourth article, by David Stern, Director of Science Libraries and Information Services at Yale University, outlines the development of more powerful user search and navigation possibilities over time. The article chronicles the development of techniques from basic Boolean searching through enhanced options such as citation analysis, natural language, exploding thesauri, customized interfaces, hyperlink connections, metadata, relevancy ranking, broadcast capabilities, and library navigational tools. Selected areas for future enhancement are discussed.

Technical Design Considerations includes more technical analyses of the digital library infrastructure components. It is our hope that this section will make STM librarians more aware of the vocabulary and technical issues involved in creating a seamlessly integrated system.

The first article, by Robert Ferrer, a Research Programmer currently with the Digital Library Initiative at the University of Illinois, Champaign-Urbana, addresses the requirements for an integrated and federated network of resources. His moderately technical paper highlights the concepts that support such distributed systems: client-server, middleware, communication protocols, DBMS conventions, including those associated with loosely-coupled and tightly-coupled federated database architectures, and the advantages gained through object-based technology. He also discusses the benefits and issues in the use of SGML for full text indexing and searching, including hyperlink and metadata capabilities, processing for normalized vocabulary and thesauri schema, difficulties with SGML entities, and graphical display concerns. Punctuating his discussion is a description of various NSF DLI projects that bring to reality the concepts described throughout the article. He concludes with an analysis of these and other federated projects.

The second article, by Daniel Chudnov, IAIMS Assistant and Librarian, Cushing/Whitney Medical Library, Yale University, addresses the enhanced integration of information storage, retrieval, and delivery systems made possible by the XML and RDF standards. He provides two enhanced seamless database scenarios in which data and metadata are integrated for more powerful manipulation within and among multiple databases.

The third article, by Steve Mitchell, Sciences Reference Librarian and INFOMINE Co-Coordinator and Co-Founder, Library, University of California, Riverside, provides a review of interface possibilities and design considerations. Topics include present interface trends, design principles and techniques, underlying database structure implications, taxonomies of interface types, and enhancement possibilities developed through the use of metaphors and interactive techniques (e.g., direct manipulation and autonomous agents). An excellent bibliography for further reading accompanies this article.

The fourth article, by Eric H. Johnson, Research Programmer, Community Architectures for Networked Information Systems (CANIS), Graduate School of Library and Information Science, University of Illinois at Urbana-Champaign, demonstrates the many enhancements possible using an object-oriented interface. This IODyne system provides an impressive example of powerful new paradigm visualization search techniques using metaphor, idiom, and drag-and-drop object manipulation approaches. He describes the benefits of replacing traditional search *commands* and *modes* with the idea of *objects* that have *properties* and display *behavior*. Advantages include modelessness, direct manipulation of screen objects, immediate feedback, object persistence, idiomatic object manipulation, cross-repository searching, and multiple simultaneous connection capabilities.

Example Scenarios includes two short reviews of existing digital library systems. The first article, by Patrick McGlamery, Map Librarian, Map and Geographic Information Center, University of Connecticut, addresses the development of a state-wide GIS mapping clearinghouse. Issues considered include staff support, hardware and software selection, scope of the database and services provided, organization of the materials, conversion of raw data into suitable patron files, and integration with the local and national community.

The second article, by Timothy Lee Wherry, Assistant Dean of Academic Affairs for Information Services, Penn State Altoona, addresses the digital libraries available in the area of patents. He describes some of the alternative search and delivery systems created to supplement the United States Patent and Trademark Office system.

Areas that call out for future analyses, but which time and space did not allow, include search engine comparisons, underlying database structures, archiving issues, pricing models, packaging of related data, integrated media, educational technology, post-search software packages, and new paradigms of information storage and retrieval (i.e., timestreams) and research techniques (citation and linkage analysis).

Librarians have been talking about the inevitability of ejournals diverging from print journals as the benefits of multimedia are added. I came across my first real life example of that in Optics Express. Go to http://www.osa.org, choose Optics Express, back issues, and look at the article by Noel and Stroud in V. 1, #7, pp. 176-185. On page four is a Quicktime animation. I believe this is the wave of the future, and it is not too soon for librarians to become prepared and involved. I hope this volume helps to motivate our readers to further explore the collaboration opportunities for information professionals in this new arena.

David Stern

NOTE

1. Drabenstott, Karen M. Analytical review of the library of the future, Washington, DC: Council Library Resources, 1994.

SELECTED RECOMMENDED READINGS

A. Clearinghouses of Digital Libraries Sources

Library of Congress Digital Library Resources and Projects
http://lcweb.loc.gov/loc/ndlf/digital.html
This site includes links to many of the major digital library inititiatives.

DigLibns Electronic Discussion List
http://sunsite.berkeley.edu/DigLibns/

"A discussion of practical issues relating to digital libraries and librarianship." Includes an excellent index to research in the field. A portion of the excellent Berkeley Digital Library SunSITE. Another excellent portion of this site is the CURRENT CITES bibliography.

Scholarly Electronic Publishing Bibliography
By Charles W. Bailey, Jr.
http://info.lib.uh.edu/sepb/sepb.html
This bibliography covers all areas of electronic publishing, special interest
would be in 6.2 Digital Libraries–
http://info.lib.uh.edu/sepb/lbdiglib.htm

Digital Library Federation (previously: National Digital Library Federation)
http://lcweb.loc.gov/loc/ndlf/
Fifteen of the nation's largest research libraries and archives have agreed to
cooperate to explore areas of mutual interest.

Net Projects
http://www.public.iastate.edu/~CYBERSTACKS/Projects.htm
This portion of CYBERSTACKS demonstrates various approaches to the
organization and visualization of large information databases.

B. Selected Digital Libraries Projects

National Science Foundation DLI projects:

Digital Libraries Inititiative site (UIUC)
Summaries of projects
http://dli.grainger.uiuc.edu/national.htm

University of California at Berkeley
Environmental Planning and Geographic Information Systems
http://elib.cs.berkeley.edu/
University of California at Santa Barbara
The Alexandria Project: Spatially-Referenced Map Information
http://alexandria.sdc.ucsb.edu/

Carnegie Mellon University
Informedia Digital Video Library
http://www.informedia.cs.cmu.edu/

University of Illinois at Urbana-Champaign
Federating Repositories of Scientific Literature
Engineering Testbed
http://dli.grainger.uiuc.edu/

University of Michigan
Intelligent Agents for Information Location
Earth and Space Sciences Testbed
http://www.si.umich.edu/UMDL/

Stanford University
Interoperation Mechanisms Among Heterogeneous Services
http://walrus.stanford.edu/diglib/

Canadian Initiative on Digital Libraries
http://www.nlc-bnc.ca/cidl/

C. Selected Writings

CURRENT CITES
http://sunsite.berkeley.edu/CurrentCites/
A portion of the excellent Berkeley Digital Library SunSITE, the CURRENT
CITES bibliography provides an archive and listserv capabilities for those
wishing to receive an annotated monthly bibliography of selected articles,
books, and electronic documents on information technology.

Digital Libraries: A Selected Resource Guide
Information Technology and Libraries
Volume 16, Number 3, September 1997
KATHARINA KLEMPERER AND STEPHEN CHAPMAN
http://www.lita.org/ital/1603_klemperer.htm
An excellent bibliography and gateway to some of the most interesting digital
projects."This "electronic literature review is an introduction and summary
of the state of the art for those who have not been intimately involved in the
evolution of Digital Libraries."

Okerson AS and JJ O'Donnell "Scholarly Journals at the Crossroads: A
Subversive Proposal for Electronic Publishing, An Internet Discussion about
Scientific and Scholarly Journals and Their Future", Washington DC: Office
of Scientific & Academic Publishing, Association of Research Libraries,
June 1995, pp. 242, ISBN 0-918006-26-0
A collection of electronic mail discussion items from the VPIEJ-L listserv
that address many issues related to the economics and theoretical paradigm
shifts allowed given the enhanced possibilities of electronic communication
between peers.

Why Publish a Journal On Line?
THE JOURNAL OF ELECTRONIC PUBLISHING,
September 1, 1997.
http://www.press.umich.edu/jep/03-01/index.html
Editors of eight electronic-only peer-reviewed scholarly journals answer that
question and discuss the enhancements available via ejournals.

PHILOSOPHIES

The Organization of Digital Libraries

Michael E. Lesk

SUMMARY. A digital library must focus on access and service, not buildings and volumes. Libraries will support users in their searching and acquiring of information, and their organization will reflect services rather than physical location. Technology, law and economics are all becoming more important for libraries, requiring new expertise in library staff. Perhaps the most important issues for the long term will be the ability of libraries to cooperate in the delivery of new services. *[Article copies available for a fee from The Haworth Document Delivery Service: 1-800-342-9678. E-mail address: getinfo@haworthpressinc.com]*

KEYWORDS. Digital libraries, access, organization, technology, law, economics, cooperate, new services

INTRODUCTION

In the early years of computing, machines were so expensive that nobody had more than one of them. Douglas Hartree speculated in 1951 that the

Michael E. Lesk, PhD, is Head of the Division of Information and Intelligent Systems at the National Science Foundation.

[Haworth co-indexing entry note]: "The Organization of Digital Libraries." Lesk, Michael E. Co-published simultaneously in *Science & Technology Libraries* (The Haworth Press, Inc.) Vol. 17, No. 3/4, 1999, pp. 9-25; and: *Digital Libraries: Philosophies, Technical Design Considerations, and Example Scenarios* (ed: David Stern) The Haworth Press, Inc., 1999, pp. 9-25. Single or multiple copies of this article are available for a fee from The Haworth Document Delivery Service [1-800-342-9678, 9:00 a.m. - 5:00 p.m. (EST). E-mail address: getinfo@haworthpressinc.com].

United Kingdom might need a total of four computers [Corn]. We now have a world-wide digital library, the Web. Computers are cheap, and libraries have many of them. How should a library be organized today?

The digital library contains both many different media and many different subjects. In a traditional library, it is common for the top level organization to be by form: photographs, sound recordings, maps, and so on are stored separately, rather than placing each photograph of an individual next to that person's biography in the bookshelves. The materials in a digital library, however, are all in equivalent formats. A library may use various digital media: disk, tape, cartridges, and so on; but these are interchangeable for storage of bibliographic citations, text, images, or sounds. Thus, the conventional special collections in a library might well be unified with the book collections in similar subject areas.

Digital libraries focus less on collections than on access. Since material is likely to be available with almost equal speed from any online site, librarians will be using their expertise much more to find material outside their physical location, as well as knowing what is directly stored in their building or under their control. The organization of a digital library will reflect what users want rather than what the librarian has been able to afford to buy. A digital library will try to provide support for searching and acquiring information, and get more involved in the overall user information needs. Whether libraries will charge for any of the information fetching services is not yet known and will depend on the individual library and individual information requests.

Many undergraduates today rely heavily on the World Wide Web as their information source. With about two terabytes of text on line, or the equivalent of perhaps two million books, this is a full-text indexed free library. It is increasing in size by a factor of ten every year, and is likely to catch the Library of Congress next year (see Figure 1).

As a collection, it is strong in areas like disk drive prices, current gossip, new technical reports, and corporate ads; however it is weak in traditional scholarship (and anything before 1995). But it is open 24 hours a day, convenient, and the exclusive source of information for some people; to quote one Cornell undergraduate asked to look something up in the traditional way, "I don't do libraries." Given the Web, we no longer can ask whether we should have a digital library; we're just arguing about its content. What libraries may find themselves doing is giving more help and advice to those who are less competent to evaluate the content and utility of what they have found so easily.

CURRENT LIBRARY ORGANIZATION

Libraries today are seeing critical problems associated with cutbacks in their general funding. For example, UK universities typically spent about 4%

FIGURE 1. Web Size

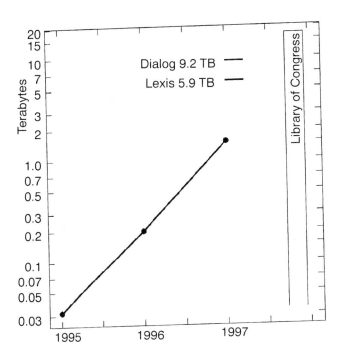

of their budget on libraries in 1980-81, but only 3% in 1991-92 [Follett]. UK libraries spend 53-58% of their funds on staff costs. US libraries are similar in their expenditures, with materials and acquisitions costs about a third, salaries about half, and other expenses about 15% now and growing steadily [Mellon]. Some libraries spend much more on staff; the San Francisco Public Library spent 74% of its money on personnel and 11% on acquisitions [SFPL].

Three major new subjects are imposing themselves on libraries; they are technology, law and economics. Each will have effects on digital libraries and how they are organized.

TECHNOLOGY

The new technology is being used for a variety of functions, which range from finding aids to video delivery. From the familiar OPAC to the online journal delivery system, people are accustomed to using workstations to obtain information. What does the library have to do?

The library must maintain descriptions of the information it holds, in whatever format. This is typically stored in the form of MARC records and delivered via a commercial OPAC. Sometimes integrating these systems with actual information delivery is hard; they are designed for, and specialize in, the description of printed books. It is more likely that the catalog system will be linked to a book circulation system than that it will be linked to an online delivery system. The input to the description system is more and more likely to come from central sources such as national cataloging authorities; cataloging, as a skill, is exercised less frequently in libraries now that records are routinely retrieved from central cataloging files.

Online delivery is often done off the premises of the library. Reference libraries need seating for their users; a typical guideline in the United States is that the number of seats in the library should be at least 1/4 the number of students on the campus. Nowadays it is expected that most students have computers in their dormitory rooms and they are connected to the campus network. The number of people physically present in the library is no longer a good measure of how many people are using the library's services. Not only may electronics help with the need for ever more bookstack space, it might alleviate the need for chairs and tables as well.

Whether the demand for seats actually goes down depends on whether access to primary material on the desktop starts to replace reading in the library. Until now most people have done bibliographic work on their terminals but then read online. Don King suggests that searching takes perhaps 1/5 of the time engineers spend with information, with 4/5 of the time spent reading. Thus, the improved bibliographic search capabilities of computer catalogs have often increased the time users spend in libraries, since they find more things to read. However we now see people reading more and more material on their desktop (or at least printing it outside the library). As this spreads, the need for libraries to provide places to read will decline.

Thus, what does the library need technologically? It needs above all networking capacity. A future organization calling itself a library might have no physical site with shelves and reading rooms. Instead, a physical complement of routers, and a personnel complement of people knowing where to find things, could make a virtual library effective. The online bookstore Amazon.com does this for retail sales; there is no shop, no stock, and only remote access.

The machines involved can be located anywhere; there is little reason to use an expensive central-campus building with impressive architecture to hold machines only a few staff ever see. Nor do reference personnel working mostly over the telephone need to be anywhere central; some computer companies provide their telephone support for all of Europe from a single site in Ireland. So the digital library needs less attention paid to its physical space (admittedly today this function is often provided elsewhere in an academic organization), and considerably more to its technology–disk drives, computers, routers, tape storage units, and the like.

In the past, a major problem with digital library implementation was the need to deal with the variety of computer hardware possessed by different users. Today, the Web has defined the standard interface which everyone must support, and we no longer have arguments about whether or not we can expect users to have graphic capability. Nevertheless, many OPACS are still designed for extremely dumb terminals, and will be phased out in favor of more attractive Web-based systems.

There are still incompatibility questions, of course. Some models of the digital library involve image scanning of printed material, particularly for retrospective conversion; others involve ASCII-based text. In principle, much of the image-scanned material can be converted through OCR, and such projects as JSTOR do this; but there are still other materials which are provided as images and which may be hard to search. With time, though, the advent of standards will decrease the various conversion problems that plague us today.

LAW

If a digital library needs to obtain much of its material from other sites, it needs to know what it can do with such material. Various rules such as "fair use" have meant that for traditional printed books most use in research libraries is permitted without additional charge beyond the original purchase. This situation is likely to get much more confusing, partly because digital information may not have the permissions associated with paper, partly because multimedia information already has different rules from printed paper, and partly because there are many revisions in the law under consideration.

The purchase of digital information often involves a license rather than a traditional purchase, even though it looks like a purchase to the library. In a recent case (*Pro CD v. Zeidenberg*) the U. S. courts have upheld shrink-wrap licenses, even when the material protected by the license would not normally have been protectable by copyright. Licenses may limit the people allowed to access the material, and they may require accounting of how many accesses are made, or even payments proportional to either the number of users or the time required.

Libraries need to worry about some of the requirements vendors may try to place upon the use of their material. In particular, U. S. libraries protect the privacy of the records of which patrons use which information resources. Information vendors are often very anxious to find out who their users are and libraries may have to be careful about contracts which might ask for delivery of user data. The most difficult issue to date has been the definition of the library's user community. Many libraries serve an extended community which may, for an academic library, include alumni and even members of the public (often state universities or land-grant universities have obligations to serve the general public in some area). Publishers are particularly anxious that remote use be limited to some reasonable extension of students, staff and faculty.

What this means to the organization of a library is that considerable effort must be spent tracking the library's activities with respect to the contracts signed with information vendors. The library will be trying to persuade publishers to agree to unlimited use site licenses, and the publisher may prefer some kind of pay-by-use (although many publishers also prefer flat-rate licenses to avoid the administrative costs and to get their money ahead of use rather than afterwards). The library may prefer to join a consortium for purchasing digital material as a way of decreasing administrative costs and increasing bargaining leverage.

The problems with non-print material are already difficult. There is no "fair use" on recorded music, for example, so that libraries should not in general be making copies of published sound recordings without obtaining permission. Video material is often involved in a great many complex copyright difficulties, and little of it is actually old enough to be in the public domain. Perhaps the best known example is the movie "It's a Wonderful Life" whose copyright holder neglected to renew it after the first 28-year term. When television stations, realizing that this movie could be played free, broadcast it so frequently that it turned into a cult favorite, the studio investigated and found that although the movie copyright had not been renewed, the publisher of the story on which the movie was based had kept the story in copyright, and so it was possible to recapture control. Each new technology has created new legal problems, since the courts have typically held that contracts to publish in one format do not transfer the right to future formats. The result has been a rash of language in copyright forms about every format now known, imagined, or to be invented, some of which may be valid.

Proposed changes to the United States law raise further difficulties. Among the important issues to libraries are digital fair use, registration, digital preservation, moral rights, data base protection, and liability for plagiarism, libel, and incorrect information.

Digital fair use. The White Paper proposed last year for copyright revisions would have declared there to be no fair use of digital materials (and also clarified that digital transmissions were indeed an infringement of copyright). Potentially, this requires negotiations with copyright holders for virtually all digital use, imposing a heavy burden on libraries and their users for what may now be thought of as commercially insignificant uses. The proposal was not adopted (partly because Congress simply ran out of time), but its proponents have not gone away.

Copyright notice and registration. Under the Berne convention, already in force in the United States, published works no longer need to be registered with the Copyright Office nor need they carry a statement identifying the copyright owner and date. Any material is protected from the date of creation. This means that in the future a librarian may be faced with a printed document which contains no author name or date, and yet need to know whether the author has been dead for fifty (or perhaps 70) years. Fortunately this problem will not arise until about 2038; few works going out of copyright before then escaped the earlier notice requirements, with an exception for certain European materials.

Digital preservation. The current copyright law allows libraries to copy deteriorating materials for preservation purposes, but only to make facsimile copies. It is proposed that the next change in the law permit digital copying for preservation, but this is of course uncertain. There are actually two separate issues, both now requiring permission: one is the scanning of deteriorating paper material to convert it to digital form, and the other is the conversion of one digital form to another as technologies become obsolete and we need to convert, let us say, CD-Rs to DVD.

Moral rights. The United States has started to adopt the principles of "moral rights" in which even after selling the copyright, the creator of a work retains certain rights, particularly an entitlement to be identified as the author and to prohibit some kinds of changes. This is already true for visual works in the U. S. The law will have to develop to be clear whether this constrains libraries. As an example of what the adoption of extended European concepts might mean to U. S. libraries, consider the effect on an architecture school library of the French rule that you cannot copy a picture of a building without the permission of the architect.

Database protection. The WIPO treaties proposed last year, but not yet ratified, would have provided that factual information in databases would again be subject to copyright, restoring the situation somewhat to the rules that prevailed before 1991. The treaty did provide for exemptions for excerpts from databases, but nevertheless it was attacked by many who felt that academic research would be severely constrained. With many revisions likely before anything like these treaties become law, it is not clear what the impact on libraries will be.

Liability. Traditionally, libraries have not been responsible for the content of the books they give their patrons. In a digital world it is not clear whether this will change. There are at least three issues: plagiarism, libel and tort liability. The plagiarism risk is that a change in the law may make people other than the original publisher responsible for copyright violations. Publishers are asking for this as a way of dealing with the amount of material that may be placed in digital form by individuals with minimal financial resources, who are not worth suing; they hope to place a responsibility on intermediaries to at least block plagiarized material, even if not to pay damages. The libel risk is the possibility that distributors of information will be sued as well as originators. In the United Kingdom, John Major recently recovered damages from the newsstand operators W. H. Smith and John Menzies for a libel published in a magazine with few financial resources. So far, this is not a problem in the United States. Tort liability is the risk that someone who gets bad information from a publication (e.g., bad investment advice or health advice) will try to sue the library as well as the author or publisher. An example is the lawsuit brought against the publisher of an aeronautical chart with a claim that the chart was badly designed and contributed to an accident. Again, this is not a problem for libraries today. However, as libraries become more ambitious in their provision of services, they may start to look more like publishers (recommending what to read, putting together packages for students in classes, etc). As they do this they will run the risk of increased legal responsibility for what is chosen.

The message from all of this is that the digital library involves a larger legal effort than does a more traditional effort, and the organization of the library will have to reflect that.

ECONOMICS

The ease with which digital libraries can transmit material from one location to another make sharing of subscriptions and similar cooperative activities very attractive. Users are hardly able to tell whether an Internet site is located five minutes walk or 5,000 miles from where they are located. The problem, of course, is that publishers have traditionally been the ones who provided distributed access to information, selling multiple copies of journals to different libraries at different universities.

A digital library, able to obtain material from remote sources, will be regularly purchasing things on-demand rather than entirely by payment in advance (what is called "just in time" rather than "just in case" obtaining of information). This will certainly mean a great deal of transactional purchasing. Whether the library also needs to do transactional selling, i.e., chargebacks to its users, is not clear. Many libraries believe strongly that charging users is a bad idea, whether for reasons of tradition, or because they fear discouraging the use of information, or because feel that centralized provision is a more efficient practice.

However, as libraries become involved in more and more specifically priced services, some of which are very expensive, it will be tempting to do chargebacks. This is certainly standard economic wisdom. Experience is, however, that ordinary users place a value on predictability; they shy away from services with per-minute pricing where they cannot know what they will wind up spending. Telephone companies have found in the past that people often choose flat rate service rather than measured service even if measured service would be cheaper; they fear that some month they will make an unusual number of calls and wish that they had flat rate pricing. Libraries are large organizations, and may be a good place to provide for averaging of these costs.

In fact, the new economics of publishers offer an opportunity for libraries or consortia of libraries. The typical publisher is small, selling 1.2 journals. Our familiarity with (and the high public profile of) Reed Elsevier and Wiley cause us to overlook the large number of small societies that publish one magazine. These societies are as frustrated as libraries by their inability to understand how they can thrive in the electronic environment of the future, and it may make sense for libraries to act as the agent for managing their distribution. The Stanford University Library, for example, has set up High Wire Press as an electronic printer for several journals, most notably the *Journal of Biological Chemistry.* Table 1 lists some numbers from the American Economic Association, which publishes three journals:

Crudely speaking, advertising plus individual sales come to 43% of their revenue, so that if the users could simply grab the papers off the Web, the Association might lose over 40% of their revenue, while saving at most the 23% they spend on printing and mailing. They might well try to continue selling to libraries and individuals at different prices, with some time or format difference causing individuals to wish to continue a personal subscription. If they felt that they were too small a publisher to maintain such a complex operation, they might be interested in joining forces with libraries or other groups, just as they do not cut their own typefaces nor operate rotary presses.

TABLE 1

Revenues		Expenses	
Membership	38%	Editing	36%
Libraries	20%	Typesetting	15%
CD-ROM sales	19%	Headquarters	27%
Advertising	5%	Printing	23%
Miscellaneous	18%		

The future economics of libraries are very unclear. If libraries are going to obtain information on demand from other sites, and deliver it to people on their office desktops, they begin to sound as if they will compete with bookstores. If they are going to provide detailed advice on what kinds of things to read, they become more like teachers. And if they provide descriptions of information, they become more like publishers. Libraries have always had these different roles, but they had in the past been entirely subordinate to the basic job of choosing and accumulating printed matter. When the basic primary information may be available online, these other functions will become more important. This will affect how libraries are funded and how they budget, and may force them to consider charging for some of the new services and reorganizing to emphasize support over storage and selection.

In all of the discussion about charging and copyright, do not forget that much of the material in libraries is not published for a fee. University dissertations, technical reports, government documents and other sources make up much of what scholars use today and will continue to use. Libraries should not, however, be encouraging their patrons to use second-rate or erroneous material just because it is available without charge. Again, some degree of judgment and assistance will be required in the digital library, just as it is today.

In summary, economics is another topic that will occupy more and more attention in libraries, and require a greater presence in the organization chart.

CENTRALIZATION AND COOPERATION

A more dangerous economic topic is the possibility that libraries may begin to compete with each other. As long as geographic separation determined the audience of libraries, they had little to fear from each other. We are now likely to see continual "outsourcing" by organizations which feel that in an electronic age referring their members to somebody else's library is now feasible and offers a chance of savings. Yet at the same time cooperation among libraries, as a way of sharing electronic resources, makes a great deal of sense.

Libraries need to cooperate for several reasons. First, it spreads the need for expertise and resources over a larger group of institutions and thus lowers the burden on all of them. Secondly, it increases the bargaining power of the libraries against others who may try to capture the benefits, particularly the commercial benefits, of the new technology exclusively for themselves. Thirdly, it encourages the development and adoption of standards to make everybody's training problems easier. The new technology not only pushes towards cooperation for these reasons, but also makes it feasible.

The same technology, of course, is encouraging cooperation among other groups. In the first half of the 1990s the fraction of papers with a British first author and a second author from some other country doubled, according to Derek Law. Another study is shown in the chart below (Figure 2), which was made by examining multi-author papers in one particular journal, and counting the fraction of times all authors were from the same institution. This measure dropped in the 1990s.

If groups are going to work together over longer ranges, will they be unified or cooperating? Will we find that larger libraries buy up smaller ones, the way chains of drugstores or hardware stores replace individual businesses? Or will we find a set of cooperating but still independent operations? Even within one university, will we find that staff costs and operations cost make it less reasonable to operate many small libraries, and instead start to concentrate effort in a few large places?

In academic libraries, I expect cooperation to win out. Most university administrators still consider their libraries to be a particular institutional strength, and are unlikely to be willing to forfeit this distinction in favor of simply being a branch location of Library-Mart or some such vendor. Librarians also have a strong tradition of cooperation, dating from interlibrary loan and cooperative cataloging. I hope that academic libraries can build on this history, and develop a sufficiently smooth and rapid cooperation so that administrators above them see no reason to try to outsource the library.

Centralization within a campus, however, is another matter. Here there

FIGURE 2. Percent Co-Authored from One Site

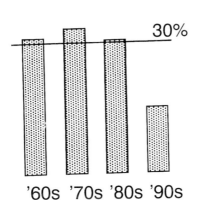

30%

'60s '70s '80s '90s

may well be cost savings without any perceived impact on the reputation or independence of the organization, and the value to the users of a small local branch library may not be defendable as electronics makes more services available at a distance. Furthermore, to the extent that separate libraries are supporting different kinds of collections (photographs, sound recordings, etc.) the electronic storage devices that support all of them decrease some of the reasons for keeping such libraries independently housed. A particular point where centralization or cooperation may be very important is preservation. In the digital world, just as in the traditional paper world, libraries will have to keep material around. Sometimes publishers may provide this service, but sometimes libraries will find themselves wishing to maintain digital files. This involves some degree of simple systems maintenance, and some reformatting for new software. Libraries may well find that it is more efficient to do this only once per document throughout at least the nation, if not the world, and need to organize how preservation responsibilities will be handled. A likely strategy, for example, is that only one library converts a document to a new format and then distributes copies to a few other sites to be safe against earthquakes, floods and hurricanes. The recipient sites would verify the copies and then absorb them. This saves effort at the expense of organization.

One example of cooperation is the United Kingdom system of purchasing site licenses for the entire academic community through the UK Office of Library Networking (UKOLN). This has given the UK libraries greater bargaining power with the commercial publishers, albeit at the expense of some flexibility for individual libraries. Cooperatives such as this also save administrative costs, and are likely to grow.

ORGANIZATIONAL STRUCTURES

The implications of digital technology, as explained here, are that physical acquisition, storage and circulation become less important. Training, searching, on-demand purchase, and other subjects become more important.

The top-level organizational units of the Cornell library, as posted on the Web, are shown in Table 2.

Even smaller libraries tend to have acquisitions, cataloging, circulation, and reference. Table 3 shows some other sample library organizations, sometimes with a more subject-oriented structure. What will happen to these activities in the future?

Certainly we will still have accounting, human resources, shipping/receiving, and development/public affairs. Human resources are likely to be more important as the range of skills needed in libraries increase. Acquisitions and Cataloging may change their focus to emphasize evaluation and helping

TABLE 2

Accounting
Technical Services: cataloging, ordering, receiving
Collection Development
Development and Public Affairs
Facilities
Human Resources
Access Services
Library Technology
Photocopy Center
Preservation/Conservation
Shipping/Receiving
Technical Services Support

users, rather than operating entirely behind the scenes. Collection development may become a more difficult task, given the need to consider the wide variety of stuff on the Internet and help users judge what is useful. Facilities, Photocopies, and Access Services (library cards) are likely to become less important, along with circulation, as more and more people use the library without walking in the door. Preservation will have a whole new set of problems, but will still be there. Library Technology and support will similarly face new problems but larger ones. And as mentioned before, efforts in legal matters and economics will probably be added to the plate, along with greater needs for reference services and training.

Cornell maintains a variety of specialized libraries in such topics as the Hotel School, Industrial and Labor Relations, Africana and Veterinary Medicine. Whether or not it makes sense to keep separate buildings for these subjects, the staff still needs expertise in the areas of staffing, budgeting, and cooperation.

STAFFING, BUDGETING, AND COOPERATION

Since no one foresees any lessening of the economic pressures on universities in general, libraries will still see severe budget limits. Yet the digital library movement adds a need for staff trained in computer technology, who

TABLE 3

Victoria University Wellington, NZ	Davidson Library, University of California Santa Barbara	Peking University Beijing, China	HK UST, Hong Kong
Architecture	Acquisitions	Acquisition	Acquisitions
Circulation	Arts	Ancient Books	Archives & Special Collections
Collection Management	Cataloging	Audio-visual	Cataloging
Law	Circulation	Automation	Circulation
Periodicals	Library Personnel	Branch Libraries	Collection Development
Reference	Map and Imagery	Cataloging	Document Supply
Technical Services	Reference	Circulation	Media Resources & Microfilm
	Sciences and Engineering	Document Services	Reference
	Serials	Logistics	Systems
	Special Collections	Reading	
		Reference	
		Serials	

are expensive, and any staff reductions seem mostly likely to occur among the relatively lower-paid staff who do physical materials handling. Reference work, and other interactions with patrons, will remain important. Libraries today are seeing increased traffic and circulation as a result of online catalogs; this also puts general burdens on buildings and staff.

Libraries may wonder where they can find technically trained staff. The number of computer science bachelor's degrees given in the United States dropped from 39,000 in 1985 to 24,000 in 1994. In fact, the general level of computer literacy is increasing greatly, and people can be found with the necessary skills, but not at the salaries traditionally paid for library assistants. As libraries become part of a vaguely defined "information industry" they will find themselves competing for staff with telecommunications companies, broadcasters, and publishers, plus new industries such as website maintenance. So they will need to pay higher salaries at a time when total budgets will continue to feel pressure.

What can libraries do about this? One possibility is charging for services as a way of boosting revenues; another is to try to cut costs further. Charging for services is disliked by a great many librarians (and some university administrators). There are new services in the digital world that don't correspond directly to services now provided free (e.g., delivery of information to dormitory rooms), but it seems unlikely that university students or university research grants are suddenly going to turn into a source of funds for library support.

Reducing costs seems more practical. If a few computer nerds can replace a great many shelving clerks, their higher salaries may still cost less in total. More practically, libraries might be able to cooperate in the provision of support services as well as in sharing collections. If library consortia could develop shared software packages, and perhaps maintain shared computer centers, this might help keep down costs at individual libraries. We might see a world in which what we now think of as a library is really just a staffed outlet, a branch, to some kind of backroom operation shared among several universities. The hope would be to minimize the amount spent on computer and backroom staff, in favor of money on reference staff and others providing direct service to the patrons.

An alternative to providing technical support to many libraries at once would be to try to share technical efforts with other parts of the university (as libraries now share building maintenance). Even today university administrative computing often supports libraries. The special needs of libraries (and for that matter of administration) are likely to render this rarer in the future. As the cost of computing becomes less and less hardware, and more and more software, the advantages of sharing co-located hardware decrease, while the advantages of sharing software with other libraries increase.

The easiest form of sharing is of course among branch libraries in the same university system. As more and more work is done in student rooms, and less and less in library buildings themselves, and as the need for special collections and special handling decreases, we can expect that reducing the effort spent in maintaining many branches will decline. Branches might become bookless "clinics" devoted only to help and assistance, or might be supplanted by telephone help-lines, perhaps using groupware programs to simplify the job of assisting a student. Again, as the physical location of more and more material becomes irrelevant, libraries will save money by not buying multiple copies of material, but by buying access rights and actually storing materials only in a few sites, located where land is cheap. The purpose of central campus buildings will increasingly be to provide personal contact for patrons, not storage of objects.

The organizational structure of the digital library thus looks more centralized in some areas and more distributed in others. Acquisitions and storage merge into a general capacity for information provision. That is probably managed centrally for groups of libraries, perhaps spreading across universities. Some of the provision is obtained by buying new electronic publications; some by converting older materials in the possession of the individual library; and some by licensing access from other libraries. Technical services becomes a computer program, run perhaps at a distance. Reference and training, however, are still local functions, and more important than ever, as it will be a while before the use of electronic resources is as transparent as that of books. Libraries will have to train their users in searching, in judging the value of what is found, and in the debugging of computer network problems.

Library budgets and administration are thus entering a time of flux. We can imagine a future in which virtually everything is digital, stored at sites related not to where they are used but where they can be found. Libraries spend their efforts helping patrons and not taking care of books, since the care and feeding of disk drives has been relegated to the remote centers. More of what librarians do will look like teaching, and it will deal more with people and less with buildings and materials stored in the buildings. Moving from this world to that one will be difficult in a time of limited budgets; substitution of electronic purchasing, closing of branches, cooperative agreements, and innovative ideas for services will all be needed.

CONCLUSIONS

The traditional library selects, stores and supplies information. Those functions are still around in a digital world. However, the selection will be increasingly on-demand, the storage may be off-site, and the supply may be electronic webpage delivery. These new techniques are more complex to the user, and will require extra training, assistance, and help. Perhaps the most difficult change libraries will face is persuading the administrators above them that they need to be valued and supported in different ways. Success as an academic library in the future is not a matter of piling up books, but of satisfying readers. The traditional metrics of books and chairs ("bums on seats," in the British phrase) won't make sense. Libraries need to be encouraged and funded to provide assistance to readers rather than raw material. They need to be evaluated on their success in reference questions, training, and not on acquisitions. Changing the administrative view that universities have of their libraries may well be harder than anything to do with CPUs or bytes.

AUTHOR NOTE

Michael E. Lesk, PhD in Chemical Physics, worked in the computer science research group at Bell Laboratories, until 1984. From 1984 to 1995 he managed the computer science research group at Bellcore, then became a chief research scientist there.

He is best known for work in electronic libraries, and his book "Practical Digital Libraries" was recently published by Morgan Kaufmann. His research has included the CORE project for chemical information, and he wrote some Unix system utilities including those for table printing (tbl), lexical analyzers (lex), and inter-system mail (uucp). His other technical interests include document production and retrieval software, computer networks, computer languages, and human-computer interfaces.

During 1987 he was Senior Visiting Fellow of the British Library, and he is currently Visiting Professor of Computer Science at University College London.

REFERENCES

[Corn] Joseph Corn, Imagining tomorrow: history, technology, and the American future, MIT Press, Cambridge, Mass. (1986); pages 58 and 190.

[Follett] Sir Brian Follett et al., Joint Funding Council's Libraries Funding Review Group: Report, HEFCE (Higher Education Funding Council for England), Coldharbour Lane, Bristol BS16 1QD (1993).

[Mellon] Anthony Cummings et al.,University Libraries and Scholarly Communication, Association of Research Libraries for the Andrew W. Mellon Foundation, Washington, DC (1992). Chapter 4.

[SFPL]. Elizabeth Reveal et al., San Francisco Public Library Strategic Audit, Coda Partners, Washington, DC (1997).

Collection Development
in the Digital Library

Daniel Jones

SUMMARY. Collection development of electronic resources presents added dimensions to the traditional library collection development model for printed materials. The basic functions of collection development in the digital library remain the same as for the traditional STM library. Applying these functions to electronic resources at this time requires increased collaboration and a broadening of the skills and experience of collection development personnel. A primary objective of collection development is to give structure to a collection of resources by organizing them in a meaningful manner. New approaches are being used to define what the collection is. *[Article copies available for a fee from The Haworth Document Delivery Service: 1-800-342-9678. E-mail address: getinfo@haworthpressinc.com]*

KEYWORDS. Digital library, collection development, electronic resources, basic functions, collaboration of skills, broadening of skills, organizing

In their book *From Print to Electronic: The Transformation of Scientific Communication*, Crawford et al. identify activities underway which suggest a very different type of library after the transformation has occurred. However, an underlying theme in the book is that the transformation to the totally digital library is far from complete; in fact, it may be very distant into the

Daniel Jones, MLS, AHIP, is Assistant Library Director for Collection Development, Briscoe Library, University of Texas Health Science Center, San Antonio, TX.

[Haworth co-indexing entry note]: "Collection Development in the Digital Library." Jones, Daniel. Co-published simultaneously in *Science & Technology Libraries* (The Haworth Press, Inc.) Vol. 17, No. 3/4, 1999, pp. 27-37; and: *Digital Libraries: Philosophies, Technical Design Considerations, and Example Scenarios* (ed: David Stern) The Haworth Press, Inc., 1999, pp. 27-37. Single or multiple copies of this article are available for a fee from The Haworth Document Delivery Service [1-800-342-9678, 9:00 a.m. - 5:00 p.m. (EST). E-mail address: getinfo@haworthpressinc.com].

future, and that STM libraries currently have a foot in both camps. On the one hand, they continue to provide the traditional print materials while, on the other hand, also incorporating electronic resources into the range of services they provide.

Collection development of electronic resources presents added dimensions to the traditional library collection development model for printed materials. Perhaps more than ever before, it requires a far greater level of collaboration within the library, with producers and distributors, and with library users. This article will address the range of considerations involved in the process of building a STM library collection that includes digital resources.

BASIC FUNCTIONS OF COLLECTION DEVELOPMENT

The basic functions of collection development in the digital library remain the same as for the traditional STM library. They are (1) identification of materials, (2) selection of materials, and (3) decisions related to the retention of materials previously collected. Applying these functions to electronic resources at this time requires increased collaboration with other areas of the library operations, and a broadening of the skills set and experience of collection development personnel.

Identification

Identifying basic information about a resource is essential before a collection decision can be made. Abundant resources are available from which to determine basic information (i.e., title, publisher, date, and price) about books, journals and other print materials. This is possible because print materials exist in a physical form, and a distribution system has developed to efficiently move them from the producer to the library. With electronic resources it is not always as simple. In some cases electronic resources are distributed similar to print materials and can be identified using the same resources. However, many electronic resources are distributed only by the producer, frequently a small software company, a society or an individual, with limited marketing and distribution resources or expertise, and thus they may not be available through established distribution channels making them difficult to identify.

Even when basic information about an electronic resource can be identified, additional information will usually be needed before a collection decision is possible. For example, one only need know that shelf space is available when selecting a book or journal for the library, but when selecting electronic resources it is essential to know if the library has the technical resources required to support it. Thus, additional factors must be determined such as computer platform and operating system, initial storage capacity and rate of growth, requirements for client software or other software necessary to manage the product, frequency of updates, network capability, user interface, medium in which it is distributed, pricing options, maintenance costs, user limitations (stand-alone, single- or multi-user), site limitations, etc. Frequently this information can only be found by talking with the producer, and it is possible the producer has not considered all these factors so that a process of negotiation may begin with the initial contact. Some electronic resources are accessed remotely and are not actually installed on library computer equipment, so the collection development staff may need to determine how this will be managed both by the library and the producer. The availability of opportunities to evaluate the product in advance of purchase should also be determined.

The identification process for an electronic resource can be time-consuming and laborious. It requires an understanding of the library's existing and planned computing and network environment, as well as an understanding of trends in the development of electronic information resources. Familiarity with traditional bibliographic tools must be supplemented with resourcefulness in using other information resources in order to have sufficient information to make a selection decision.

Collection development librarians and bibliographers need to understand and be conversant in the technical infrastructure required to support digital resources, and library systems and computing staff who manage this infrastructure need to find ways of keeping them informed as it evolves.

Selection

Traditional selection criteria, such as subject area and relation to the teaching and research programs the library supports, also apply to the selection of electronic resources in the digital library. In the STM library this is usually not difficult to determine. Other criteria which need to be considered in the selection decision include content, user interface, equipment needed, and licensing. The alternatives of local implementation versus remote access should also be considered. Any of these factors can halt, or at least stall, a selection decision. Consultation, evaluation and communication among interested parties such as potential users (including library staff and clients), subject specialists, and technical support personnel regarding the selection process needs to be coordinated in reaching a decision whether or not to select an electronic resource for the digital library.

Content

Content of a digital resource is a primary consideration. Factors to consider include the quality of the data or images, accuracy of the information, completeness with which it covers a topic, and the authority of the producers of the product. Subject specialists can usually advise the library in this regard, especially for non-bibliographic resources. For bibliographic resources the library should determine the coverage of the relevant literature in consultation with bibliographers and subject specialists. In STM settings current information is usually considered a priority by clients, so the currency of the contents of an electronic resource can affect a selection decision. For example, a database that is updated weekly or continuously may be preferred over one that is updated monthly, quarterly or annually. On the other hand, currency of content may not be a concern for finite data sets such the U.S. Census, or a database of chemical or physical constants.

In the case of full text databases the relation to existing print materials should be assessed to determine to what extent the electronic product corresponds with the print product, and whether or not this is a concern. For example, a full text database may only contain selected articles (frequently original research) and may not include review articles, correspondence, or news items. This may affect the selection decision if the library is seeking to replace a print product with an electronic one.

Interface

The interface is the point at which the product and its user interact. The interface should be appropriate to the product and the users needs. While a graphical user interface (GUI) is becoming more common, the character-based user interface (CHUI) may also meet the needs of the library and its users. Circumstances may also require that both types of presentation to the user are needed for certain electronic resources.

Whether or not the producer provides a user interface should be determined. The lack of a producer-supplied user interface may not necessarily be a decisive factor, especially if the library has the capability of providing a standard or locally developed one. For example, if the product is Z39.50 compatible it may be desirable to use a common search interface already owned by the library and already familiar to the users. Similarly, a hypertext markup language (html) file may be easily accessed using the inherent capabilities of a common web browser.

Compatibility with existing equipment must be considered. It is important to know the type of equipment that the intended users will be using. An interface that requires distributing client software to the user workstation may provide logistical challenges for users who do not have the appropriate workstation platform, operating system, memory or storage capacity. Even after client software is distributed one must consider the need for properly installing it, configuring it and updating it as new versions become available.

Assuming the appropriate presentation is provided, attention should be given to the ease of use and functionality of the interface. The needs of beginner or occasional users should be balanced with the needs of the advanced or frequent user. The ability to set a default interface for beginners with an advanced user option may be considered essential. The option to print or to control printing may be an important consideration, as could be the availability of downloading or forwarding retrieved results by electronic mail. An overriding concern should be the extent of training and instructional materials required for the user to successfully use the product, as this may have a significant effect on the utility of the product.

Equipment

Selection decisions for electronic resources can hinge on the availability of appropriate equipment. Alternatively, the availability of equipment may have little bearing on the selection decision if the resource is to be accessed remotely. Collection development issues associated with selection of remotely accessed resources will be discussed later.

All resources in a digital library need not necessarily be online at all times. The collection development process may result in acquisition of digital products before there is a demonstrated need. Such resources might be stored on a shelf until required by the user. Ultimately, when a user needs to access it, the availability of equipment will need to be addressed.

Certainly, a goal of the digital library is that all resources are stored online and always available in a networked environment. For selection purposes it is important to understand storage equipment requirements before a decision can be made. If the product is stored and runs from one or multiple CD-ROMs, then it may be necessary to acquire additional CD-ROM drives. If the product can be installed to memory on a server hard drive, then it is important to know how much space it will occupy in case additional storage capacity is needed. Some products are distributed on magnetic tape and the availability of tape drives for certain size tapes could have a bearing on how easily they can be stored online. Some legacy data may be stored on 80 column punch cards, so a card reader may be needed. While this may be an extreme example, it illustrates the importance of having the appropriate equipment to support a digital library collection and illustrates another issue, the need for migrating data to be compatible when new equipment, operating systems or software are implemented.

Digital storage is one end of the equipment continuum; the user workstation is the other end. The selection decision needs to take into consideration the number and availability of appropriately configured workstations to provide access to a digital product. This does not necessarily mean that all existing workstations should be able to access a product before it can be selected. A very desirable product may only require a single properly configured workstation to justify adding it to the collection. In any case, it is essential to anticipate the availability of adequate workstations to use a product effectively.

While collection development work does not require operational level understanding of computer systems and networking, a broad familiarity with these activities, and a close collaboration with people who are responsible for them will facilitate effective collection development in the STM digital library. Such familiarity will be invaluable to collection development personnel for effective communication with producers and interested users of electronic resources.

Licensing

Most electronic resources are distributed after negotiating a license, a written agreement that explains how they may be used. Usually, payment for a product covered by a license is a payment to *use* the product, not an outright purchase of the product or ownership of all rights to the product. This is a fundamental difference from traditional information resources, usually print material, provided by libraries. The result is that the library can have very specific, limited rights to the electronic product. A full understanding by appropriate library personnel of the terms of license agreement is essential before a selection decision can be made.

There are currently no standards for licenses, so each one needs to be reviewed carefully before it is signed. The primary objective of the library should be to negotiate a license that it can actually accept. It is common practice for libraries to seek changes in license agreements before they are accepted.

Proposed license agreements should be reviewed objectively. One should first determine if institutional or corporate support already exists for negotiating license agreements. The goal should be to identify what should be changed, added or removed from the proposed license. Care should be given to the definitions section, especially the term "authorized user." Changes or negotiations are frequently needed in sections of licenses that address where or how the product may be used, or how the library will control access to it, and responsibility for the actions of users. A proposed license may not grant the basic user rights allowed under copyright law, so the library should seek inclusion in the license rights needed for scholarship and research, educational uses and those rights considered fair use for print materials.

The following internet sites provide useful information on licensing electronic products:

- Association of Research Libraries. "Intellectual Property: an Association of Research Libraries Statement of Principles." http://arl.cni.org/scomm/copyright/principles.html

- University of Texas System. "Online Resources for Software and Database License Review." http://www.utsystem.edu/ogc/intellectualproperty/contract.htm
- Yale University. "Licensing Digital Information: A Resource for Librarians." http://www.library.yale.edu/~llicense/ index.shtml

Ownership

The concept of ownership of digital products can be complicated. In general, one owns what the license agreement states, which is often only a limited right to access and use a product. It is possible that the library does not even own the medium on which the product is distributed, such as magnetic tape or CD-ROM. Thus, an important part of the selection process is to understand the conditions associated with an electronic product in order to support it effectively.

Remote Access vs. Local Implementation

A final selection issue may be the option to choose between remote access and local implementation of an electronic resource. Remote access in this case means to provide access, usually via the Internet or a leased communications line. In general, the electronic product is stored and managed by the producer, or by a third party. Selection of this option allows the library to provide access to a resource but to avoid much of the overhead costs, such as equipment and staff, associated with providing access to it. Local implementation of an electronic resource may require significant infrastructure investments, both computing and network resources, and local technical expertise. In a large academic or corporate setting the infrastructure may be available for local implementation, whereas in a small specialized setting remote access may be the only realistic option. Security issues are frequently a significant concern in corporate settings, and so this may also be a factor in deciding for a local implementation if possible.

Another aspect of the remote access vs. local implementation issue is the expected use and desired response time for users. Response time over the Internet is not always predictable and at times access can be totally blocked by many factors. Where rapid and dependable response time is essential, such as in the case of a poison control center or a hospital emergency room, then a local implementation may be required.

Summary of Selection Process

The selection process is the initial phase of providing electronic resources in the STM library. Selection of electronic resources requires more than an understanding of subject matter. It requires a broad understanding of user requirements, of new categories of materials, and of the technical aspects of providing access to them. Especially in a large academic setting, this provides opportunities to expand the roles of subject specialists and bibliographers, and provides avenues for greater collaboration with library users and with their colleagues responsible for computer and network operations.

Retention

Decisions whether or not to retain print material in a library collection are usually associated with its inherent, enduring value and utility. Retention decisions about electronic materials require additional considerations. A primary factor to consider is the requirements of the license. If the license does not allow retention beyond a certain point and it cannot be renegotiated, then the library must comply with the license. Beyond the obvious license requirements, however, there are other factors to consider.

One of the great advantages of electronic products is the potential to monitor their use. Exactly what constitutes "use" can be debated, but assuming that the library can obtain meaningful use data, this can be used to determine whether an electronic resource will be retained.

Compatibility with evolving technology can also be a factor. Maintaining and supporting aging technology simply may not be feasible and therefore may force a situation where an electronic resource can no longer be provided. For example, it may not be possible to convert a whole information system written for an aging mainframe to a new computer platform. However, a data set such as physical constants may be easily transported to new media and new computer platforms. Thus, just as technology is an important selection criterion, it also can determine whether on not an electronic resource continues to be provided by the library.

CATEGORIES OF ELECTRONIC RESOURCES COMMON IN THE STM LIBRARY

Indexes

Electronic databases of many of the standard printed indexes have been available for a number of years. These databases contain references and usually abstracts of journal articles and a method for searching and printing references from the database. Databases commonly available in STM libraries include *Chemical Abstracts, Science Citation Index, MEDLINE, Current Contents, Biological Abstracts, Psychological Abstracts*, etc. They are available via dialup or Internet access, or are distributed for local implementations. Some are only distributed through third-party vendors with specially designed search interfaces.

Aggregations of Articles and Other Full Text

A fairly recent development has been the availability of aggregations of journal articles in databases. These are sometimes referred to as electronic journals or full text databases. In some cases they contain only selected articles from selected print journals and from selected books and pamphlets. Some only contain the text of articles and exclude illustrations, figures, etc. Distributors of aggregations include Information Access Company, EBSCO, and University Microfilms (UMI), and some society publishers.

Electronic Journals

The term "electronic journal" can mean many things. A common form has been an annual CD-ROM of articles from a print journal. There are currently no standards for their production and often each publisher has developed a unique approach. Because of this they represent many challenges for libraries and have not been widely incorporated into the concept of the digital library. A more recent trend has been the aggregation of journal titles into collections by various vendors, including OCLC's Electronic Collections Online and Blackwell's Navigator. These vendors provide electronic access, usually via the Internet, to a list of journals from which the library may select specific titles. Many STM journals are not yet available in this manner.

A trend among some commercial and society STM journal publishers has been to create their own electronic journals and provide access to them via the Internet. In most cases these are electronic versions of their print journals, but in some cases there is no print equivalent. One of the first STM publishers to do this was Academic Press (IDEAL). Others include Elsevier, Springer-Verlag (LINK), the Institute of Physics, the IEEE and the ACM.

Another variation has been for some journal publishers to contract with an electronic publisher to produce the electronic edition of their journals. An example of this type of collaboration is the partnership between a number of society journal publishers and the HighWire Press, a unit of the Stanford University Libraries.

Having described these various forms in which electronic journals are produced, it is important to point out that because many of them are available via the Internet, that DOES NOT MEAN that access is free. Nor does it mean that the electronic version is available at the same time, or sooner, than the print version. In most cases, the cost of the electronic version of a journal is dependent on the library having a subscription to the print version. In addition, access to the electronic version may cost a premium in addition to the cost of the print subscription. And some publishers, such as the American Association for the Advancement of Science (AAAS) which publishes *Science*, provide electronic access only to individual subscribers, and not to institutional subscribers.

Electronic Books and Reference Materials

The printed monograph is not dead. However, the role of the electronic book is evolving, especially in the STM disciplines. The time required to publish a book is growing shorter, but still it can take too long for developing areas. Electronic books can be updated and distributed rapidly. Many of these are still distributed on CD-ROM for local implementation, but Internet access to them may also develop. Some examples include *Scientific American Medicine*, a major medical text, and the *Current Protocols in . . .* titles of John Wiley & Sons.

These are a selection of the major categories of electronic resources provided in STM libraries. Other categories include data sets, image files, computer-based instruction programs, and test banks. They represent additional resources, not necessarily replacements for printed materials, that constitute the collections of the digital STM library.

ORGANIZATION AND PROMOTION OF ELECTRONIC RESOURCES

A primary objective of collection development is to give structure to a collection of resources by organizing them in a meaningful manner. The traditional methods of cataloguing and classification have been the primary tools for achieving this objective. These same tools should also be applied to collections of electronic resources. However, by their nature, electronic resources enable the library to expand the concept of the collection. No longer is it tied to a location on a shelf in a specific building. New approaches are being used to define what the collection is. The development of the web-based catalog allows direct links from the catalog record for a title to its content. In addition to the library's organization, bibliographers, subject specialists, faculty and individual users can apply their own organizational principles to key resources in their discipline on their personal webpages.

One of the challenges of providing electronic resources in a library setting is alerting users that they are available. Frequent users will be aware that a particular resource is available, but the needs of the occasional user or new user must also be considered. All users need to be alerted as new resources are added, and as significant changes or updates occur for existing electronic resources. Collection development can have a role here by preparing the text for press releases and electronic alerts to be used by the library to promote the availability of electronic resources. In addition, by providing bibliographers and subject specialists advance opportunities for learning to use new resources before they are made widely available, Collection Development can help assure a successful implementation of new electronic resources.

CONCLUSION

Collection development in the digital library applies many of the skills used to develop print collections. Resources must be identified, selected and decisions must be made about their retention. However, the nature of electronic resources presents new challenges for persons responsible for collection development. They need a greater understanding of technology, including hardware, software and network communications. And they must be effective in evaluating and negotiating licenses, and in communicating the terms of licenses that have been negotiated.

In addition, collection development in the digital library requires broadening of the degree of collaboration with subject specialists who frequently identify and instruct users in the use of new resources, and with technical personnel who are responsible for enabling them. And finally, they need to be effective in communicating with users about the full range of resources provided by the library.

AUTHOR NOTE

Daniel Jones is a graduate of Clemson University and Emory University, and is a distinguished member of the Medical Library Association's Academy of Health Information Professionals. He has served on the editorial board of *Serials Review*, and the *Newsletter on Serials Pricing Issues*.

Usability Evaluation
of Digital Libraries

Barbara Buttenfield

SUMMARY. This paper distinguishes evaluation procedures in a physical library from those in a digital library, reviewing usability evaluation work within a taxonomy of system design, development and deployment. Usability evaluation of digital libraries should follow two evaluation strategies. The first a convergent methods paradigm. Evaluation data are collected throughout the system life cycle using several different methods. Where comparable interpretations result, evaluators can make confident recommendations for system revision. A second strategy assesses not only the digital library, but the evaluation methods themselves. This self-referring analysis is termed a "double-loop paradigm" and allows evaluators to identify relative efficacy of particular assessment methods for specific library situations. The paper will present evidence for adopting these two strategies, drawing upon the user evaluation effort for the Alexandria Digital Library Project. *[Article copies available for a fee from The Haworth Document Delivery Service: 1-800-342-9678. E-mail address: getinfo@haworthpressinc.com]*

KEYWORDS. Evaluation procedures, digital library, usability evaluation, system design, development, deployment, convergent methods, system life cycle, self-referring analysis, double-loop paradigm, assessment methods, Alexandria Digital Library Project

---

Barbara Buttenfield is Associate Professor of Geography at the University of Colorado in Boulder.

This paper forms a portion of the Alexandria Project, funded jointly by NF, ARPA, and NASA (NF grant IRI-94-11330). Matching support from the University of Colorado is also gratefully acknowledged.

[Haworth co-indexing entry note]: "Usability Evaluation of Digital Libraries." Buttenfield, Barbara. Co-published simultaneously in *Science & Technology Libraries* (The Haworth Press, Inc.) Vol. 17, No. 3/4, 1999, pp. 39-59; and: *Digital Libraries: Philosophies, Technical Design Considerations, and Example Scenarios* (ed: David Stern) The Haworth Press, Inc., 1999, pp. 39-59. Single or multiple copies of this article are available for a fee from The Haworth Document Delivery Service [1-800-342-9678, 9:00 a.m. - 5:00 p.m. (EST). E-mail address: getinfo@haworthpressinc.com].

I believe it is time we take much more seriously the important responsibility we hold in adopting the technologies now rolling out of Silicon Valley workshops. We need to evaluate them carefully before we buy [into] them. (Nielson, 1981: 112)

INTRODUCTION

How can one tell if a digital library is any good? What are the criteria, what are the procedures for assessment, and how do results of an evaluation inform subsequent refinements of system design? Many books identify the challenges of user needs and assessments (see recent examples in Nielson and Mack, 1994; Rubin, 1994; Norman and Draper, 1986). The literature is particularly rich in the case of evaluations for computer systems and software testbeds. In the HCI community, a literature going back more than a decade points to a chronology of development, with ethnographic and empirical advances (Greenbaum, 1988; Strauss and Corbin, 1990; Dervin, 1992; Nielsen, 1993; Rubin, 1994; Bowker et al., 1997) paralleling technological progress (Laurel, 1990; Bricken, 1990; Cooper, 1995; Ntuen and Park, 1996: Shneiderman, 1998). See for example any of the CHI Conference Proceedings in recent years for a wealth of papers evaluating specific projects. The bibliography at the end of this article forms a sample, not a census: the list is too long to enumerate comprehensively.

This paper distinguishes evaluation procedures in a physical library from those in a digital library, and presents these distinctions as an argument for two evaluation strategies that should be followed. The first is the use of a convergent methods paradigm, whereby evaluation data are collected throughout the system life cycle using several different methods. Where comparable interpretations result, evaluators can be more confident in recommending design revisions. Allowing the various evaluations to converge has a second advantage, namely the assessment not only of the digital library, but of the evaluation methods themselves. This self-referring analysis is termed a "double-loop paradigm" and allows evaluators to identify relative efficacy of particular assessment methods for specific (classroom or library) situations. The paper will present published and anecdotal evidence for adopting these two strategies, drawing upon the author's experience leading the user evaluation effort for the Alexandria Digital Library Project.

HOW IS EVALUATING A DIGITAL LIBRARY DIFFERENT?

Evaluation procedures for traditional libraries were established (Lancaster 1977; 1993) long before network and computing technology could support digital libraries. Lancaster (1995) points to three general types of services that traditional libraries provide. Document delivery, question answering, and database searching each can be assessed in terms of effectiveness, cost per successful transaction, risk of incorrect information or a failed search, and benefit of a successful search. The expectation in a physical library is that over time, evaluation procedures will stabilize, and knowledge will gradually accumulate about what does and what doesn't work effectively.

> The author postulates that, while the digital library implies some fundamental conceptual differences, most obviously document access instead of document delivery, user objectives and evaluation criteria will not change *in substance* even where contents of the digital library may differ most profoundly from those of a traditional library (e.g., non-static items versus static items, items with fuzzy boundaries versus items with precise boundaries). Lancaster (1995, p. 1)

At the time Lancaster made this statement, digital library construction and evaluation were relatively new undertakings (Siegal, 1991). The concerted efforts spearheaded by the National Science Foundation's Digital Libraries Initiative had been underway roughly one year. Based upon limited efforts on these and other digital library work, it was reasonable to expect that the complexities of a physical library were understood well enough to anticipate their recurrence in a digital environment. Likewise, it was assumed that evaluation procedures could be re-drawn from the sketchpads of physical library evaluation. As with the physical library realm, patron needs for information will modify as they gather information. Patrons expect to focus on topical interests, not in struggling to learn the library organization (Kemeny, 1965). The intention is to shorten the learning curve. This drives the logic underlying physical library organization (books in the main stacks, current periodicals in a special reading room, maps and large or heavy artifacts in the basement, etc.).

Several assumptions about digital libraries stand out in particular contrast to the traditional library. First, the assumption is illogical that user needs in the digital library mimic the needs in a traditional library. A digital library is more than a physical library in electronic form. DeBuse (1988) for example, documents an electronic version of Robert Burns poetry with mouse click functions to convert words from the original Scottish dialect into everyday (American) English. As electronic documents can take on multivalent characteristics, formats, and functions (Phelps and Wilensky 1996), the boundaries between main collections and special collections become blurred. Patrons use a digital library for tasks that are not feasible in a traditional library. As discussed below, they sometimes use the digital library in ways that are not anticipated by system designers. Evaluation of the digital library must accommodate these important differences, in addition to Lancaster's traditional "cost, benefit, risk, and effectiveness" quartet. Second, it's important to remember that a digital library has something a traditional library does not have, namely an interface. This turns out to be something of a disadvantage. In fact, for the patron, it amounts to a "giant step backwards." It could be argued that in a traditional library, a reference librarian is a very intelligent, advanced "interface." That position not only patronizes and objectifies the librarian, it misses the point. The librarian can sense, respond, and interact with a user's elation, confusion, or frustration. The software interface cannot accomplish this, in spite of best intentions. Even though the interface may connect users with omniscient search engines, extensive map and metadata browsers, thesauri or gazetteers, it cannot "tell" the user where is the "best" Internet site to locate requested information, nor how to refine a query to insure success. The interface cannot in fact differentiate between a search returning wanted items from a search returning unwanted items.

Moreover, to most users, the interface IS the system. It cannot be said that the reference librarian IS the physical library. Patrons can work in a physical library without consulting a reference librarian. The patron in the physical library can often go into the catalog or stacks and work independently. In the case of the digital library, the interface is a gatekeeper to the collection. If the interface isn't understandable, or doesn't work, the digital library holdings remain essentially inaccessible.

Third, there are the so-called "moving target" issues that distinguish evaluation of a digital library. Particularly for Internet-based document delivery, one can predict with confidence that technology will change rapidly. None of the six awardees of the Digital Libraries Initiative Award foresaw the extent to which Internet accessibility would grow. In looking through the original proposals drafted in 1993 (NF, 1996), nearly all of the proposed testbeds were based on local network technology, not on the Internet. By June 1995, all six had shifted primary emphasis to coding in html. Two years later, in June 1997, all six had migrated wholly or in part to Java. Each technology provides new functionality, and likewise, new architectures. Patron needs tend to change in the face of new functions. Interface designs must also change, often dramatically. Knowledge accumulated under one technology may not be directly transferable to the next, and users may have to learn a lot with each successive version. Landauer (1997, p. 144) comments "Everybody is in a constant state of computer illiteracy."

Taken as a whole, these issues contradict Lancaster's statement above that the "document delivery, user objectives and evaluation criteria will not change in substance. . . ." In a digital environment, the assumptions of physical library evaluation do not necessarily hold true. Therefore, the knowledge base is thin for determining what evaluation methods are most effective. The

technology can and will migrate over time. New technologies will generate
new functionality, and possibly mandate modifying evaluation procedures.
Added interface functions can be expected to steepen the learning curve
while generating patron requests for additional functionality (Markusson,
1994). The dilemma is to evaluate a library which has not been completed
and which is expected to become functionally more complex, using methods
whose efficacy cannot be determined absolutely, and which may in fact not
be appropriate. Moreover, the results of evaluating one system iteration may
not prove repeatable for future iterations. At first glance, these seem insur-
mountable odds. In practice, the evaluator's situation turns out to be most
advantageous.

A TAXONOMY OF EVALUATION METHODS

Landauer (1997) distinguishes usability (ease of operation) from useful-
ness (serving an intended purpose), commenting that the two are hard to
separate in the context of evaluation. Strauss and Corbin (1990) argue to
involve the user on the premise that establishing the "situation of use" is
mandatory for rigorous assessment of needs and requirements. ". . . [S]ys-
tems development must explicitly include not only theories of use, but actual
users and instances of use" (Anderson and Anderson, 1995, first page). A
variety of evaluation methods have been developed, and variously referred to
under the rubric of user-centered design, user-centered evaluation, participatory design, socially grounded engineering, usability engineering, usability
inspection, or usability testing. The terms are not precisely equivalent (Nielsen, 1993). Throughout this paper, these terms will be referred to according
to the terminology adopted by various authors.

Four categories of methods evaluate usability of computer systems in
general. In automatic evaluation, usability measures are computed using
specialized software. Formal evaluation methods calculate usability measures using exact formulaic models. These two methods are not applicable to
highly interactive interfaces (Nielsen and Mack, 1994). Empirical evaluation
(usability testing) employs actual users; this type of method is used mostly
for summative evaluation. Informal evaluation (usability inspection) can be
applied to both formative and summative assessment, and relies on ". . . rules
of thumb, and the general skill, knowledge, and experience of the evaluators"
(Nielsen and Mack, 1994, p. 2). Both types of evaluation have been applied
to digital libraries, and where possible, that literature will be cited in the
discussion that follows. However, published evaluations of other computer
systems are far and away more numerous. Results of these bodies of literature
will be included where they clarify the discussion.

User evaluation methods could be categorized as being formative (intended to advise on system revision) or summative (intended to determine how good a system is overall, or in comparison to another system). They could be organized on the basis of Norman's (1986) seven stages of user activities, or upon the types of usability problems one expects to encounter (Cuomo and Bowen, 1992). Karat (1994) adopts a dichotomous categorization of empirical usability testing and informal usability inspection, distinguished on the basis of the degree of experimental controls placed on the social and technical environment created for the evaluation.

A taxonomy of usability evaluation methods develops naturally within the chronology of system design, development, and deployment. Design is the aggregate of all the thought processes to formulate a problem, draft and refine a set of operations to solve that problem, analyze the sequence to ensure operability, and decide upon the resulting (sub)set. One can design products, environments, or messages (Dent, 1990, p. 24). Development is the implementation of the architecture, generation of code, and establishment of links between various operations. A sequence of development often includes development of requirements, development of specifications, development of individual modules, and integration of modules. Because of the *Principle of Synthesis* (Mayall, 1979) that things working in isolation do not always work in integration, development tends to iterate with design. Deployment puts the solution into the hands of end-users. In actual use, additional system refinements may be identified and necessitate further iterations of design and development.

Evaluation During System Design

In principle, system design occurs in response to an identified need. The need to test an emerging technology is one type of identified need. This paper will focus on needs identified by users. User-centered design is driven by articulated needs for information, computation, or services (for example, browsing and retrieval from very large data archives). Most often user-centered design is based on "needs and requirements" study, or in ethnographic paradigms. Semi-structured interviews, videotaping, and observation are commonly integrated to establish needs. The assumption is that the impacts of a particular computing functionality are as much a product of social configurations as a consequence of technology alone (Kling, 1992; Star, 1992; Suchman, 1994). The goal is to define the everyday working environment, and representative types of activities. Insights about the social environment are considered significant factors in user-centered design. Justification for this position is based in the argument that *how* the software integrates into someone's daily workflow is as important as what someone does with software. "Design is accomplished by interacting with the world the system is about to join" (Anderson and Anderson, 1995, first page).

Examples establishing needs and requirements by methods of ethnographic evaluation (also called institutional ecology) may be found in diverse contexts: genetics (Star and Ruhleder, 1996); museum science (Star and Greisemer, 1989), nursing interventions classification (Timmermans et al., 1995), library catalog search (Cochrane, 1984) and digital libraries (Covi, 1996). Kling and Jewett (1994) and others (for example, Gasser, 1986) argue that new computing technologies and computing environments foster new forms of routine work. Evaluation based on social practice and ethnographic appraisal fits naturally at the design stage, since it is here that software functions are fit together with user needs and requirements. These methods also adapt to evaluating a deployed system (discussed below).

Task analysis studies provide a second type of evaluation that is appropriate to the system design phase. Potential users describe the steps and requirements for specific tasks that the system should accomplish. Tasks may be defined in the form of scenarios (Nielsen, 1987) representing specific examples of how the system has been or could be used. Scenarios control the emphasis of attention during evaluation to specific intended use (Gluck, 1996). Scenarios are mandatory for cognitive walk-throughs (described below) to structure the search for relations between user goals and user actions. Nielson (1987; 1994) argues that in some situations, scenario provision can constrain evaluation unnecessarily. Even when scenarios are not provided, evaluators will tend to create their own task orientation which is an ad-hoc form of scenario building.

Heuristic evaluation provides a third type of evaluation applicable at either the design or the development phase. The method is relatively easy to apply, does not require that the design be implemented except on paper, and requires very few evaluators: Nielsen (1994) recommends no more than five or six plus an observer. The procedure involves training the evaluators according to a set of heuristic principles (Nielsen 1993). Subsequently, each evaluator takes two passes through the interface design, searching for usability problems and components inconsistent with the heuristics. Evaluators work independently; the observer collates their separate evaluations, which inform the design revision. Jeffries et al. (1991) find that heuristic evaluation tends to detect a larger number of usability problems than do other methods; other authors (e.g., Cuomo and Bowen, 1992) dispute this finding.

Evaluation During System Development

When the system goes into development, a second class of methods can be applied. Characteristic of these methods is they may be adapted to the first pencil-and-paper version of a design; neither the system nor the interface need to function, necessarily. While the design is fluid, innovative ideas and scenarios for use can easily emerge. Actual users, potential users, and system designers can all be reasonably included in the evaluation subject pool.

Cognitive walk-throughs evaluate ease of use, and logical flow; evaluation is directed at the interface (Polson et al., 1992). Potential users work with paper mock-ups or screen shots. Interviewers guide users through a scenario and solicit discussion and questions about the interface response. Scenarios can be generated following results of ethnographic study, for example, if the development is partially implemented. The intention is that user response (acceptance, confusion, etc.) guides subsequent interface refinement. Helping users learn software utilizing scenarios that are specific to their intended use of the system ". . . insures that the cost of learning a new feature is in part determined by the feature's immediate benefit to the user" (Wharton et al., 1994: 105).

Lewis et al. (1990) note that the cognitive walk-through is narrowly focused; the advantage is that evaluators gain in-depth information specifically about the success of users specifying a sequence of actions. Other criticisms (summarized in Wharton et al., 1994) relate to the severity and specificity of identified problems, and to the nature of problems (usability, consistency throughout the interface and recurrent versus first-encounter problems). To stay on track during a walk-through, evaluators must keep extensive records of users' peripheral comments for later discussion. Even so, the method takes more time than others.

Similar in organization and rationale are requirements walk-throughs and code walk-throughs, where the developers of one or more system components step through the sequence of intended use. A group of peers offers critique and suggestions for refinement. The evaluation is narrowly focused, as with cognitive walk-throughs. Standards inspection and consistency inspection (Wixon et al., 1990; Wixon et al., 1994) provide other methods in this evaluation category. Here, the system is inspected by developers of similar systems for conformance (respectively) either to a given standard, or by relative comparison (one system against others). Both types of evaluation identify the developers' conception of using the system. In contrast, the cognitive walk-through evaluates the end-user's conception.

Evaluation During System Deployment

Deployment involves actual implementation, use and maintenance. Software engineers refer to "alpha-" or "beta-" testing, which mark the earliest deployment to end-users. Major design changes become more difficult following deployment, and it is at this stage that tensions tend to develop between evaluators, designers and developers. One hears a good deal of anecdotal evidence that evaluation in these cases did not begin until the deployment phase (Jeffries, 1994; Landauer, 1997). Evaluation should not originate at deployment, but should build upon prior evaluation originating at earlier phases.

Evaluation during system deployment can involve both usability testing and usability inspection. Many of the techniques previously described are applicable. The defining characteristic for this category is that evaluation involves actual use and actual users. Deterministic evaluation by means such as transaction logging and reverse engineering become appropriate at this phase. Transaction log analysis (Wildemuth 1993; Buttenfield and Kumler, 1996; Buttenfield, 1997; Gay and Mazur, 1993), also referred to as online monitoring (Birbeck, 1986; Borgman, 1995; Rice and Borgman, 1983; Penniman and Dominick, 1980), has a checkered chronology. A transaction log contains a timestamped sequence of every mouseclick or keystroke plus a timestamp of the complete system response. Patterns of transactions can be studied to identify specific typical and atypical behaviors, for example, cycles of searching action, instances of confusion (cycling back and forth between two options), and recurring misuse of system commands (Wildemuth et al., 1992; 1993). Proponents claim the method is ". . . unobtrusive, provides large volumes of data at relatively low cost, can be used to build quantitative models, and can assist in qualitative interpretations of quantitative models" (Borgman, 1995, first page). Critics argue that transaction logging tends to require large amounts of pre-processing before interpretation may begin, and that (particularly on the Internet) it is difficult to isolate individual users and individual sessions without adding special administrative code (user-ids, session counters). Moreover, network delays on the Internet can obscure timestamp patterns of use (Buttenfield, 1995).

Usability inspection methods adapt well to a deployed system. Talk-aloud protocols become practical once the development phase reaches the point where the system is actually "up-and-running" (Wixon et al., 1990, Lewis, 1982). Subjects work online, describing as much as possible what runs through their mind as they work with the system. Choosing a set of goals, setting priorities, selecting a sequence of interface functions, moments of confusion, etc., tend to emerge. Without some prior training, talking aloud in the midst of performing a task turns out to be more difficult to do than to describe. Commonly, subjects either stop talking, or stop working with the interface. An alternative that improved the data stream during the author's Alexandria Digital Library evaluation is to videotape a subject using the interface, and immediately ask the subject to talk aloud as they view the videotape. This elicits information from a different source, cognitively speaking, and it is important to keep the time short between videotaping and video playback.

Entry and exit surveys provide another method for evaluating deployed systems. A significant problem with Internet surveys is the high subject loss rate. Buttenfield and Hill (1997) note that the slightest perceived impediment to accessing pages in a complex Internet site can cause a user to terminate the session. Users are sensitive to overly long entry surveys (especially those involving self-identification, user-ids and passwords). Exit surveys show a particularly low response rate; many users simply jump out of the website. An alternative is to identify users and contact them off-line. Where possible, this method can inform evaluators on many levels. Bishop and Squire (1995) interview users of an online art gallery. Their data describe as much about using the gallery interface as about the pros and cons of putting any large archive on the Internet. Galleries ". . . face loss of revenue and control and the need to restructure operations throughout the organization, while creators face the loss of formal recognition and reward . . ." (Bishop 1995, third page).

Two other inspection methods should be mentioned. Pluralistic walk-throughs are ". . . meetings where users, developers, and human factors people step through a scenario, discussing usability issues associated with dialogue elements involved in the scenario steps" (Mack and Nielsen 1994: 5). As with walk-throughs, the scenarios chosen will guide the scope of discussion. Focus groups demonstrate a system to a group of potential or actual users, and subsequently record the semi-structured discussion that ensues. An alternative focus group technique briefs groups of individuals with diverse backgrounds about a software product. This evaluation may be completed during the design phase, well before deployment. The intention is to determine viable target user groups while the system is still under design. This method is often used for marketing surveys (Greenbaum, 1988). Focus groups need a good facilitator to manage group dynamics and stay on task (Wharton et al., 1994).

Evaluation by Convergent Methods

Evaluation should be incorporated throughout a system life cycle. Regular cycles of evaluation and testing are the expected norm for development of cars, dishwashers, and factory machinery, but software development most often operates contrary to this principle (Landauer, 1997). Often, the evaluation of a software testbed does not begin until deployment. Evaluation after deployment is of course important to validate intended function. But the need for evaluation during design and development is pragmatic. It is easier to modify a design in progress, and often requires less re-coding to revise a system early in the cycle. Evaluation early on can improve usability. For example, Landauer (1997, p. 282) cites development at Bell Labs of a voice-messaging system where cognitive walk-throughs on a system mock-up reduced use error to less than 1%.

Several authors compare application of the same evaluation method to different systems (Jeffries et al., 1991; Nielsen and Mack, 1994; Cuomo and

Bowen, 1992). Their comparisons are limited to usability inspection methods. None explicitly report the system status at the time of testing. Karat's (1994) comparison of usability testing with usability inspection includes a section on timing. She cites Whitten (1990) that the ideal positioning would include two walk-throughs during design and two iterations of usability testing during deployment. Noting that system life cycles often change unexpectedly, she recommends a "tool kit" of usability inspection and usability testing methods: "Having the flexibility to choose among methods and knowledge of the trade-offs in the different methods should give practitioners a good opportunity for success" (Karat, 1994: 217).

When multiple evaluation methods are applied, several outcomes can occur. When the results converge, interpretations from one method confirm the findings of the other. When equivalent methods are applied over and over to a single system, comparability is relatively straightforward. When differences occur, validity of comparisons is harder to establish. Differences may occur in the methods, the system, the target user groups, or in composition of the evaluation team. Particularly when a system life cycle spans several years, one must expect some differences. This is often the situation with a digital library testbed.

The *convergent methods* paradigm is applied in social science when one is uncertain that statistical assumptions can be met, or when one's focus is upon analyzing a technique as opposed to analyzing a data set (Blalock, Johnson). Instead of comparing a single method across multiple systems, one applies multiple methods to a single system, independently, and compares findings. The paradigm is not intended for confirmatory validation: the point is not to reject a null hypothesis at some given significance level. It is an exploratory venture, whose goal is to uncover similar patterns in the data using multiple tools. The complication for a software testbed under construction is that it changes continuously. Over time, it is not really a "single" system. Applying multiple methods to multiple systems can become pretty complicated, pretty quickly, as least as far as interpretation goes. One of the variables must remain constant. Therefore, convergent evaluations must be performed concurrently. This requires not a single evaluator, but a team.

The primary advantage is that results are comparable, within a design, development or deployment phase. Over time, patterns of findings tend to emerge. Repeatability of results lends credence to recommendations for revision, and sidesteps the issue of technology drift that is endemic to digital libraries, and other computing systems. As shown in the case study, an additional advantage is gained. One can not only assess the usability of the system but also can assess how informative is a particular evaluation method at a particular phase of the system life cycle. This characteristic has come to be known by the author's evaluation team as a "double loop paradigm," in the sense that its methods can serve not only as tools but as objects of evaluation.

CASE STUDY–THE ALEXANDRIA DIGITAL LIBRARY PROJECT

The Alexandria Digital Library (ADL) delivers comprehensive library services for distributed data archives of geographically referenced information stored on map sheets and series, photographic and satellite images, atlases, and other geographic media. "Distributed data" means the library's components may be spread across the Internet [http:// www.alexandria.ucsb.edu], as well as coexisting on a single desktop. "Geographically referenced" means that items are associated with one or more regions ("footprints") on the surface of the Earth. Geographically referenced information has been traditionally treated as a separate problem by librarians and data archivists, due to complexities of spatial ordering, layering, and spatial and temporal autocorrelation. Our intention is to eliminate the traditional distinctions made in libraries between general collections of books and text with special collections such as maps and photos. (Buttenfield and Goodchild, 1996, page 2)

ADL is a collaboration between the University of California-Santa Barbara, the University of Colorado-Boulder, and numerous federal agencies and private corporations active in spatial data production and dissemination. The project includes development of an operational software testbed, usability evaluation, and basic research to address technical impediments to the adoption of digital library technology. The system life cycle officially began in 1994, when ADL was named as one of six NF/ARPA/NASA Digital Library Initiative awards. The original NF solicitation articulated a requirement that 25% of the effort should be devoted to system evaluation and testing. A good portion of this 25% effort has gone into usability inspection and usability testing. The Alexandria Digital Library offers a vision and experience for usability evaluation over the past four years, and explains how and why convergent evaluation works.

It was clear at the outset that the fast pace of software development would necessitate a lag between evaluation and code revision. A decision to "freeze" testbed versions at various points to allow evaluation without slowing the software production was adopted. A simple plan, but difficult at first to implement. Early in the project, the freezes were composed of hypermedia mock-ups of preliminary screen designs. Curiously, results of cognitive walk-throughs of the mock-ups were criticized by funders at the six month review, who argued (contrary to all the literature) that walk-throughs could not be considered credible if based upon mock-ups. An unfortunate outcome was that the walk-through method was set aside until a digital catalog, working interface, etc., had been implemented. Valuable evaluation insights that should have been collected during system design were lost as a result.

The second "freeze" attempt was equally problematic. This time, the problem did not relate to a lack of understanding about usability inspection methods, but to problems of technology migration. ADL collaborated with ESRI (a major GIS software vendor) to produce a Windows CD-ROM version of the first, UNIX-based prototype. The intention was to put the Alexandria testbed into the hands of librarians who could not access UNIX. The interface was a multiple window GIS design with a Tcl/TK query dialog. Almost immediately after distribution of fifteen hundred CDs nationwide, Microsoft marketed Windows95. Major incompatibilities hung the CD-ROM version every time a Tcl/TK query was launched; usability evaluation was stymied once again. Soon after, the testbed was migrated to Internet technology. Using html, it became easier to freeze versions on a regular basis. A frozen version was ported to a public URL for usability testing, reserving an internal Web site for implementing new code. Periodically, a newly frozen version would appear on the public URL; to end-users, the process had the appearance of incremental change.

To be honest, the multiple method strategy was implemented as a consequence of the repeated usability inspection problems, not because of an initial theoretically-based intention to converge evaluation results. During the initial design phase, methods included ethnographic surveys of the University of California Map and Imagery Library (MIL), and cognitive walkthroughs of interface screen snapshots. During the development phase, videotaping volunteers and ADL team members was initiated. Online user surveys and focus groups to elicit user requirements augmented other methods. Following deployment, beta tester demographic data were collected to determine the user population, and later to define three target groups (earth scientists, information mediators (librarians and data archivists), and teachers of middle- and high-schools. Transaction logging was initiated at the deployment phase to monitor actual use patterns, and to create statistical models of the "average" user in each target group.

Informal evaluation methods to establish user requirements included tape recording conversations of reference librarians helping patrons at the University of California Map and Imagery Library (MIL), and focus groups at Santa Barbara and at Boulder Colorado with librarians, professionals in environmental sciences, teachers and students at all grade levels. The convergence of user needs and requirements informed design of ADL queries, allowing users to constrain their search by location, time, and theme (for example, "what ADL holdings display airports constructed on existing wetlands prior to 1975?").

An especially vivid convergence arose from comparison of videotapes with the transaction log data and exit surveys. Analysis of the transaction logs often showed patterns of disorientation, following initial deployment of the html Web testbed. This was not surprising, given that the version contained more than one hundred webpages. In exit surveys, users commonly reported feeling "lost in the library" as well as being confused about "where they were" in the process of constructing a location-time-theme query (in that version, a full query could not be completed without visiting at least seven different Web pages). Evaluators were videotaping an ADL system analyst about that same time. In a particularly endearing video clip, the analyst turns to the camera with a perplexed look; in response to his question "Hmmm. Where am I?", the evaluator chuckles and responds, "Why, you're in Santa Barbara, of course!" (Rae, 1995). The point of the story is not to poke fun at the systems developer, but rather to note the convergent information from transaction logs, videotapes, and exit surveys. The interface design was revised as a result of this convergence; one major change was the implementation of different colors of Web wallpaper to alert users to having entered the Library catalog, gazetteer, map browser, tutorial pages, and so forth. When usability testing demonstrated that disorientation still occurred, the catalog, gazetteer, and map browser were collapsed to a single "place" in the Library (all three functions are currently available within a single Java frame).

Scenario-building (also referred to as task analysis) provides another excellent example where results from multiple methods converged. Scenarios were collected by explicit and implicit methods. In interviews with patrons at academic map libraries (Buffalo, NY, Seattle, WA, and Boulder, CO) and at the U.S. Geological Survey Library in Reston, VA, the author recovered seventy-five scenarios by asking explicitly for activities using a digital library. At a design review meeting hosted by the ADL Evaluation Team in Leesburg, VA in 1995, participants contributed thirty additional scenarios. Online email available within the ADL testbed returned dozens of messages with scenarios embedded implicitly in questions asking for technical assistance. Scenarios were generated explicitly and implicitly during ADL consistency inspections: every six months, NF hosted a two day meeting for the six Digital Library initiative awardees to demonstrate and critique each others' software testbeds. Regular consistency checks allowed the developers to become users, for a short time, and provided a valuable source for evaluators to understand usability from the developers' perspective. Sitting near the software demonstration workstation where system engineers from other projects questioned ADL engineers, the evaluation team annotated dozens of scenarios woven into comments and questions ("How does your system respond to a request such as . . .").

More than one hundred fifty scenarios were collected in four years, with a good many duplicates or near duplicates. Commonalties emerged consistently between scenarios generated by explicit and implicit methods, summarized in the following categories of user requests for data:

1. of specific type (show maps of seismic activity);
2. about a specific place (tell about Juneau Alaska);
3. having a specific characteristic, such as data resolution (is 30 meter digital terrain data available);
4. to locate a place given a placename (I'm looking for my parents' hometown, I think it was called Heiderville);
5. that is historic (maps before the Gold Rush);
6. that allows change detection (advance of deforestation in the Amazon Basin).

User suggestions for adding system functionality provided two additional scenario categories:

7. interface display (animate water filling the land behind the Glen Canyon Dam); or
8. analysis and interpretation (compute the number of acres lost to agriculture when the land behind the Dam had completely filled).

A final area where convergence has played a significant role in evaluation can be seen in comparing the results of transaction log analysis with talk-aloud protocols and exit interviews. The convergence is that data are collected on what people say they are doing, *and* on what they actually do. Timestamps allow specific users to be identified during specific sessions, and have aptly demonstrated the double loop characteristic effectively. First, one can clearly identify and label use patterns in the logs, comparing transaction sequences with talk-aloud sessions. Second, one can use identified transaction streams to automatically parse other instances of similar behaviors from the log data. Automatic parsing can dramatically reduce the large data volume problems so often mentioned. Third, with exit interviews, one can distinguish between user delay and network delay, simply by asking the user what happened. This can eliminate data artifacts that could otherwise bias analysis of the logs. Lastly, sequences of user behavior in the logs can insure robust target group formation, and in some cases, avoid data loss. Preliminary analysis indicates that transaction patterns for the librarian target group differ from other groups, for example. One way to place a newly registered user in this target group relies on the beta tester demographics collected when a user first registers and gives their occupation. If they do not report an occupation, it may be possible to assign them to a target group on the basis of similarity with aggregated group patterns, instead of discarding the data or assigning it to a miscellaneous category. Resolution of this problem forms an ongoing research interest.

SUMMARY AND PROSPECTS

Marchionini and Maurer (1995) identify three broad roles of libraries: to share expensive resources, to organize artifacts and concepts, and to bring together people and ideas. All three roles support human activity. A digital library must surmount incredible challenges to meet all three roles, with changes to be anticipated in technology, intended purpose, and target user groups. At the heart of the design, development and system deployment lies usability evaluation, which establishes that the three roles have been achieved, and that user needs are supported. Ideally, one would prefer a self-evaluating and self-modifying system, as for example described by Stephenson's (1992: 107) "self-aware" Digital Librarian. "Even though he's just a piece of software, he has reason to be cheerful; he can move through the nearly infinite stacks of information in the Library with the agility of a spider dancing across a vast web of cross-references." A major contribution of digital library technology may be to advance knowledge and skill about usability evaluation closer to the point where humans may navigate digital archives with equal agility.

The Alexandria Digital Library offers a vision and experience over the past three years that demonstrates several important reasons why digital library evaluation cannot be based in the traditions of the physical library. The interface under development is unstable, due in part to ongoing development and in part to technology migration; thus each cycle of usability evaluation is performed essentially on a new product. As a consequence, the effectiveness of usability inspection and usability testing methods at particular phases in the software life cycle are difficult to determine. Moreover, technological changes can render knowledge gained from previous evaluations obsolete. The situation cries out for evaluators to keep an open mind, to explore their data rather than rely upon conventions established within much more stable constraints.

Convergent methods evaluation has been proposed as a paradigm to surmount these obstacles. Two advantages are cited, that evaluation data may be collected throughout the system life cycle using several different methods but without requiring complete knowledge about earlier system phases results to proceed. Recommendations for design revision should be made with confidence. Allowing the various evaluations to converge can be utilized not only to establish confidence in the digital library, but also to evaluate efficacy of the evaluation methods themselves. This provides a self-referring analysis, termed a "double-loop paradigm," which can lead to a streamlining of evaluatory methods. Over time, as the interface becomes increasingly functional, the double loop characteristic may be relied upon to determine particular situations in which a particular evaluation method can best inform system revision.

For a double loop, self-referring evaluation to develop, it is essential that a workable feedback process is established between evaluators and system designers. This will not happen through lip service to the principle, but by direct attention to self-study, as evaluators. "One way of dealing with these questions may be not 'just' to develop new methods and techniques, and focus on the practical level, but also to enrich our theoretical understanding of the user-designer-technology relations, and how they are constructed in various methods for user-centered design" (Markusson, 1995: second page). The dynamic tension between system design, usability evaluation, and system revision must be maintained through all phases of the digital library life cycle, if the priority of responding to user needs is to be maintained. The evaluators elicit user confusion, frustration, or recurring problems. The developers acknowledge the problems, and recognize that a number of additional problems will emerge as a consequence of fixing them. The designers protect against compromising a holistic conceptual solution. All three corners of this triangle should have equal credibility in resolving usability problems at this stage. The balance between what is imaginable, what can be implemented and what users expect is preserved by mutual sensitivity, respect, and acceptance that team efforts involve a lot of compromise. This is the ideal, at least.

AUTHOR NOTE

Barbara Buttenfield's research interests include cartographic knowledge formalization, spatial data delivery on the Internet, and information design for geographic modeling. A current project to evaluate the user interface for the Alexandria Digital Library is funded jointly by NSF, ARPA, and NASA. She is a member of the Mapping Science Committee at the National Research Council. Barbara is Past President of the American Cartographic Association, and serves on the editorial boards of *Transactions on GIS*, *Cartographic Perspecties*, and *Computers Environment and Urban Systems*.

REFERENCES

Anderson, W. L. and Anderson, S.L. 1995. Socially Grounded Engineering for Digital Libraries. *Proceedings*, 37th Allerton Institute, Graduate School of Library and Information Science, University of Illinois, Champaign-Urbana, 29-31 October 1995 (no page numbers).

Birbeck, V.P. 1986. Unobtrusive Testing of Public Library Reference Service. *Refer*, vol. 4(2): 5-9.

Blalock, H.M. 1979. *Social Statistics*. Revised 2nd Edition. New York: McGraw-Hill.

Borgman, C.L. 1995. Online Monitoring Methods for User-Based Design and Evaluation for Digital Libraries. *Proceedings*, 37th Allerton Institute, Graduate School of Library and Information Science, University of Illinois, Champaign-Urbana, 29-31 October 1995 (no page numbers).

Bowker, G.C., Star, S.L., Turner, W., and Gasser, L. (eds) 1997. *Social Science, Technical Systems, and Cooperative Work: Beyond the Great Divide*. Hillsdale, NJ: Erlbaum.

Bricken, M. 1991. Virtual Worlds: No Interface to Design. In: Benedikt, M. *Cyberspace: First Steps*. Cambridge, Massachusetts: MIT Press: 363-382.

Buttenfield, B. P. and Kumler, M.P 1996. Tools for Browsing Environmental Data: The Alexandria Digital Library Interface. *Proceedings*, Third International Conference on Integrating Geographic Information Systems and Environmental Modeling. Santa Fe, New Mexico, January 21-26, 1996 (no page numbers). Paper is also on the Web at http://www.ncgia.ucsb.edu/conf/SANTA_FE_CD-ROM/sf_papers/buttenfield_babs/babs_paper.html.

Buttenfield, B.P. 1995. Evaluating User Requirements for a Digital Library Testbed. *Proceedings*, AUTO-CARTO 12, Charlotte, North Carolina, 27 February-1 March: 207-214.

Buttenfield, B.P. 1997. Delivering Maps to the Information Society: A Digital Library for Cartographic Data. *Proceedings*, 17th Conference of the International Cartographic Association, June 1997, Stockholm, Sweden: 1409-1416.

Buttenfield, B.P. and Goodchild, M.F. 1996. The Alexandria Digital Library Project: Distributed Library Services for Spatially Referenced Data. *Proceedings*, GIS/LIS '96, Denver, Colorado, November 1996: 76-84.

Buttenfield, B.P. and Hill, L. 1997. *The Second Alexandria Design Review: Report on the Workshop*. Santa Barbara, California, 19-21 February 1997. On the Web at http://www.alexandria.sdc.ucsb.edu/public_documents/papers/adr2

Cochrane, P. A. 1984. The Library is a Growing Organism in the Era of Online Public Access Catalogues and Communication Networks. In: Mohanrajan, P.A. (ed.) *New Trends in International Librarianship*. New Delhi: Allied Publishers: 199-206.

Cooper, A. 1995. About Face: *The Essentials of User Interface Design*. Foster City, CA: IDG Books.

Covi, L. 1996. Social Worlds of Knowledge Work: Why Researchers Fail to Effectively Use Digital Libraries. *The Information Society*, vol.11(4): 261-271.

DeBuse, R. 1988. So That's a Book . . . Advancing Technology and the Library. *Information Technology and Libraries*, March 1988: 7-18.

Gasser, L. 1986. The Integration of computing and Routine Work. *ACM Transactions on Office Information Systems*, vol 4(3): 205-225.

Gay, G. and Mazur, J. 1993. The Utility of Computer Tracking Tools for User-Centered Design. *Educational Technology*, vol. 1: 45-59.

Gluck, M. 1996. Geospatial Information Needs of the General Public: Text, Maps and Users" Tasks. In: Smith, L.C. and Gluck, M. *Geographic Information Systems and Libraries: Patrons, Maps and Spatial Information*. Champaign, Illinois:

Graduate School of Library and Information Science, University of Illinois at Urbana-Champaign 151-172.

Greenbaum, T.L. 1988. *The Practical Handbook and Guide to Focus Group Research.* Boston: D.C. Heath.

Jeffries, R. 1994. Usability Problem Reports: Helping Evaluators Communicate Effectively with Developers. In: Nielson, J. and Mack, R.L. (eds.) *Usability Inspection Methods.* New York: John Wiley, 273-291.

Johnston, R.L. 1978. *Multivariate Statistical Analysis.* London: Longman.

Karat, C. M. 1994. A Comparison of User Interface Evaluation Methods. In: Nielson, J. and Mack, R.L. (eds.) *Usability Inspection Methods.* New York: John Wiley, 203-233.

Kemeny, J.G. 1965. A Library for 2000 A.D. In: Greenberger, M. (ed.) *Computers and the World of the Future.* Cambridge, Mass: MIT Press, pp. 135- 162.

Kling, R. 1992. Behind the Terminal: The Critical Role of Computing Infrastructure in Effective Information Systems' development and Use. In: Cottermna, W. and Senn, J. (eds.) *Challenges and Strategies for Research in Systems Development.* New York: John Wiley & Sons.

Kling, R. and Jewett, T. 1994. The Social Design of Worklife with Computers and Networks: An Open Natural Systems Perspective. *Advances in Computers,* vol. 39. New York: Academic Press, 240-293.

Lancaster, F.W. 1977. *The Measurement and Evaluation of Library Services.* Washington D.C.: Information Resources Press.

Lancaster, F.W. 1993. *If You Want to Evaluate Your Library . . .* Champaign: University of Illinois Press.

Lancaster, F.W. 1995. Are Evaluation Criteria Applied to "Traditional" Libraries Equally Applicable to Digital Libraries? *Proceedings,* 37th Allerton Institute, Graduate School of Library and Information Science, University of Illinois, Champaign-Urbana, 29-31 October 1995 (no page numbers).

Laurel, B. 1990. *The Art of Human-Computer Interface Design.* Reading, Massachusetts: Addison-Wesley.

Lewis, C. 1982. *Using the Think Aloud Method in Cognitive Interface Design.* IBM Research Report RC 9265 (#40713) IBM, Thomas J. Watson Research Center, Yorktown Heights, NY.

Lewis, C. and Norman, D. 1986. Designing for Error. In: Norman, D. and Draper, S. (eds.) *User Centered System Design: New Perspectives on Human-Computer Interaction.* Hillsdale, N.J.: Erlbaum.

Lewis, C., Polson, P., Wharton, C. and Rieman, J. 1990. Testing a Walkthrough Methodology for Theory-Based Design of Walk-Up-and-Use Interfaces. *Proceedings* ACM CHI '90 Conference, Seattle, 1-5 April, 1990: 235-242.

Markusson, R. 1994. Dilemmas in Cooperative Design. In: Trigg, R., Anderson, S.L. and Dykstra-Ericson, E.A. (eds.) *Proceedings* Participatory Design Conference, Chapel Hill, N.C., 27-28 October, 1994.

Markusson, R. 1995. "What Do We Mean by User-Centered?" *Proceedings,* 37th Allerton Institute, Graduate School o Library and Information Science, University of Illinois, Champaign-Urbana, 29-31 October 1995 (no page numbers).

Mayall, W.H. 1979. *Principles of Design.* New York: Van Nostrand Reinhold.

Nielsen, J. 1993. *Usability Engineering*. Boston: Academic Press.

Nielson, B. 1981. Technological Change and Professional Identity. In Smith, L.C. (ed.) *New Information Technologies–New Opportunities*. 18th Clinic on Library Applications of Data Processing, Champaign-Urbana, 26-29 April 1981: 101-113.

Nielson, J. 1987. Using Scenarios to Develop User-Friendly Videotex Systems. *Proceedings*, NordDATA'87 Joint Scandinavian Computer Conference, Trondheim, Norway 15-18 June 1987: 133-138.

Nielson, J. 1994. Heuristic Evaluation. In: Nielson, J. and Mack, R.L. (eds.) *Usability Inspection Methods*. New York: John Wiley: 25-61.

Nielson, J. and Mack, R.L. (eds.) 1994. *Usability Inspection Methods*. New York: John Wiley.

Norman, D. and Draper, S. 1986. *User-Centered System Design: New Perspectives on Human-Computer Interaction*. Hillsdale, NJ: Erlbaum.

Ntuen, C.A. and Park, E.H. (eds) 1996. *Human Interaction with Complex Systems: Conceptual Principles and Design Practice*. Boston, MA: Kluwer.

Penniman, W.D. and Dominick, W.D. 1980. Monitoring and Evaluation of Online Information System Usage. *Information Processing and Management*, vol. 16(1): 17-35.

Phelps, T.A. and Wilensky, R. 1996. Multivalent Documents: Inducing Structure and Behavior in Online Digital Documents. *Proceedings* of the 29th Hawaii International Conference on System Science, Maui, Hawaii, January 3-6, 1996. ftp://ftp.cs.berkeley.edu/ucb/people/ phelps/papers/mvd_hicss96.s.gz

Polson, P., Lewis, C., Rieman, J., and Wharton, C. 1992. Cognitive Walkthroughs: A Method for Theory-Based Evaluation of User Interfaces. *International Journal of Man-Machine Sutides*, vol. 36: 741-773.

Rae, M.R 1995. Personal Email Communication with the Alexandria Digital Library Videotape Archivist.

Rice, R.E. and Borgman, C. L. 1983. The Use of Computer-Monitored Data in Information Science and Communication Research. *Journal of the American Society for Information Science*, vol. 34(4): 247-256.

Rubin, J. 1994. *Handbook of Usability Testing: How to Plan, Design, and Conduct Effective Tests*. New York: John Wiley and Sons.

Shneiderman, B. 1998. *Designing the User Interface: Strategies for Effective Human-Computer Interaction*. Third Ed. Reading, MA: Addison-Wesley.

Siegal, M.A. (ed.) 1991. *Design and Evaluation of Computer/Human Interfaces: Issues for Librarians and Information Scientists*. 28th Clinic on Library Applications of Data Processing, Champaign-Urbana, 5-7 April, 1991.

Star, S. L. and Griesemer, J. 1989. Institutional ecology, Translations, and coherence: Amateurs and Professionals in Berkeley's Museum of Vertebrate Zoology, 1907-1939. *Social Studies of Science*, vol. 19: 387-420.

Star, S.L and Ruhleder, K. 1996. Steps Toward an Ecology of Infrastructure: Design and Access for Large Information Spaces. *Information Systems Research*, vol. 7(1): 111-134.

Star, S.L. 1992. The Trojan Door: Organizations, Work and the "Open Black Box." *Systems Practice*, vol. 5(4); 395-410.

Stephenson, N. 1992. *Snowcrash*. New York: Bantam.

Strauss, A. and Corbin, J. 1990. *Basics of Qualitative Research: Grounded Theory, Procedures and Techniques*. Newbury Park, CA: Sage Publications.

Suchman, L.A. 1994. Working Relations of Technology Production and Use. *Computer Supported Cooperative Work*, vol. 2; 21-39

Timmermans, S., Bowker, G.C. and Star, S.L. 1995. The Architecture of Difference: Visibility, Control, and Comparability in Building a Nursing Interventions Classification. In: Mol, A.M. and Berg, M. (eds.) *Differences in Medicine: unraveling practices, techniques, and bodies*, 1998.

Wall, P. and Mosher, A. 1994. Representations of Work: Bringing Designers and Users Together. In: Trigg, R., Anderson, S.L. and Dykstra-Ericson, E.A. (eds.) *Proceedings* of the Participatory Design Conference, Chapel Hill, N.C., 27-28 October, 1994: 87-98.

Wall, P. and Mosher, A. 1994. Representations of Work: Bringing Designers and Users Together. *Proceedings* of the Participatory Design Conference, Chapel Hill, NC: 87-98.

Wharton, C., Rieman, J., Lewis, C. Polson, P. 1994. The Cognitive Walkthrough Method: A Practitioner's Guide. In: Nielson, J. and Mack, R.L. (eds.) *Usability Inspection Methods*. New York: John Wiley: 105-139.

Whitten, N. 1990. *Managing Software Projects: Formula for Success*. New York: John Wiley & Sons.

Wildemuth, B. M. 1993. Post-positivist Research: Two Examples of Methodological Pluralism. *Library Quarterly*, vol. 63: 450-468.

Wildemuth, B.M., de Bliek, R., and Friedman, C. 1993. Measures of Searcher Performance: A Psychometric Evaluation. *Information Processing and Management*, vol. 29: 533-550.

Wildemuth, B.M., de Bliek, R., He, S. and Friedman, C. 1992. Search Moves Made by Novice End Users. *Proceedings*, 29th Conference of the American Society of Information Science, Pittsburgh, PA, 26-29 October: 154-161.

Wixon, D. Holztblatt, K. and Knox, S. 1990. Contextual Design: An Emergent View of System Design. *Proceedings* ACM CHI'90 Conference, Seattle, Washington 1-5 April 1990: 329-336.

New Search and Navigation Techniques in the Digital Library

David Stern

SUMMARY. The introduction of technology into library information systems has provided new and enhanced search powers in the following areas: the speed of searching large individual and federated databases, keyword access, access to value-added metadata, customized interfaces (that relieve the burden of difficult techniques for sophisticated options), combinatorics for citation and semantic analysis, post-search relevancy analysis, release from the cost recovery scenario, and smart agent assistance. These advances save time, provide new research possibilities, and create new data relationships and research areas. However, there are still many areas in which improvements are needed: filters for handling information overload, cross-database searching standards, subject schema normalization, and balancing the need for subject-specific customization and cross-disciplinary standardization. Regardless of the technological advances, there will always be a need for critical thinking skills in order to perform an adequate research search. *[Article copies available for a fee from The Haworth Document Delivery Service: 1-800-342-9678. E-mail address: getinfo@haworthpressinc.com]*

KEYWORDS. Search and navigation techniques, digital library, enhanced search powers, metadata, customized interfaces, citation and semantic analysis, post-search relevancy analysis, smart agent, subject schema normalization, standardization

---

David Stern is Director of Science Libraries and Information Services, Yale University.

[Haworth co-indexing entry note]: "New Search and Navigation Techniques in the Digital Library." Stern, David. Co-published simultaneously in *Science & Technology Libraries* (The Haworth Press, Inc.) Vol. 17, No. 3/4, 1999, pp. 61-80; and: *Digital Libraries: Philosophies, Technical Design Considerations, and Example Scenarios* (ed: David Stern) The Haworth Press, Inc., 1999, pp. 61-80. Single or multiple copies of this article are available for a fee from The Haworth Document Delivery Service [1-800-342-9678, 9:00 a.m. - 5:00 p.m. (EST). E-mail address: getinfo@haworthpressinc.com].

61

PAPER BASED SEARCHING

Traditional paper-based library searching for monograph and journal materials involved searching for author, title, and subjects using card catalogs and indexing and abstracting tools. Advanced search techniques utilized controlled vocabulary/hierarchy arrangements and key-word-in-context (KWIC) listings. Some tools even incorporated unique card filing and sorting using holes in cards and rods or overlay screening techniques. Review articles and monographs (e.g., Annual Review of . . ., Advances in . . .) were also important tools for researchers attempting to stay current within specific disciplines. Browsing the full text of current and archival materials, and table-of-contents services, was another important way of discovering material.

FIRST GENERATION ONLINE SEARCHING

The major advantage provided by the first generation of online searching tools was the ability to search for keywords from any and all fields in a record. This ability to use Boolean AND/OR/NOT commands within selected fields of MARC and A&I records provided powerful finding aids and research opportunities for scholars. The searching of keywords within the usual selection of paper-based access points was an important advance, but searching was also significantly enhanced through the ability to search other fields such as dates, media type, language, and publication type (e.g., reviews, articles, conferences). The ability to explode and combine subject thesauri terms allowed for the development of even more sophisticated search strategies. Full text searching provided additional access points, but demonstrated a need for greater precision techniques such as relevancy analysis.

This proliferation of advanced search options created confusion for all searchers, and was a serious deterrent to creating enduser searchers. The proliferation of nonstandard conventions for basic searching across different vendor products made the search process even more perplexing for any searcher regardless of theoretical understanding or experience with the variety of systems. Basic protocols such as the codes for search(find)/print/limit, the truncation symbol, the way to limit to specific fields, and the default set of fields were often quite different and online help was hard to find. Some services even had very archaic programming conventions such as the OCLC 4,2,2,1 entry of letters from title words. Online searching was not intuitive. A great deal of time and effort went into the explanation and documentation (i.e., cheat sheets) of searching techniques. Classic lookup tables of equivalent commands were taped above search terminals in most libraries (right beside the phone numbers, passwords, and instructions for how to dial-up via modem).

The migration from dumb terminals to personal computers allowed for some automation of tasks associated with this complex online process. The development of better auto logon telecommunications software that could script logons and capture search sessions to disk made the search process much easier–searchers could then concentrate on the search itself rather than the process. The creation of search strategies using the various protocols was quite time and labor intensive, and often required a conference with the researcher before going online. Most searchers strongly recommended that researchers attend and collaborate during the actual search session.

Often these command mode operations were performed under the added pressure of cost considerations. While online library catalogs were free, many of the first generation A&I services were billed on a cost-recovery transactional basis. Costs were determined by a combination of online time, number of search statements entered, and number of results viewed. Even the speed of a modem could significantly affect the cost of a search. There is not a worse way to learn to search than when you are worried about the cost involved in (1) typographical mistakes, (2) the need to reenter search statements in various combinations, and (3) reviewing titles for relevancy while the clock is ticking in the background. Even the development of pre-search strategy building software did not completely remove this pressure since the great majority of good searches are based upon an interactive process which requires a real-time online session.

An attempt to provide a less stressful search environment was the introduction of a new set of pricing models and interfaces aimed directly at the enduser. The major search services marketed easy to use interfaces for specific enduser groups such as the medical community and corporate searchers. After-hour discounts were also offered for certain sets of databases, primarily in the academic community. (These easy to use interfaces naturally migrated to the WWW over time.) Many of these enduser services offered discounted prices by providing less powerful search systems, either through stripped down options (e.g., no truncation or field limits) or through offering subsets of the complete databases.

The next major change in user searching occurred due to the development and distribution of a new technology: the Compact Disk-Read Only Memory (CD-ROM) device. This personal computer device allowed for relatively inexpensive stand-alone local storage and searching of large data sets in an apparently free (to the user) scenario. This unlimited, unpressured search capability allowed users to spend much more time exploring the capabilities of these search engines and databases. Many users began to skip the intermediary librarian searcher and perform their own searches. This resulted in some very knowledgeable endusers, and also some very bad search strategies. At this point librarians began to emphasize the creation of appropriate search strategies within instruction sessions in much more detail than they had when patrons were using paper indexes. A learning curve was developing in response to both the added power and the return of control of the research process to the enduser.

The development of the Windows operating system made the user interfaces to these CD-ROM tools much more intuitive. Pull-down options replaced memorized command-code key combinations. Search, mark, and print options were clearly presented on the screen with context sensitive help (see Figure 1). Unfortunately, not all Windows based interfaces were equal; many proprietary protocols were developed that confused the users of more than one product, some had terrible design and performance, and many assumed the user had previous experience with and an understanding of Windows.

Unrelated to the CD-ROM technology, and often limited to the traditional "online" remote systems, were other improvements such as the development of cross-index searching, cross-database searching, and the related ability to

FIGURE 1

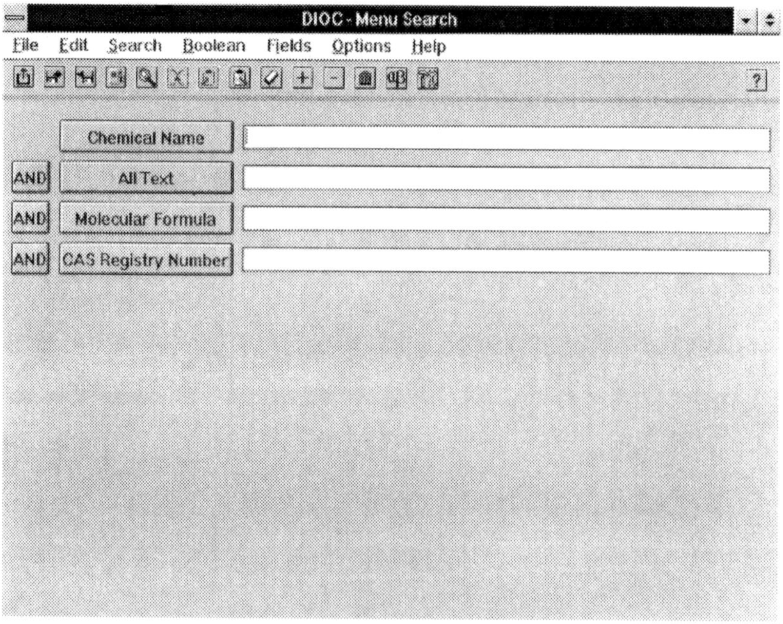

remove or cluster duplicates. Cross-index searching, the ability to quickly and cheaply search multiple indexes in order to identify the most appropriate databases from among the ever increasing list of resources, was the first attempt to address the alarming issue of information overload. The ability to search related databases at one time was an early attempt to provide in-depth interdisciplinary investigation across subject-based tools. Issues not resolved through this approach included the normalization of database-specific thesauri, variances in indexing practices across databases, cross-database searching of resources provided on different proprietary systems, and even variances in the searching of the same database over different time segments.

The local mounting of supplemental A&I databases on library OPACs resulted in the creation of search interfaces which often mimicked the traditional online catalog options (see Figure 2). These Z39.50 compliant interfaces often offered severely limited capabilities when compared to dedicated A&I search systems. The loading of full text files onto OPACs, with indexing which was designed for MARC records, often further reduced or obscured the implementation of possible search options.

The first generation of online search tools could provide a great deal of

FIGURE 2. A vt100 OPAC interface to a locally mounted database.

```
                        Expanded Academic Index
                              Introduction
-----------------------------------------------------------------
             INTRODUCTION TO EXPANDED ACADEMIC INDEX (ACAD)

Expanded Academic Index (ACAD) is an index to citations in the fields of
the arts, humanities, social sciences, and general sciences. It covers over
1500 scholarly and general-interest English-language publications, including
the New York Times, and contains information from 1985 to the present. The
database is produced and copyrighted by the Information Access Company and
is updated monthly.
             SEARCH OPTIONS:        TYPE:
             TITLE OF ARTICLE       t=assembling california
             AUTHOR                 a=berube michael
             SUBJECT HEADING        s=political correctness
             KEYWORD                k=suffragettes and art
For an explanation of title (t=), author (a=), subject (s=), or keyword (k=)
searches, type exp t, exp a, exp s, or exp k.
-----------------------------------------------------------
             Enter search command
             NEWs


NEXT COMMAND:
```

power, but required a good deal of effort to perform sophisticated searches. This steep learning curve probably resulted in many users unknowingly obtaining valuable but incomplete information. Another result was the frequent lack of searching for any data earlier than that found online. Through a combination of misinformation, in part due to unreasonable user expectations about what is actually available on computers, and human nature, the average searcher often failed to locate important information from important paper-based information sources. There are many dangers in expecting computer databases and software to adequately reproduce the comprehensive research and identification work of scholars.

SECOND GENERATION SEARCHING

The first generation of online search tools were based upon improved technology. Enhancements were found in online telecommunications software, PC applications software, faster hardware, local storage devices, etc. The result of this evolution was better interfaces providing easier librarian and enduser searching (see Figure 3).

The second generation of searching was dependent upon a combination of improved technologies and enhanced data. New techniques for identifying relevant or related items became available in generic and customized database applications. Often these were the result of better computer combinatorics capabilities. Other improvements were due to improved interface or network capabilities. Significant improvements were also due to the addition of (or access to) value-added data within the primary database(s). The recent development of object-oriented databases now allows for new types of user-database interactions.

The following section highlights selected examples of advances in this second stage of online searching.

Bibliometric Analysis

One of the most important supplemental tools to keyword searching is that of bibliometric analysis. While there are many factors that must be considered when using these techniques, it is undeniable that cluster analysis of citation data and patterns is a powerful way to identify related items. The use of citation techniques to identify quality is a much more complex and controversial topic that is covered elsewhere. The ISI Citation Indexes, in their many formats and manifestations, have provided a variety of relational links between journal articles. Individual articles have served as the roots of tree structures of historical citations, in this way identifying the development of

FIGURE 3

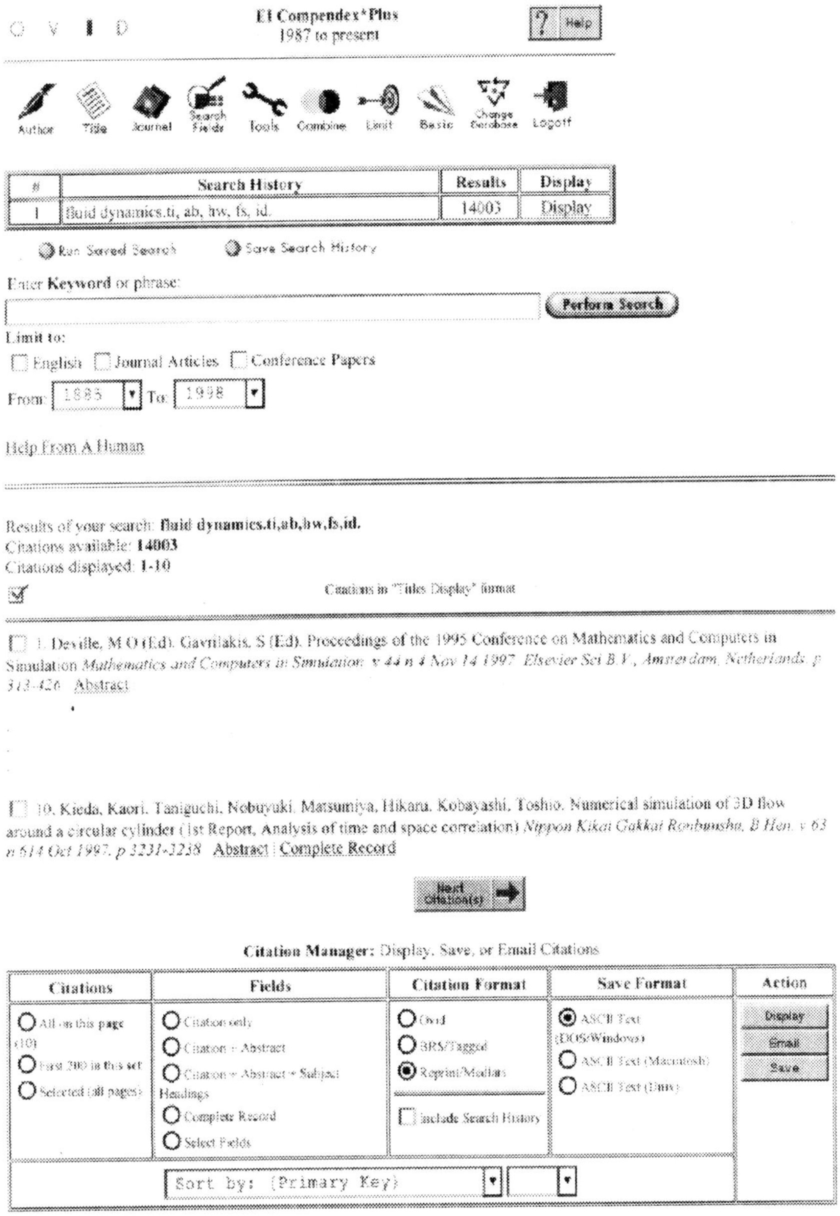
O V I D
Ei Compendex*Plus
1987 to present
? Help
Author Title Journal Search Fields Tools Combine Limit Basic Change Database Logoff
Search History Results Display
1 fluid dynamics.ti, ab, hw, fs, id. 14003 Display
Run Saved Search Save Search History
Enter Keyword or phrase:
Perform Search
Limit to:
English Journal Articles Conference Papers
From: 1885 To: 1998
Help From A Human
Results of your search: fluid dynamics.ti,ab,hw,fs,id.
Citations available: 14003
Citations displayed: 1-10
Citations in "Titles Display" format
1. Deville, M O (Ed). Gavrilakis, S (Ed). Proceedings of the 1995 Conference on Mathematics and Computers in Simulation Mathematics and Computers in Simulation v 44 n 4 Nov 14 1997 Elsevier Sci B.V., Amsterdam, Netherlands p 313-426 Abstract
10. Kieda, Kaori. Taniguchi, Nobuyuki. Matsumiya, Hikaru. Kobayashi, Toshio. Numerical simulation of 3D flow around a circular cylinder (1st Report, Analysis of time and space correlation) Nippon Kikai Gakkai Ronbunshu, B Hen. v 63 n 614 Oct 1997. p 3231-3238 Abstract | Complete Record
Next Citation(s)
Citation Manager: Display, Save, or Email Citations
Citations Fields Citation Format Save Format Action
All on this page (10)
First 200 in this set
Selected (all pages)
Citation only
Citation + Abstract
Citation + Abstract + Subject Headings
Complete Record
Select Fields
Ovid
BRS/Tagged
Reprint/Medlars
Include Search History
ASCII Text (DOS/Windows)
ASCII Text (Macintosh)
ASCII Text (Unix)
Display
Email
Save
Sort by: (Primary Key)

research fronts. Using author citations one can explore the earlier stages of these same fields. Related records find non-cited articles through an analysis of other cited reference lists. Additional searchable keywords are added to records through a similar analysis of cited titles (see Figure 4).

ISI also markets spin-offs of these analyses as separate products for administrative use. Institutional and departmental rankings by number of articles, number of citations, and impact factors are provided in customized

FIGURE 4

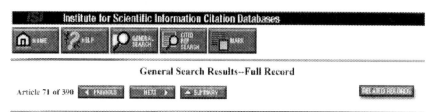

Institute for Scientific Information Citation Databases

HOME   HELP   GENERAL SEARCH   CITED REF SEARCH   MARK

General Search Results--Full Record

Article 71 of 390   ◄ PREVIOUS   NEXT ►   ▲ SUMMARY   RELATED RECORDS

SGML DOCUMENTS - A BETTER SYSTEM FOR COMMUNICATING KNOWLEDGE
STERN D
SPECIAL LIBRARIES
86: (2) 117-124 SPR 1995

Document type: Article   Language: English   Cited References: 3   Times Cited: 1

Abstract:
The use of SGML-based (Standard Generalized Markup language) documents and databases can provide enhanced access and display capabilities when compared to the files and indexes now available through most local or remote databases. These options are increased tremendously due to the structured nature of the SGML files. This article will attempt to outline some of the basic features of SGML and discuss their implications when compared to the utilities of other document and database types. It will also attempt to identify the areas needing further development in order to allow these SGML knowledge information systems to improve researchers' searching, display, and manipulation of electronically stored data. Particular emphasis will be placed upon possible enhancements to the currently limited print display imitation of most current electronic journals.

Addresses:
STERN D, YALE UNIV, SCI LIB, NEW HAVEN, CT 06520.
YALE UNIV, INFORMAT SERV, NEW HAVEN, CT 06520.

Publisher:
SPECIAL LIBRARIES ASSN, WASHINGTON

IDS Number:
QU457

ISSN:
0038-6723

Article 71 of 390   ◄ PREVIOUS   NEXT ►   ▲ SUMMARY

reports or as a portion of the University Science Indicators product. Individual author rankings can be generated for purposes of promotion and tenure documentation. The Journal Citation Reports product can be used to evaluate the citation patterns for individual journals.

Information specialists have utilized increasing computer capabilities to supplement and enhance the traditional search and evaluation processes. In particular, the use of these citation links was an innovative attempt to overcome the problems of differences in vocabulary within interdisciplinary searching. Of course the success of this approach does depend to a certain extent upon the authors crossing boundaries in their initial citations when semantic analysis produces few matches.

SDI

Another powerful tool for searching is the use of Selective Dissemination of Information (SDI) profiles. These strategies are created once and then saved and run against each new load of information into the identified databases. Search results are automatically delivered to the enduser. This classic online searching technique has recently become popular in the general literature under the term "push technology."

There is a strong demand for technology that proactively filters information for researchers with little time to browse and/or read the overwhelming amount of data within even their own areas of specialization. The increase in specialty journals is partially the result of researchers developing a paper-based way of filtering the most important published information for their particular needs from within the larger universe of their discipline. Of course there is a danger of becoming too isolated if this is the only way in which you see new ideas, as it has been shown that research benefits from the infusion of new ideas from other disciplines. The access to pre-publication material is becoming a very important information channel that is left out if one only reads paper-based peer reviewed material. Searching online A&I databases and Internet sites could simultaneously search pre-print and non-peer review material.

Customized Interfaces

Customized interfaces, made possible by improvements in both client and server software, have resulted in simple user options allowing for advanced searching of complex databases. One example is the pull-down ability to identify and search for property data in certain A&I databases. Endusers can now browse thesauri and field data possibilities for numerical and chemical properties in the INSPEC database. Property measurements such as temperatures can be automatically converted online (i.e., from degrees Celsius to degrees Kelvin). The Astrophysics Data System allows searching by a variety of astronomical properties (e.g., brightness, position, variability). The chemistry databases allow for property searching on many fields (e.g., molecular formulas, preparations, reactions, synonyms, and substructure searching).

The chemistry databases have also developed another very important client search enhancement: image drawing and searching. The ability for chemists to use the latest chemical drawing programs to help identify the desired search "term" is essential for this complex field. New chemistry search interfaces either build these drawing capabilities into their products or allow for the import of drawn figures from other drawing programs (see Figure 5). This enhanced capability comes with a cost-there is a need for proprietary software that resides on each workstation. This is a step backward from the

FIGURE 5

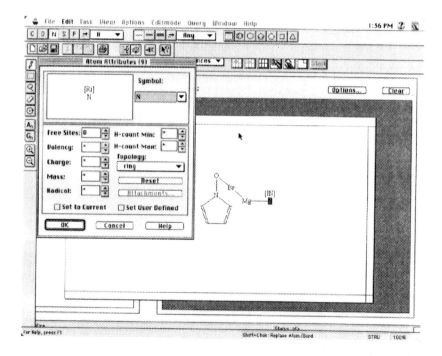

goal of open standards software (such as the current WWW browsers) that requires no centralized support and upgrades. In the future (Java) applets will provide such complex capabilities within the open standard scenario.

The ability to refine searches using more advanced interface options is an important enhancement when searching more complex databases. These sophisticated options provide an important competitive advantage when searching the increasing amount of value-added (non-bibliographic) data found in online databases.

Relevancy Ranking

The enormous amount of information that is now available from computer databases has transformed the original intent of search engines from that of identifying all relevant information into that of filtering for only the most relevant information. Imagine how much more important this relevancy filtering would be if all recorded knowledge was available online. In response to this situation, a number of relevancy algorithms have been developed. Some base their relevancy upon simple frequency analysis of search terms. Other systems perform much more complex semantic analysis using subject thesauri, positional considerations, and/or citation analysis. Regardless of the initial techniques, many systems also allow users to perform a second level of analysis by identifying selected items for further analysis. This "find similar" approach has proven quite helpful and is appearing on a number of services.

Here we see computer assistance advancing from simple matching processes to facilitator applications.

Full Text Searching

Full text databases have increased retrieval power through the ability to search for much more information than is available in standard bibliographic A&I services. This power also comes with a cost-languages have many peculiarities which are not considered until one attempts to create viable search and retrieval strategies. Simple concepts can be represented in many ways in any language, and therefore good search strategies must be broad enough to find all possibilities and still be specific enough to highlight exact needs. Below we will consider just a few examples of difficult language issues: Specifying the proximity of terms can be a valuable way to identify highly significant relationships, but natural language can create problems for inexperienced searchers. Many people would expect to find articles on automobile accidents by using the terms "automobile accident?" or "car accident?". However, Boolean searching for these strings will miss very relevant articles in which the author has written "car and motorcycle accidents." Searching for the terms (automobile or car) and accident? within three words of each other in any order, or within the same paragraph, sentence, or title might be better ways to locate relevant articles in full text databases that do not use authority subject headings. Most searchers never think of these approaches.

The use of acronyms, synonyms, and local terminology also creates problems for users. Most users do not consider the full range of alternative entry terms when performing searches. The normalization of these possibilities is often not an option in full text files, especially those without added-value indexing. Even if indexing were provided, many endusers are not familiar with the advantages of thesauri and controlled vocabulary.

Most full text files do not adequately handle the storage and retrieval of non-text information such as mathematical notations and images. At best there might be a rough approximation of the textual portions or a caption describing the image. The ability to search for valuable information contained in these data elements is extremely important for many fields of study, and the inclusion of enhanced metadata indexing is being explored for this information in a variety of disciplines.

The multiple meanings of words can often create problems of precision even when using combinations of terms. An example would be searching for "plasma" and "components" in an interdisciplinary science file. Plasma can mean both a blood component in biology and a state of matter in physics. The inexperienced searcher will browse many false hits until discovering what is happening and then creating a filtering technique. Often the employed technique is one in which many good hits are unintentionally removed–such as limiting search results to a known journal title. This immediately removes one of the great advantages of online searching, the identification of many relevant items from lesser known sources that might only be found through the efficient online searching of full universes of resources.

Most full text files do not have metadata subject indexing for the placement of the specific topic within its larger context. There is a great deal of assumed knowledge of the general topic and therefore explanations of basic terminology and techniques are often not provided. This lack of context can make searching difficult for those attempting to identify either specific items (imagine trying to locate an article discussing the current endorsements of the former basketball player Kareem Abdul Jabbar, not the football player of the same name) or for larger issues (imagine trying to locate all mathematical analytical approaches that might be relevant for a specific problem when the choice of technique is often not discussed or explained in mathematics articles).

These are just a few examples of the problems novice and experienced searchers encounter when attempting to search in full text data files. Most searchers are never aware of these issues, or of the implications of ignoring these considerations. There are a number of possible techniques under investigation to overcome these difficulties. One area of exploration that will address these concerns, as well as many others, is the use of artificial intelligence within search engines.

Artificial Intelligence

Fuzzy logic and natural language searching are examples of AI techniques in use within search interfaces. Both techniques perform a number of manipulations of the entered data terms. Common manipulations include auto-truncation, autospelling checkers, thesauri matching, word frequency analysis, and more sophisticated semantic analysis. Many systems also provide relevancy ranking of search results. The potential for a combination of artificial intelligence techniques and post-search interactive refinement of search results could provide a powerful search capability for those endusers without an interest or need to learn the intricacies involved in creating powerful search strategies.

Object-Oriented Search Interfaces

The recent adoption of Structured Query Language (SQL) databases in the information world means that the powerful relational database infrastructure can be mined for new possibilities. Advances in SQL-compliant search interfaces has allowed for the development of new and creative visualization opportunities that will involve the enduser in more interesting, interactive, and productive search sessions. Entirely new search processes will be developed through this paradigm shift in search interface tools. See the article by Eric Johnson in this volume for a more detailed discussion of this area.

An example of a visualization interface methodology, in this case for displaying results from a PubMed database search, is the INFORMATION VISUALIZATION system available at URL http://tamas.nlm.nih.gov/

Hyperlinks

Another new technique that has rapidly gained universal acceptance is that of point-and-click linkage between objects. The hypertext link made popular by the WWW protocol has created a population of users that expect simple connections between various visual entities. These links create online avenues for browsing related items. In addition to their convenience in linking full text items directly over the networks, these links differ from traditional paper-based citations in the fact that they are dynamic, allowing for additional related links to be appended over time to create an intricate web. The ability to search across the Internet and create on-the-fly pages of related connections has revolutionized access to large sets of distributed data. New products of this technology include threads of online discussion groups, online errata, personal and group commenting capabilities, and the distribution of large sets of supplementary materials for traditional paper based journals (i.e., the *Journal of Industrial Ecology* at URL http://mitpress.mit. edu/journal-home.tcl?issn=10881980). Many of these items are not found in the traditional A&I services and therefore there is a need to create indexes to these wide ranging and disparate databases and individual items.

SEARCHING HETEROGENEOUS DATABASES

This multi-database searching of independent but federated databases, known as "broadcast" capabilities, is best exemplified by the Northern Light search service at URL http://www.nlsearch.com/

This search engine seamlessly explores a great percentage of the data available from many sectors of the Internet. Searches cover material on locally created popular sites, official government sponsored sites, and commercial and freely available scholarly sites. Examples of data entries include peer reviewed published items, trade publications, society sponsored materials, vanity press items, online news sources, personal and group web page items, library pathfinders, and unpublished material from preprint servers.

A whole new world of information is easily published and shared through the simple process of loading data on the Internet. Using tools such as Northern Light, access to current scholarly information is expanded tremendously in areas such as university curriculum, staff, and current events information. The ability to perform a federated search of many out-of-print book dealer inventories is another example of the power of the Internet. Even more amazing is the ability to find popular information from individual and group sites. Imagine how long it may have taken to find information on the most effective ways to amplify an accordion in the days before the Internet. Now this type of information is shared for thousands of hobbies and activities. It is this federation of information resources that will create the Digital Library of the future.

This new power to search the entire Internet, or at least a great deal of the Internet at one time, is fraught with problems. The reliability of any site, the depth and scope of each search engine, and the applicability of the common search engines for particular discipline needs are among the issues that need to be considered. Many search engines now provide relevancy ranking and subject classifications for their results. The search protocols for many services differ, and the behind the scenes "black box" nature of these helper applications often confuse and disguise incomplete or irrelevant results. Results often differ from session to session on the same service. Accountability regarding the information covered and the exact services provided need adequate documentation in the near future. Trickery and misrepresentation of site contents by both commercial and personal page designers is another frustration. The inability to regulate or screen selected Internet sites by content may provide problems for certain segments of the population.

For those more interested in browsing than keyword searching, there are subject classification schemes such as that provided by Yahoo (URLhttp://www.yahoo.com). There are also peer reviewed pathfinders; one example, the Argus Clearinghouse (formerly known as Clearinghouse for Subject-Oriented Internet Resource Guides) serves as a central access point for value-added topical guides which identify, describe, and evaluate Internet-based information resources (URL http://www.clearinghouse.net).

The same issues of reliability of any site, the depth and scope of each browser index, and the logic of the classification scheme exist for these finding aids. What we have is an embryonic situation similar to the early A&I scenario with its diversity and proprietary chaos, but on an even larger scale with even less of a control mechanism or authority.

One possible solution for this aspect of Internet information overload, which might also mimic that of the online A&I industry, may be the utilization of customized interfaces for specific user populations. User groups with well defined niches have seen the development of various levels of subject-specific information systems. One example is the commercially available Engineering Information Village (URL http://www.ei.org/eihomepage/village/intro.html) created by Engineering Information (Ei), the producers of the Engineering Index and Compendex engineering A&I database services. In addition to serving as a gateway to their A&I product, this service provides pointers to a variety of related engineering resources on the Internet. The indexing of thousands of Internet sites is a very helpful tool for engineers in a variety of settings. One interesting aspect of this service is the inclusion of a selection of these records in the online A&I database. This information is not currently included in the Compendex database loads from other service providers (see Figure 6).

The CoDAS search system (URL http://www.iop.org/EJ/codaswelcome), provided by the Institute of Physics in cooperation with a number of other publishers and A&I services, attempts to create a self-sufficient full text environment for peer reviewed material in the area of condensed matter physics. In addition to this linkage between somewhat competing services, a fascinating aspect of this service is the ability to create an individual "virtual

FIGURE 6

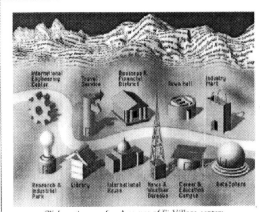

For a close-up look at the kinds of information you'll be able to browse through or search for in Ei Village once you're a resident, click here on the various centers. (Once you're a member, you can also find answers by using the Directory search engine.) Sign on for a free 30-day trial at any time during this tour by clicking on Free Trial.

Click on the map for close-ups of Ei Village centers.

Ei Home Page ... Free Trial

file cabinet" for favorite search strategies, online article links, and hyper-linked comments.

An even further extension of a self-sufficient and integrated knowledge system is found in the Astrophysics Data System (ADS) at URL http://adswww.harvard.edu This NASA funded project integrates bibliographic citation databases with full text journal images and nonbibliographic databases (e.g., star catalogs, data archives) in the areas of stellar and extragalactic research.

This new paradigm of integrated information demonstrated by the ADS and CoDAS services is quite exciting and useful to researchers in their fields, but the proprietary nature of the infrastructure presents difficulties in terms of federated searching and linkage, as well as presenting major concerns relating to salability issues. The system designers are well aware of the need to comply with the newly developing open standards (such as SGML and DOI) and are converting and migrating their materials in anticipation of future considerations.

Regardless of whether one is searching traditional online databases or those on the WWW, there is a constant tension between the need for power-fully customized subject-specific search systems and less powerful but inter-disciplinary search services. As we have seen, there are certain legitimate reasons to desire niche solutions. However, there are also times when the ability to search across a number of related databases is the most important option. In many cases simple keyword searching across these related databases may be satisfactory, but there are times when one would like to use controlled vocabulary and/or subject hierarchy schema. In these instances one would need either a concordance for manual matching of equivalent terms or an automated matching system.

Until metadata descriptors from various systems are normalized searchers will need to find innovative ways of using the presently available relational tools. Some obvious approaches were mentioned earlier: bibliometric citation analysis, word frequency analysis, and hypertext links. Another approach that is under exploration is the creation of "concept spaces" in which multiple thesauri and metadata descriptors are semantically analyzed in order to create and present clusters of related headings which can be used to link similar concepts across different schema. The Interspace Research Project is developing a prototype environment for semantic indexing of multimedia information in a test bed of real collections. The semantic indexing relies on statistical clustering for concepts and categories (URL http://www.canis.uiuc.edu/interspace/)

FINDING THE RIGHT PLACE TO SEARCH

Often the appropriate database(s) are available but users fail to identify or locate them within the confusing set of options on networked and/or stand-alone workstations. What is necessary, in addition to personal help from a trained information specialist, is a top level pointer and filter system for first time users. A number of such navigational tools are now being developed. These filters may point to metasearch indexes, subject-specific indexes, web pages, or a combination of these services. Three examples are presented below.

The **INFOMINE** search system provides links to Internet resources. The specific resources are indexed in a SQL database and the search engine locates terms within the librarian generated descriptions. This tool provides an excellent start for identifying selected items on the Internet (URL http://lib-www.ucr.edu/).

The **CHEMINFO** system helps users find and learn how to use chemistry information resources on the Internet and elsewhere. CHEMINFO provides links and/or information about both Internet and locally held chemistry information sources. Both online and paper-based tools are covered. This is an excellent in-depth subject-based information resource locator. In particular explore the experimental Chemical Reference Sources Database (CRSD) interface which is designed to allow for easy queries on chemistry reference materials (URL http://www.indiana.edu:80/~cheminfo/).

In contrast to these pointer approaches, the NAVIGATOR expert system at the Yale University Science Libraries emulates a reference librarian interview and attempts to match specific needs to a particular resource using the "type" of information desired as the deciding factor. Examples of information "types" may be short news items, a state-of-the-art review, the most current peer reviewed item, a definition or a property. The system is built upon nested web pages, but will soon be migrated to a SQL database. Eventually the results will be displayed in a hierarchy according to an algorithm of prioritized metadata tags using XML (URL http://www.library.yale.edu/scilib/help/sources.html).

There are many ways to begin a search for information; even searching for search engines or starting points can be overwhelming. Most of this article has only considered searching for known concepts or items. Browsing requires entirely different methodologies and interfaces. Perhaps a new approach to gathering information is required.

THIRD GENERATION SEARCHING

An entirely new approach to information gathering has developed as the information technology industry expands its focus toward the enduser market. The creation of smart agents, software applications that automatically perform a series of complex user-configured functions, means that some of the daily burden of information search, retrieval, filtering, and classification can be performed without direct user involvement. Customized search strategies are created once and automatically run across a number of regularly updated subject databases. These search results, be they full text, citations, or data sets, are then run into a personal database management system in which the records are read, indexed, summarized, and placed in folders for future access. This software exists today in various levels of sophistication and integration.

These smart agent techniques are found by searching for terms such as deductive databases, data mining, and knowledge discovery within the larger concept of data warehousing. One good starting point is the Data Warehousing Information Center. (URL http://pwp.starnetinc.com/larryg/index.html) Another selection of Intelligent Software Agents can be found at URL http://www.sics.se/isl/abc/survey.html

Udo Flohr writes in "OLAP by Web," (*Byte*, Sept 1997) (http://www.byte.com/art/9709/sec6/art6.htm):

On-line analytical processing (OLAP) . . . programs make up a category of business software that lets users manipulate a data warehouse. Typical OLAP operations include consolidate, drill-down (i.e., query refinement), slice, dice, and pivot. . . . Results can be reported in traditional or tabular database formats, as well as in graphical charts. Although this output might be in a fixed format, it often allows the user to directly manipulate the data for further analysis, such as identifying trends, correlations, or time series.

An example of an intelligent agent for information handling is the "Lifestreams" software created at Yale University. This software attempts to record not only the data that is searched and retrieved, but it also captures and links other important life events at the time. This approach which creates "a time-ordered stream of documents combined with several powerful operators" allows a searcher to retrieve information from non-obvious links such as "it was around the time when I went to Acapulco." This is a truly integrated application (URL http://www.cs.yale.edu/HTML/YALE/CS/HyPlans/ freeman/lifestreams.html).

Another approach to finding information is utilizing the concept of shared preferences across a previously identified information domain. A number of computer users enter their preferences on a topic into a database, and when new searches match these preferences suggestions are made for other interesting sites. This system is being tested on web sites in areas such as music and book selection (BookMatcher on Amazon.com is found at URL http:// www.amazon.com/exec/obidos/bookmatcher/enter/7453-7278070-250700).

A variation on this approach is the Alexa (URL http://www.alexa.com/ download/index.html) suggestion bar at the bottom of a web browser page. Users of this plug in application are offered two related web sites for each page they view based upon previous visitor page histories.

These are just a few examples of how smart software can change the entire "information search" process. In some cases there is no actual search operation in sight. In other scenarios the search is actually performed on locally stored knowledge databases of relevant but previously unseen data. Searching will never be quite the same once these new technologies are available as a normal part of the information network.

BEYOND THE TECHNOLOGY

Regardless of how deeply technology becomes integrated into your life, and how smart it becomes in automatically handling your data, the most difficult part of information retrieval is still the formation of the most appropriate question. There is no algorithmic substitute for good critical thinking. The creation of precise search strategies is very dependent upon a variety of difficult to define considerations. Often searching the most specific data element will not provide the easiest or most efficient path to a desired item. An example below will explain this counter-intuitive situation.

A researcher is interested in the guests and the topic on tonight's edition of *Politically Incorrect,* a television show hosted by Bill Maher on the Fox network. Common sense might say enter the most specific information: Bill Maher and *Politically Incorrect.* You will get pages of data about Bill Maher and pages of material on the topic of political correctness, perhaps limited to only tens of pages by combining the two concepts. The much quicker way to find this information is to search for the broader concept of Fox television and broadcast schedule. It will be much easier to find the information on this well organized page. The logic and appropriateness of this approach would be hard to explain in a generalizable way, but it is absolutely correct in many cases. A computer program capable of these interpretations is not yet available, and it will years before they store and relate the critical threshold of information necessary in many fields to perform such actions.

CONCLUSION

The search process has changed dramatically since the introduction of automation. Much of the early change was due to sheer speed and power, but more recent technological innovations have created new approaches to data and schema analysis and presentation. Traditional search methodologies have been significantly enhanced, and new possibilities for research exist as a result of these techniques being applied to large Digital Libraries of information.

AUTHOR NOTE

David Stern's research involves the development of seamless electronic retrieval and transmission systems, focussed primarily upon scholar workstations. He is currently involved in the development of enduser search systems for both local and remote hosts.

TECHNICAL DESIGN CONSIDERATIONS

University of Illinois the Federation of Digital Libraries: Interoperability Among Heterogeneous Information Systems

Robert Ferrer

SUMMARY. This paper briefly reviews some of the trends and issues now challenging today's digital library that need to be addressed in successfully federating multiple heterogeneous databases. Trends include the development of loosely-coupled federations that combine object technology with client-server architecture. Issues include those dealing with heterogeneity, especially the problems associated with schema translation and integration. The paper also addresses the benefits of SGML in facilitating the searching of full-text documents with a

Robert Ferrer is a Research Programmer with the Digital Library Initiative, University of Illinois, Champaign-Urbana, IL.

[Haworth co-indexing entry note]: "University of Illinois the Federation of Digital Libraries: Interoperability Among Heterogeneous Information Systems." Ferrer, Robert. Co-published simultaneously in *Science & Technology Libraries* (The Haworth Press, Inc.) Vol. 17, No. 3/4, 1999, pp. 81-119; and: *Digital Libraries: Philosophies, Technical Design Considerations, and Example Scenarios* (ed: David Stern) The Haworth Press, Inc., 1999, pp. 81-119. Single or multiple copies of this article are available for a fee from The Haworth Document Delivery Service [1-800-342-9678, 9:00 a.m. - 5:00 p.m. (EST). E-mail address: getinfo@haworthpressinc.com].

high degree of precision. *[Article copies available for a fee from The Haworth Document Delivery Service: 1-800-342-9678. E-mail address: getinfo@haworthpressinc.com]*

KEYWORDS. Federation of digital libraries, interoperability, trends and issues, multiple heterogeneous databases, loosely-coupled federations, object technology, client-server architecture, schema translation and integration, SGML, full-text documents

INTRODUCTION

The information needs of today's library patron is complex. Users often require a multitude of information from many different sources. Nowhere is this more evident than in today's science and technology libraries. These libraries simply cannot keep up with the plethora of publications that emerge each year from new sources as diverse as the disciplines that comprise science and technology. The cost of subscribing and housing even current publications becomes prohibitive. Libraries are faced with the daunting task of meeting the ever-increasing information needs of the patron while remaining fiscally responsible, especially under diminishing budgets.

Downsizing has become a popular business trend. For many companies this has resulted in the decentralization of business units and a leaner organizational structure. The same can be said about today's libraries. Collection Development is shifting away from a philosophy of acquisition to one of access. The decentralization of business units has increased the establishment of remotely located information warehouses independently organized in dissimilar environments. They are faced with the challenge of connecting and coordinating the "islands of the archipelago" not only to be able to share information but also to provide control in the areas of data integrity and security. Libraries too are faced with the challenge of being able to interconnect different computers and software in order to access the information needed by patrons. This paper briefly reviews some of the trends and issues now challenging today's digital library that need to be addressed in successfully federating multiple heterogeneous databases.

MAINFRAME ARCHITECTURE

Much has changed since the mainframe architecture in which the original information retrieval services, such as Dialog and BRS, maintained their data. Dumb terminals connected to a large high-end computer allowed users to enter commands and display output one line at a time (Figure 1). The mainframe handled all other aspects of a search session. A centralized server managed communications, user query interaction, database management and data presentation. The data from different sources had to be converted into a single homogeneous structure and organization.

CLIENT-SERVER ARCHITECTURE

The development of client-server architecture is the major enabling technology behind distributed computing and the driving force towards federating heterogeneous networked databases.[5,8] Unlike mainframe architecture, workload is balanced between the client and server (Figure 2). The client handles the user interface-query formulation and results presentation. User-friendly graphics-based client software offers a consistent interface regardless of the underlying support structure. Today's PC-based client can also manage multiple tasks, such as maintaining simultaneous connections to a variety of sources. The result is transparent access to information sources

FIGURE 1. The mainframe computer manages all aspects of a session including communications, user query interaction, database management and data presentation.

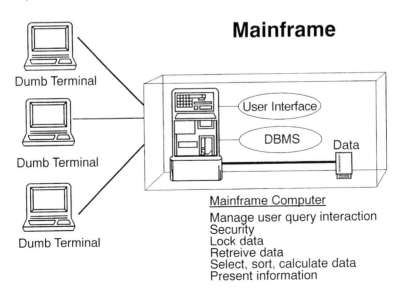

Mainframe

Dumb Terminal

Dumb Terminal

Dumb Terminal

User Interface

DBMS

Data

Mainframe Computer
Manage user query interaction
Security
Lock data
Retreive data
Select, sort, calculate data
Present information

FIGURE 2. Workload is more balanced in client-server architecture. Middleware software standardizes communications protocol allowing clients and servers to interoperate regardless of the different hardware and DBMS software involved.

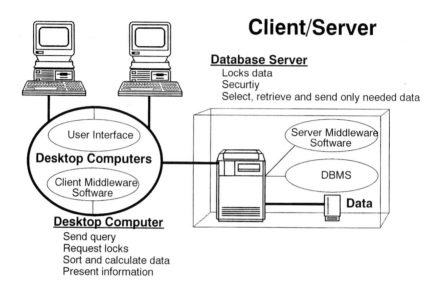

regardless of location. The server handles the database management tasks and the processing of requests.

Middleware

Connecting the client to the server is a class of software known as middleware. The software components that comprise middleware physically reside on both the client and server. Middleware insures that the client can communicate or interoperate with the server regardless of the different hardware and software involved. Clients and servers generally communicate by using a standardized sequence of messages known as a protocol. A message can be a request from the client for the server to perform an operation, such as search a remote database. A message from the server can be a response to the client, such as the results of a search. The Application Programming Interface (API) is the middleware component that facilitates the transferring of messages between the client and server based on a protocol.

The API protocol defines a set of messages that both the client and server understand (Figure 3). The client's API translates a message into a form independent of either the client or server that permits travel across the net-

FIGURE 3. The Application Programming Interface (API) is the middleware component that facilitates the transfer of messages across the network. The client query is converted into a standardized form that the server's API can translate and submit to the DBMS. Results are likewise converted into a form that the client's API can present to the client program.

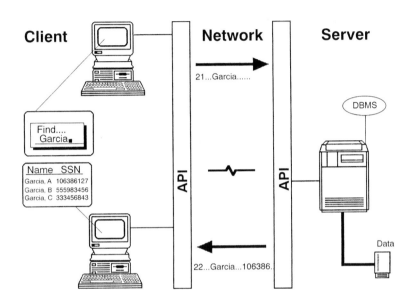

work. The server's API receives the message and translates it into a form that the server understands. The message is processed, and a response is sent to the client via the server's API. The client's API transforms the response into a form that the client understands, and thus completes the transaction.[3]

Depending on how the API is implemented, messages can be sent either synchronously or a synchronously (Figure 4). Synchronous models are generally session-oriented. A connection is established and maintained for the duration of a session. A telephone call is based on a synchronous communications model where a connection is maintained for the duration of a conversation. For client-server, a session can be the exchange of a sequence of requests and responses in order to accomplish a specific task. The advantage of this is that the session is stateful. The client and server can use what has previously transpired in the messages that are exchanged and operations that are performed. This is particularly useful in an iterative activity such as searching.

The problem is that the connection is maintained even while the server is

FIGURE 4. In synchronous communications a connection is maintained for the duration of the session. The client is busy until the connection is terminated. In asynchronous communications the client is free to do other tasks as soon as the current task is initiated. However, there is no guarantee that the tasks will complete in the order initiated.

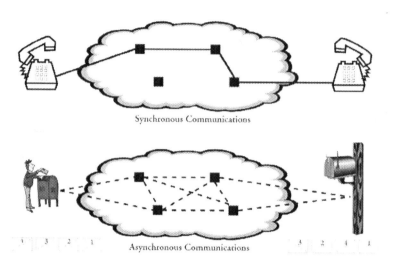

waiting for a request from the client, or vice-versa. A connection ties up the resources of both the client and server. Neither the client nor the server can do other activities while in a session, even during periods of inactivity. This may be viewed as an advantage since it insures that a sequence of messages are exchanged in proper order. Nevertheless it is inefficient, and impacts on the scalability of the system. The Remote Procedure Call (RPC) is a synchronous communications implementation common to client-server architecture where operations are executed on remote servers but appear to the client as local functions. Typical of synchronous models, the client is blocked from doing other work until the operation has completed execution and a response is received.

Alternatively, asynchronous models are not session-oriented. A message is sent but the sender does not wait for a response before doing other work. The recipient is not sitting idle waiting for a message. This is similar to sending messages via the postal system, or electronically via E-mail. Multitasking in a modern operating system involves the execution of a task without waiting for the task to complete before initiating the execution of another task. The HTTP protocol used to access information on the World Wide Web is based on an asynchronous communications model. The client establishes a connection with a server in sending a message, such as a request for information. Once the message is sent, the client is free to send messages to other servers. Once the server receives the message and sends the requested information, it closes the connection. If the client wants to send additional messages to the same server, it will have to reestablish a connection with the server. For each message a connection is established and terminated.

Resources are tied up only when needed. During periods of inactivity while waiting for messages, the client and server are free to do other activities. The server, for example, is free to service other requests. This contributes to the system's scalability. However, since a new connection must be established with each message, state information is not maintained. The server does not remember anything about the previous message. The stateless nature of the asynchronous communications model limits the level of sophistication possible in iterative activities, such as searching. Current research is focused on how to implement stateful asynchronous models.

Regardless of implementation, because the API is well defined for both the client and server, it provides unparalleled flexibility in choosing hardware and software components for both the client and server. As long as the client and server use the same API, their components can be independently upgraded or changed without critically impacting each other. Furthermore, the role of the API as represented in middleware software plays an increasingly strategic role in the evolution of network computing that enables interoperability among heterogeneous systems.

Z39.50

The Z39.50 protocol is an example of a synchronous session-oriented implementation of the client-server architecture specifically designed for database searching and information retrieval on systems that run on different hardware and software. Developed in conjunction with the Library of Congress and bibliographic service providers, the Z39.50 protocol allows databases from different information providers to interoperate. Z39.50 currently supports the search and retrieval of bibliographic records primarily in the MARC format.[7,20]

The Z39.50 standard specifies the messages that are exchanged in a session, the structure and semantics of a search query, and how results are returned to the user. The search query is hierarchically structured into sets permitting the inclusion of Boolean operators to connect the sets (Figure 5). Each set includes a search term or phrase, and any parameters that specify which attributes of the record to search, such as author, title or descriptor fields.

Currently the standards assume that the client and server communicate over a stateful connection on the Internet. The dialogue that is created by the exchange of messages between the client and server is called a Z39.50 Asso-

FIGURE 5. The Z39.50 query structure is hierarchically arranged into sets. Sets are connected by Boolean operators.

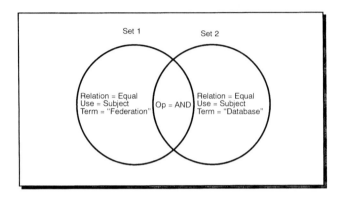

ciation. Messages are a sequence of commands and responses. The protocol establishes a set pattern for dialoguing. For each command sent by the client, the server responds with an acknowledgment or the requested information (Figure 6).

A searcher submits a query using the client interface. The middleware software module on the client is called the Origin. It translates the query into a standardized form specified by the Z39.50 protocol. The Origin initiates a session with the INIT command. The software module on the intended server is called the Target. The Target sends an acknowledgment that the session has started. The Origin sends the query via the SEARCH command. The Target interfaces with the desired database on a remote system. It responds to the query and sends the results of the query back to the Origin. The Origin interfaces with the searcher. The searcher informs the Origin which records to view. The Origin sends a PRESENT command with the specific records to retrieve. Finally, a TERMINATION command is sent to end the session.

Newer versions of the protocol are expected to better support the searching of databases with more diverse record structures. The EXPLAIN command will allow the client to ask the server to describe the contents, the record structure and supported attributes of the database it serves. A full-text document delivery service will also be provided.

Nevertheless, there are limitations to Z39.50. It cannot adequately handle searching full-text documents. Full-text documents often provide a rich and complex set of access points that go beyond those offered by the MARC record. Furthermore, the protocol cannot operate in an asynchronous communications environment such as the World Wide Web, an important source of

FIGURE 6. This is a simple Z39.50 session between the client and server.

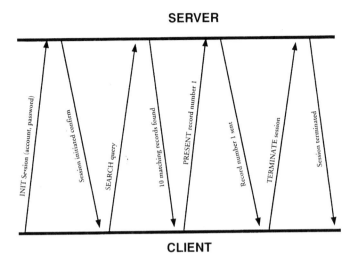

information. Session-oriented synchronous communications tie up computer resources for the duration of the session, preventing the client from simultaneously directing a query to multiple database systems. Most important, however, is that it is unreasonable to expect everyone to change existing hardware and software in order to adopt a single protocol. What is needed is the ability to federate independent database systems.

FEDERATED DATABASES

A Federated Database System (FDBS) is a group of cooperating but autonomous Database Systems (DBS). Individual component databases continue local operations as defined by their own Database Management System (DBMS), yet participate in a federation by sharing their data in response to a query. The Federated Database Management System (FDBMS) is the middleware software that controls and coordinates how the component databases cooperate. There are several characteristics of an FDBS worth noting.[19]

Data distribution and autonomy represent key characteristics of a federated database system. Data may be distributed to many locations on machines supported by different database systems. The problem of having to coordinate data distributed on heterogeneous systems arises from the fact that component databases evolved independently as standalone systems prior to forming a federation. Each component database has its own DBMS which controls its own data for local operations. In many cases, data may also reside on machines remotely located from its respective DBMS. An individual DBMS can execute local commands as well as respond to commands from the federation. It can decide if and when to respond to a request from the federation. Autonomy is also exercised by the different ways individual databases are designed, such as how the data is represented, managed and shared, and which operations are supported by the system.

Autonomy is the primary cause of heterogeneity among component systems. Handling heterogeneity is central to the tasks performed by the FDBMS. This is the feature that most accurately characterizes the interoperability of an FDBS. Heterogeneity can be attributed to differences in the basic information systems provided by different producers. This includes the hardware and software that comprise an individual DBS. For example, a particular DBMS may run under UNIX. The data for a given DBMS may reside on a Windows NT™ machine and is accessed by the HTTP protocol.

The data models that describe the structure of a database contribute to the issue of heterogeneity at the database level. One DBMS is based on the hierarchical data model. Another DBMS is based on the relational data model. A more recent database structure is based on the object model. Differences in the syntax of the query languages used to access data also contribute to heterogeneity at the database level.

Heterogeneity on the semantic level is one of the most difficult aspects of federating databases that continue to occupy researchers. The semantic level is characterized by the data schema. The schema is a description of the classes or fields that define the data and the interrelationships between them. There can be differences in the meaning, interpretation, precision or intended use of data with equivalent labels. One schema may use the label "figure" to refer to both tables and graphs, while another may use "figure" to refer only to graphs, and use a different label to refer to tables. Conversely, data with different labels may be semantically equivalent. The labels "fig" and "figure" used by two different schemes refer to the same thing. An FDBMS is required to know the different schemes that comprise the individual database systems of a federation.

In short, the FDBMS coordinates the activities among cooperating databases and their supporting protocols. It is responsible for operations, access and transaction processing. Operations involve acquiring, translating, mapping and integrating different database schemes into a federated schema. Access includes interoperating with a variety of data models and query languages. Transaction processing deals with concurrency control. Concurrency control is required when concurrent users in a distributed system want to update the same record. Without it, the actions of one user can be interleaved with the actions of another causing data inconsistencies. Although not discussed since the information systems described here are all query-based, a major challenge in the development of FDBS is the maintenance of global serializability among heterogeneous databases. Transaction serializability is a procedure for executing the actions of concurrent users so that the results are the same as if there are no other users updating the record. Transaction serializability is necessary for guaranteeing data integrity. Concurrency control is an important issue for distributed bibliographic systems that wish to include circulation and interlibrary loan transactions.

The taxonomy of a federated database system is based on the degree of integration of the component databases and the power a central authority has over them. At one extreme there is no integration. The central authority is nothing more than a pass-thru interface to allow users to connect directly to individual databases (sometimes known as a multidatabase system). On the other extreme, there is total integration. There is only a single global schema and none of the databases exhibit any autonomy (sometimes known as a distributed database system). The FDBS represents a compromise between these two extremes (Figure 7).

LOOSELY-COUPLED FDBS

A loosely-coupled FDBS categorizes a multidatabase approach. Working from a bottom-up orientation, the FDBMS does not exercise strict centralized control over the participating databases. Component databases maintain ultimate control over their operation and data organization.

A way this functions is that the FDBMS sends a "Who Are You" query to the participating databases. A recipient of the query may choose to respond by replying with a view of its schema. The FDBMS may then consult with one or more data dictionaries (i.e., thesaurus) in the attempt to construct a federated schema. There is no pre-determined process for controlling the creation of the federated schema. Basically, the focus of the FDBMS is on schema importation, a dynamically-binding process where a federated schema may be created, changed or destroyed on the fly. The "EXPLAIN" command of the Z39.50 protocol offers a simplified version of this process. More sophisticated approaches based on the concept of registries are discussed below.

TIGHTLY-COUPLED FDBS

A tightly-coupled FDBS categorizes a distributed approach. Working from a top-down orientation, the FDBMS exercises much more control over the participating databases. Component databases relinquish some autonomy in the acceptance of a central authority.

FIGURE 7. A Federated Database System (FDBS) is a group of cooperating but autonomous Database Systems (DBS). The FDBMS is the middleware software that coordinates the activities among the databases. Each component DBS has its own DBMS that defines a local schema. The export schema is a subset of the local schema since not all elements of the local schema may be available to the federation. A federated schema is created either statically by translating the integrating the export schemas before the federation is created (tightly-coupled) or dynamically by importing specific export schemas and creating a view over them on the fly (loosely-coupled). Data Dictionaries are consulted to help in the creation of a federated schema. Component DBSs may exchange data with each other.

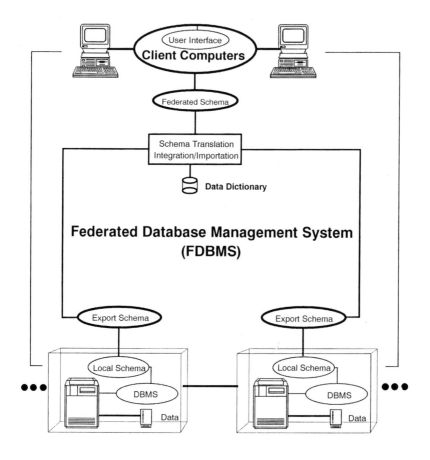

The creation of a federated schema is a statically-binding process. A global schema is created in advance. The role of the FDBMS is to map the schemes of the participating databases to the global schema. In many cases, schema integration may involve incorporating parts of the federated schema into the structure of the component databases. Regardless of the type of federated database system, the process of correlating schema objects in one database schema to schema objects in another schema is a major task not easily accomplished as is demonstrated by the case study described below.

DLI PROJECT–UNIVERSITY OF ILLINOIS

The driving force in the Digital Library Initiative (DLI) at the University of Illinois, Champaign-Urbana is the desire to federate full-text scientific and engineering literature from various publishers.[7,13] A patron should be able to pose a single query simultaneously to a group of remotely located databases. The results returned should be a list of titles satisfying the search criteria from each of the sources addressed. The results are combined and organized into a meaningful set and presented to the patron in a unified fashion for evaluation. The patron should then be able to retrieve the full-text article associated with the title complete with graphics and links to other materials referenced in the article. The article is presented not as plain ASCII text but in the full graphical format originally intended.

Full-text searching has been around for awhile. The problem with it is that it is difficult to retrieve a set of results with a high degree of precision. A match is made, regardless of relevancy, if the query corresponds to a string of characters anywhere in the article. The searcher may be looking for articles written by a particular author, but is not interested in articles written by others where the author is cited. This is a difficult search given current full-text searching capabilities. Of course, one can associate the article with supplemental metadata that acts as a surrogate to the article and re-presents the bibliographic information in clearly delineated fields. However, metadata should add information not contained in the original object. Metadata consisting of information already existing in the original object is unnecessarily redundant, even if it re-presents the information in a different format. Redundancy not only wastes space, it also forces the issue of coherency. Full-text searching offers the possibility of searching the object directly and not its surrogate. How can full-text searching be made more effective?

SGML

The DLI testbed consists of articles marked-up in the SGML format as the objects to be indexed, searched and retrieved.[6] SGML's system of tags, attributes and entities are used extensively in the publishing world to provide styling and formatting information for articles going to press. The tags also provide extensive content information. Tags are used to demarcate the various regions of an article. A region is delineated by the boundary marked by an opening tag, <body>, for example, and a closing tag, </body> (Figure 8). Front matter, body and back matter are tagged. In addition to identifying standard bibliographic information (title, author, publishing information, abstract, etc.), tags are used to identify figures, tables, citations, author affiliations, formulas, section titles and more.

The structure of an article is described by the Document Type Definition (DTD) that is provided with the articles from each publisher. The DTD defines the regions in terms of their logical structure. Regions are hierarchically defined by other regions in a particular order and occurrence. An article is completely described by its tags, in a top-down fashion, all the way to its minimal character unit. All this information is provided without having to add anything to the original article, and best of all, SGML-based materials are part of the normal products produced by most publishers as part of the printing process.

So what does all this provide us? It provides us with the tools to search for only those articles where the author is in the front section of the article (main author) and not part of a citation where article availability might be problematic. Assuming that matches in titles provide excellent results, we can look only in the article title or the section titles for hits. We can look for specific figures or tables by their captions. In short, we can now conduct a search directly on the original articles and retrieve a set of results with a high degree of precision.

The DLI group receives regular contributions of SGML-based articles from five publishers covering over sixty publications in Science and Engineering. The group has processed and indexed over thirty thousand articles to date. The DLI group has also developed both a web-based and a custom PC-based client to facilitate search and retrieval.

Each participating publisher electronically sends the group a compressed set of SGML-based ASCII files for the text of the articles, graphic files in EPS, TIF or JPEG for the figures, and a copy of the DTD. A set of these files usually comprises one or more issues of the corresponding printed version. The set is processed. Files are uncompressed and organized into sub-directories corresponding to issue and article titles. Each article directory contains both the SGML document and any graphic files associated with the document. Additional files are added to each directory that are needed to view the articles. Table of Contents files are also generated. The original SGML document is slightly modified to accommodate the implementation of digital signatures that are used to insure security, document integrity and authentica-

FIGURE 8. The DTD (left) describes the structure of the article (right). Figures are referenced by external entities that point to URLs. Citations are referenced by internal IDs that point to the back of the article.

```
<!--      MyArticle.dtd is an example of a very simple          -->
            Document Type Definition (DTD)
<!DOCTYPE article
[
<!-- Entity definitions replace entity names in the body of the DTD  -->
<!ENTITY % text "#PCDATA|%emphasis;|%fontfamily;|%fontattr;" >
<!ENTITY % fontattr "up | dn" >

<!-ELEMENT      MIN    CONTENT    (EXCEPTIONS)    ->

<!ELEMENT article      - -    (front, body, back)            >
<!ELEMENT front        - -    (title, (author)+)             >
<!ELEMENT title        - -    (%text;)*                      >
<!ELEMENT author       - -    (fnme, snme, (aff)?)           >
<!ELEMENT fnme | snme | aff   - -   (%text;)*                >
<!ELEMENT body         - -    (h1)+  +(figrp | ref)          >
<!ELEMENT h1           - -    (st, (p | h2)*)                >
<!ELEMENT h2           - -    (st, p)+                       >
<!ELEMENT st | p       - -    (%text;)*                      >

<!ELEMENT figrp        - -    (figref, fig)                  >
<!ELEMENT figref       - -    (%text;)*                      >
<!ATTLIST figref  rid    IDREF    #IMPLIED                   >
<!ELEMENT fig          - O    #EMPTY                         >
<!ATTLIST fig     id     ID       #REQUIRED                  >
                  name   ENTITY   #REQUIRED                  >

<!ELEMENT ref          - -    (%text;)*                      >
<!ATTLIST ref     rid    IDREF    #IMPLIED                   >

<!ELEMENT back         - -    ((ack)?, biblist)              >
<!ELEMENT ack          - -    (%text;)*                      >
<!ELEMENT biblist      - -    (citation)+                    >
<!ELEMENT citation     - -    ((author)+, title, ((sertitle, vol) |
                              (city, pub)), date, (page)?)   >
<!ATTLIST citation  id    ID      #REQUIRED                  >
                    type   (article | book)   article        >
<!ELEMENT vol | city | pub | date   - -    (%text;)*         >
]>
```

```
<!DOCTYPE article SYSTEM "myDTD.DTD" [
<!ENTITY f8 SYSTEM "http://--ferrer/article/fig8.tif" ndata tif>
]>
<article>
<front>
<title>Federating Digital Libraries</title>
<author><fnme>Robert</fnme><snme> Ferrer</fnme><aff>
University of Illinois, Champaign-Urbana</aff>
</front>
<body>
```

```
<h2><st>SGML</st>
<p>The DLI testbed consists of articles marked-up in the SGML format
as the objects to be indexed, searched and retrieved<ref
rid=ref6><sup>6</sup></ref>. SGML's system of tags, attributes and
entities are used extensively in the publishing world to provide styling
and formatting information for articles going to press.  The tags also
provide extensive content information.  Tags are used to demarcate the
various regions of an article.  A region is delineated by the boundary
marked by an opening tag, &lt;body&gt; for example, and a closing tag,
&lt;/body&gt; <figrp><figref rid=fig8>(figure 8)</figref><fig id=fig8
name=f8>.  Front matter, body and back matter are tagged. In addition to
identifying standard bibliographic information (title, author, publishing
information, abstract, etc.), tags are used to identify figures, tables,
citations, author affiliations, formulas, section titles and more.</p>
```

```
<citation id=ref21 type=article>
<author><fnme>Zhonghua</fnme><snme> Yang</snme></author> and
<author><fnme>Keith</fnme><snme> Duddy</snme></author>.
<title>"CORBA: A Platform for Distributed Object Computing"</title>
<sertitle>ACM Operating Systems Review</sertitle> <vol>30</vol>
<date>(April 1996) </date><page> 4-31</page></citation> </biblist>
</back> </article>
```

tion. The files and their directory structure are finally stored on web servers. The SGML browser makes use of the web's HTTP protocol to retrieve articles, graphics and other needed files stored in remote repositories.

When the patron finally requests to view a specific article the SGML browser is launched (Figure 9). It retrieves the SGML-based article, figure files, DTD document and other files that allow the browser to resolve entity declarations and render the article in its full graphical format. Articles rendered from SGML offer many value-added features that can be incorporated into the browser's functionality. The hierarchical structure of the tagging can be used to create an outline of the article's contents that users can use to quickly navigate to specific parts of the article by clicking on a particular heading in the outline. The outline can be used to facilitate note-taking. Users can simply type or cut and paste sections of the article into the outline. The browser can easily append the appropriate citations to the notes.

The tagging permits the browser to offer internal hyper-linking. A reference to a particular figure, formula or citation can take the user directly to that component by clicking on its reference-ID embedded in the article. These article components can be viewed in a separate window allowing the user to continuously refer to them as the article is read. In fact, article components are no longer restricted to static objects such as images. Any object can now be a component, including multimedia objects. Formulas and tables can easily be transferred to other applications and observed in action.

Furthermore, SGML offers opportunities to embed external hyperlinks throughout the article. Clicking on the citation can take the user directly to the article referenced by the citation. Article updates can be dynamically incorporated by linking. Links can take the user to the author's homesite where the user can explore the research environment from which the article emerged. SGML can provide support for collaborative work or groupware. Comments or annotations can be recorded and embedded as links in the document. SGML-based documents can foster a peer-to-peer cooperative work orientation emulating the federated client-server network and database environment that supports their dissemination.

The DLI project implements a tightly-coupled federated system (Figure 10). A single vendor-supplied product provides the indexing and search engine. A separate database is created for each publisher and maintained in remote locations on UNIX-based servers. Session-oriented synchronous communications to the databases are managed by the TCP/IP network protocol. The documents to which the databases point to are stored on separate Windows NT™-based servers. The NT drives are NFS mounted to the UNIX drives. Therefore, the SGML directories and files appear locally to the indexing process located on UNIX. The indexing process makes use of the elements and attributes specified in a document's DTD to automatically delin-

FIGURE 9. An SGML browser renders tagged documents. It provides a navigator to link quickly to article sections. Links to figures and references are easily accessible. Furthermore, the browser allows for the insertion of user notes.

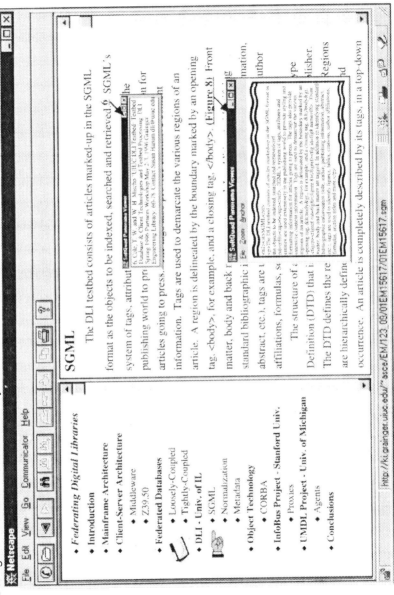

97

FIGURE 10. SGML documents are piped through a filter that strips out entities. Metadata is derived from the documents that includes the URL of the
figures. The index consists of pointers to each region in the filtered documents
and their metadata. Each export schema is a subset of the regions of the DTD
that will be normalized into a federated schema. The FDBMS handles the
steps necessary to connect, query and process results from multiple databases. Clients finally retrieve documents and figures using the URLs stored
in the metadata.

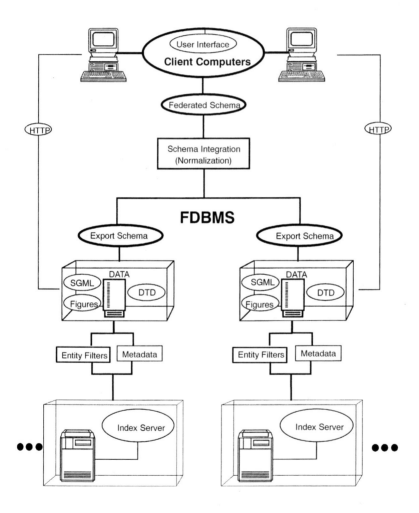

eate and create the access points used in a query. A vendor-developed proprietary query language is employed to search the databases individually.

The vendor also provides the necessary federated database management
middleware software specifically designed to simultaneously connect, query
and process results from multiple remote databases created by the same
product. All the databases participating in the federation must be known in
advance. However, the software allows for the participation of databases in a
variety of combinations. Users may select any grouping of databases to query
when initiating a search session. The multidatabase query language is virtually identical to the query language used for individual databases. Results are
returned in the same format as those from individual databases with the
addition of a label indicating from which database a given result originated.

NORMALIZATION

Despite the fact that the "S" in SGML stands for "Standardized," it is
certainly not. Experience with documents from various publishers has shown
that there are many variations in the way documents are tagged, even for
those that claim to use a DTD of a similar type. Almost all of the publishers
use a DTD of type "Article" as stated in the Doctype Declaration that
prefaces each document. The key point is that each database can operate
independently. The user simply needs to know the set of tags that provide the
access points to the data for each database. However, in order to collaborate
in a global search, the DTD of each database must be normalized and mapped
to a global schema.

There are three types of differences that must be normalized and mapped.
The first involves a simple translation of tags where the tags point to the same
logical region but use different names. One database points to the author of
the article with the tag "<author>". Another points to the same region using
the tag "<auth>". The second difference requires that multiple tags be con-
catenated as one. Some publishers distinguish between inline and display
formulas. Logically, they are the same thing. The third difference requires the
creation of a pseudo-tag. One publisher does not have a tag to denote the
bibliographic citations region. Instead a pseudo-tag is created by defining the
region based on the content of the article. In this particular case, the citations
region is circumscribed by the word "REFERENCES" that exists within a
section title region and by the next "</h1>" tag. The indexing product used
requires that the inclusion of these dynamically created regions and aliases is
integrated locally at each database site. Nevertheless this is achieved without
altering or interfering with the database's original schema or structure. Furthermore, the original SGML documents remain unchanged.

Despite all of the advantages mentioned in using SGML-based documents for search and retrieval, there are aspects inherent in SGML that can inhibit successful searches. In addition to tags that comprise the document's regions or access points, a document is also punctuated with a variety of entities and specialty tags such as processing instructions (these tags that begin with "<? Pub Tag . . ." are used to provide additional formatting information). Entities are ASCII representations of non-standard characters and symbols that will be resolved and rendered into a graphical representation when the document is retrieved and displayed. They are characterized by text that begin with an ampersand ("&") and end with a semi-colon (";"). Many of the entities are set by ISO standards such as those describing diacritics (¸), math symbols (&infinity;), Greek and Latin characters (ρ), special publishing characters ( ), etc. Publishers may also provide a set of entities created for their specific needs.

Since these special elements are part of the text of a document they can complicate a search. For example, a user is searching for the author O'Shay or Félix. They may be represented in the document as O’Shay and Fe´lix. (Actually, there are many variations that publishers use. Remember the "S" in SGML?) Users would generally enter the names as O'Shay or Oshay, and Felix. No hits will be returned.

Specialty tags may interfere with proximity searching. Let's say that a user wants "Federation" and "Scientific Literature" to be within three significant words of each other as in, "The Federation of Diverse Collections of Scientific Literature." However, the phrase is represented in the document as "The Federation of <?Pub Tag italics> Diverse Collections. . . ." Again, no hits will be returned.

A customization feature is provided at the indexing stage that permits the filtering of characters and strings. As each document is passed through the indexing stage, it is piped to a program that parses the document for entities and specialty tags. The entities and specialty tags are stripped out. Either they are replaced with spaces or apostrophes equal to the number of characters representing the entity or tag replaced. "O’Shay" is changed to "O"""""Shay," and "The Federation of <?Pub Tag italics> Diverse Collections" is changed to "The Federation of   Diverse Collections." The indexing process allows for the mapping of apostrophes to nulls. Multiple consecutive spaces are treated as a single space. This effectively squeezes out characters that might get in the way of searching. When searching, "O'Shay" is recognized as "Oshay." "Federation" is within three words of "Diverse Collections" since it is treated as "The Federation of Diverse Collections." Other mapping options include equating hyphens with spaces and uppercase characters with lowercase characters.

The resulting output that is finally indexed is a virtual copy of the document with the changes as described above. It is also of the same byte count as the original document. This allows for the ability to accurately highlight the search terms in the document when displayed since the index engine stores pointers to each word in the document based on byte displacement. The original document remains physically unaltered and is displayed in its pristine state.

METADATA

The DLI testbed makes extensive use of metadata to support search and retrieval. The document repositories reside on remote HTTP servers. The metadata provides link management to the repositories by storing the URLs to the documents and associated figures. By keeping separate URLs for each figure, users can retrieve them independently from the document.

In addition to providing document and figure linkages, the metadata also provides linkages to external sources. This includes other articles cited in the document that might be electronically available. Links to the local OPAC can provide location and availability information to printed materials. The custom client developed by the DLI group provides links to relevant INSPEC records where controlled vocabulary terms from its thesauri are displayed for each article. The metadata can provide much value added information.

The DLI testbed also relies on metadata to serve as document surrogates on the index server. The idea behind this is that the index servers are separate from the document repositories. Documents are only temporarily available locally to the index servers. A "web spider" is used to deliver documents to the indexing system in addition to FTPing. The indexing system stores pointers to the document contents. The contents are not retrievable directly from the indexing system once the documents are removed from the local environment. This makes it difficult to retrieve basic bibliographic information necessary for the display of intermediate results. There are two types of intermediate results. The first consists of just the article titles that represent the initial results set. The second consists of the bibliographic description of each article in the results set individually displayed. The description includes full title, author(s) and affiliation(s), citations, abstract, and captions and links to figures and tables.

As a result, the bulk of the metadata consists of bibliographic data parsed directly from the article. Some of the metadata actually precoordinate bibliographic information that exists in the SGML as complex constructs. For example, authors are associated to their institutional affiliations by indirection. An internal reference ID next to the author's name is resolved at the end of the article where all the affiliations are listed by reference number. The search algorithms provided by the indexing system cannot easily associate the author to the appropriate affiliation. The metadata presents the association between author and affiliation in a much simpler and easily accessible form.

The indexing system allows for the incorporation of metadata at the time of indexing. As with the filtering process described above, each file is piped to a custom program that parses the document for metadata as it is being indexed. Metadata contents as well as pointers to them are stored by the indexing system. The indexing system allows users to search both the document and its metadata as a single object. But since metadata contents are stored by the indexing system separate from the documents, they can be retrieved directly from the indexing system. Metadata is the source for the display of intermediate results.

There are problems with using metadata as document surrogates. Metadata should provide value added information, not redundant information. Redundancy contributes to the problems of scalability and data coherency. It is now necessary to use metadata to resolve complex constructs such as author-affiliation associations. However, there are commercially available SGML syntax checkers that are able to deal with these types of constructs. The checker currently used for the DLI testbed flags those cases where a reference ID does not point to its reference in the article. A future version of the index system should do the same thing as the syntax checker and automatically resolve a reference id to its reference. Finding articles where the author is associated with a specific affiliation should be easily searchable directly from the documents.

A more fundamental issue is that the metadata is filtered to display only ASCII text. This is necessary since the facility that displays the metadata as the contents of the intermediate results cannot resolve entities or specialty tags. Unfortunately, because of the technical subject matter of most of the articles that are processed, even titles are heavily punctuated with entities. Formulas are represented as complex SGML constructs or as TeX. This has the effect of rendering the metadata contents as unintelligible with as many holes and gaps as Swiss cheese.

There must be a way to render the intermediate results in graphical form. One idea that comes to mind is why not use the SGML browser to display the intermediate results. Beyond the group of titles that comprise the initial results set, the bibliographic information associated with each title is displayed one at a time. Why not fetch the original document at this point. Documents can have multiple views. The browser allows documents to be associated with several style sheets. One style sheet is used to render the document in its entirety. A second style sheet can be employed to display only bibliographic information. The style sheet can render the document to display only specified sections of the article. All other areas can be styled as hidden. Entities are resolved. Reference ids are linked to their references. In short, the bibliographic information is presented in its full graphical form.

Several issues need to be addressed in order for this approach to be made viable. The first is performance. How much time will it take to fetch and render an article where most of the article is hidden? Will it be faster than having to display the entire article? The browser fetches figures on an as-needed basis. However, many of the articles have a large number of embedded GIFs representing formulas that have been converted from the original TeX. Formulas are in TeX and not SGML because the current version of the SGML browser has difficulty in accurately rendering math in SGML. The browser cannot work directly with TeX. Therefore, TeX encodings must be parsed and converted.

Another issue has to do with the part of metadata that provides value added information such as linkages. The custom client is able to display both bibliographic information and value added information such as links to other sources since all the data originate from a single source. If the browser is used to display the bibliographic information directly from the original document, how do you integrate it with the value added information from the metadata? The browser does not inherently display data from different sources simultaneously. A separate facility must be used to display the information from the metadata. A display manager will need to be developed to handle the different "frames." These are areas that need further investigation.

OBJECT TECHNOLOGY

The static binding characteristic of tightly-coupled systems limits the degree of scalability and extensibility. What is searched and how it is searched are combined and bound together in pre-determined ways at compile time. It is hoped that the introduction of object technology can overcome these limitations. Object technology permits objects to be dynamically combined in unforeseen ways. This contributes towards greater extensibility. Object technology also offers improved modularity where changes made to one area of the system do not impact other areas. This contributes towards greater scalability.

Central to object technology is the object.[9,11] An object is a representation of real-world entities. It comprises a set of data attributes or properties defined by a data structure. It also comprises a set of operations or services that can be performed. These operations may change the state of the object's attributes. Together, an object's attributes and operations form a modular unit of information. For example, the bibliographic domain may include author, title, abstract and publisher objects. The author object may consist of attributes such as first name, last name and institutional affiliation. A set of operations that can be performed involving these attributes include search author, how many results, and retrieve documents.

There are many different ways of segmenting a particular domain into objects and defining them by a set of properties and operations. Another way to describe the bibliographic domain mentioned above would be to create objects based on access methods. One object describes accessing bibliographic information using the Z39.50 protocol. Another describes access based on the Telnet or HTTP protocols.

A key concept is that the actual implementation of an object is not known by the user of the object. The visible exterior that interfaces with the user encapsulates an inaccessible interior that supports the object's operation (Figure 11). There is a separation between a description of what the object does (exterior) and how it actually does it (interior). The interior consists of details such as data representation and the implementation of various operations. The user of the object only needs to know the specifications of the object. This is called the object's interface. The specifications that describe the

FIGURE 11. An object consists of properties and operations that can be performed. The interface functions encapsulates the object by hiding the details and actual mechanisms of the object. The object's interface and the object's implementation may reside on separate servers.

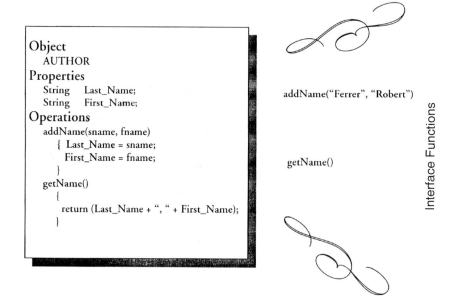

```
Object
  AUTHOR
Properties
  String    Last_Name;
  String    First_Name;
Operations
  addName(sname, fname)
    { Last_Name = sname;
      First_Name = fname;
    }
  getName()
    {
      return (Last_Name + ", " + First_Name);
    }
```

addName("Ferrer", "Robert")

getName()

Interface Functions

operations that can be performed are called the interface functions. They are also known as member functions or methods. The details of the object can be changed without affecting the object's interface. This is important for a client-server architecture where the implementation of an object may reside on a remote server and the object's interface resides on a client. Invoking a method (method invocation) is similar to sending a message to an object in which a particular operation is performed on the data encapsulated within the object.

Objects with similar characteristics may be grouped together and hierarchically arranged. Those at lower levels of the hierarchy inherit the characteristics or attributes of those objects higher up the hierarchy. Inheritance of this type permits the reuse of components that have already been defined. The characteristics of objects are extended without having to modify existing objects. Existing objects become base models for new objects.

For example, there are many types of authors (Figure 12). Just to mention a few, there are authors of books, composers of music and artists of artwork. Common to them is that they all have names which generally consist of first and last names. A base author object is composed of a first and last name. Derived from the base object are new objects characterized by the different types of authors. Each derived object accesses the name characteristics of the base author object. It can also access the functions associated with the base object, such as add Name(last name, first name). The new derived objects have properties and functions specific to the nature of their type. The composer object is further characterized by the different instruments that composers write for. The artist object is further characterized by the different media (painting, sculpture, etc.) in which artists create.

Related to the concepts of encapsulation and inheritance mentioned above is the concept of polymorphism where the same operation is applied to different types of objects (Figure 13). A base object may contain operations of a general nature. For example, the base author object contains a function that returns the genre of the author's work. Depending on the type of author, genre can have different meanings. For the author of books, genre can mean Mystery or Science Fiction. Genre can mean Classical or Jazz for the composer of music. Artists can work in the Abstract or Realistic genre. Each derived object has the same interface function as the base object to return the genre of the author's work. However the implementation of the function differs depending on the type of object involved. The results of the function may also differ.

In a client-server architecture, messages are sent requesting services via the interface. Included in the message is the type of object involved. In regards to polymorphism, the system determines how to service the request based on the type of object involved, and dynamically binds the object to a

FIGURE 12. COMPOSER and ARTIST are derived from the base object, AUTHOR. The deried objects inherit the properties First_Name and Last_ Name from the base object. The COMPOSER object also has the property Instrument. The ARTIST object also has the property Media.

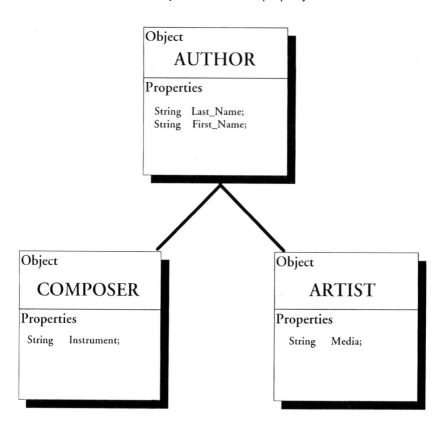

specific implementation at the time of method invocation during runtime. This is contrary to the less flexible but more efficient method of statically binding the interface with its implementation in advance at compile time. Method invocation automatically results in the execution of a specific implementation that has already been predetermined.

CORBA

Common Object Request Broker Architecture (CORBA) represents one of the more widely known models of distributed object-oriented comput-

FIGURE 13. In this example of polymorphism, isGenre() is a function where its interface is common to the derived objects, but its actual implementation varies depending on the specific object.

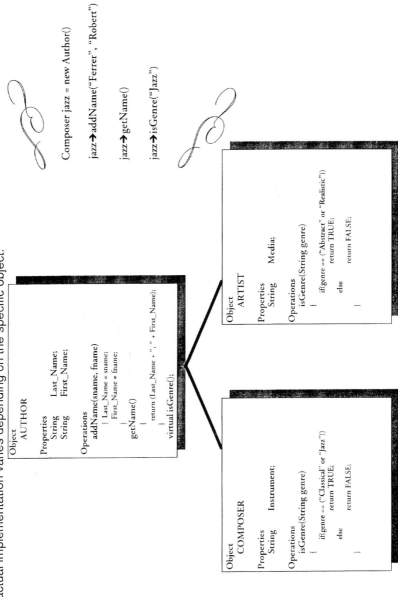

ing.[16,21] Its standards have been incorporated in the middleware of several commercially available network system products. CORBA relies heavily on the concepts that characterize both object-oriented and client-server technologies.

CORBA uses an open systems approach where designers can implement the CORBA specifications in a variety of ways depending on their needs. Designers are free to choose the most appropriate hardware and software to use for each component of the CORBA system. CORBA components may interact synchronously or asynchronously, and in any combination. Components may be distributed among different servers. CORBA specifications center on CORBA objects and begin with a request (Figure 14).

CORBA objects are abstractions of real-world entities possessing attributes and operations. The manipulation of an object is mediated by the object's interface. The object is known to the client only by what is defined by its interface. The rest of the details of the object are hidden. The Interface Definition Language (IDL) defines the different types of objects by specifying their interfaces. The IDL specifies for each object's interface a set of interface functions and parameters to these functions. It is through these functions that the object's attributes are accessed and changed. The various IDL definitions that represent the objects in a system are stored in an Interface Repository (IR). Each object definition registered in the IR is given a unique object reference ID. The object reference is used to map an object's interface to its implementation, which may reside on a remote server. CORBA specifies a global object reference structure that permits different implementations of CORBA to interoperate.

Requests for services are made from the client. The client does not know the location of the object or any of the implementation details. A request consists of a target object's reference ID, the operation to be performed, and any necessary parameters. The most common request is the type where the client knows the specific object and operation to perform as defined by the IDL. This is known as a static invocation interface since the request is incorporated into the client's code as a function call. The request is statically bound to an object and its implementation at compile time.

CORBA also provides a means to dynamically build and invoke a request at runtime. This is used when the client application does not know the object's interface at compile time and wants to discover it during runtime. This is known as a dynamic invocation interface since the request is dynamically established, and then bound to an object and its implementation at runtime. Requests are constructed from information obtained from the Interface Repository. The client specifies the type of object and operation to be performed. By repeatedly querying the IR, the client is able to discover an appropriate object, and specify an interface function along with the necessary

FIGURE 14. In this example of a CORBA implementation, the client makes two method calls. Method call 'A' is statically invoked and is associated with an Object Reference ID. Proxy 'A' is immediately created and interfaces with the Object Request Broker via the Interface Definition Language (IDL) Stub. The second call is dynamically invoked (Dynamic Invocation Interface, DII). An Interface Repository (IR) Proxy communicates with an Interface Repository until an appropriate interface function is constructed. Proxy 'B' can now be created and follow the same path as Proxy 'A'. The requests pass through the appropriate IDL skeletons on the server side where Object Adapters map object references to object implementations that reside on remote servers from information stored in an Implementation Repository. The Object Adapters implement the requests by communicating with the appropriate servers. The ORB Core handles the communications that connect the client and server via the Remote Procedure Call (RPC).

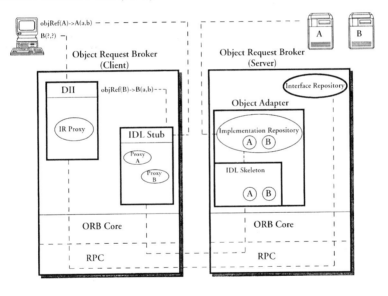

parameters. The request is treated as a function call after it is fully constructed.

Regardless of the type of request, each request may spawn what is called a proxy process. A proxy process interfaces with the CORBA network and handles the request on behalf of the client. This facilitates asynchronous operations since the client is free to do other work while the proxy is busy handling the request. The proxy interacts with the CORBA network using the more reliable synchronous RPC protocol. The proxy notifies the client when it is ready to return the results of the request. Proxies interface with the CORBA infrastructure through the Object Request Broker (ORB).

The ORB is the infrastructure that connects the clients and servers and allows for object communications. It is middleware that handles the binding of interfaces and methods that implements requests. The Object Request Broker locates the target objects residing on different servers and routes requests to them through message passing. It can relay requests across heterogeneous environments. The ORB is also responsible for getting results back to the client via proxies.

On the client side, statically bound requests, as defined by the Interface Definition Language, interfaces with the ORB via the IDL Stub. Dynamically bound requests follow a more complicated path that begins with the Dynamic Invocation Interface (DII). It is through the IDL Stub and the DII that the Object Request Broker is able to implement requests on the server side. Object implementation is handled the same way for both dynamically and statically bound requests.

Object implementation on the server side is supported by Object Adapters (OA). They are responsible for facilitating method invocation by mapping object references to object implementations from information stored in an Implementation Repository. Object Adapters are also responsible for invoking object implementations that reside on remote servers and for passing requests to ORBs that reside on different CORBA systems.

Object technology used in conjunction with client-server architecture, such as CORBA, address the need for interoperability by allowing applications to communicate with one another no matter where they are located or how they are designed. Together, they are part of a strategic arsenal capable of making the federation of loosely-coupled systems viable. This is evidenced by the two digital library projects presented below.

INFOBUS PROJECT–STANFORD UNIVERSITY

Stanford University's Digital Library Project implements the CORBA model as the distributed object network protocol to access a variety of information services. The objective, as envisioned by what the project calls the InfoBus, is to be able to multiplex a single query to any number of information providers. The InfoBus would be able to transparently maneuver through all of the protocol-level interoperability issues. The project initially focuses on accessing computing literature from Dialog, Stanford's library catalog and the World Wide Web.

Stanford defines the bibliographic domain by the service providers that facilitate access to information.[15,10] Services such as Dialog, Stanford's library catalog and the World Wide Web are objects. They are represented to the client as specialized CORBA objects which the project calls proxy objects. Proxy objects appear to have the same interface, yet are wrappers for the various implementations that speak the native protocol of the services. Requests for service are communicated by method calls based on the COR-BA IDL. A proxy implementation executes the method call using the appropriate protocol of the service. There are proxies for the World Wide Web (HTTP protocol), Stanford's library catalog (Z39.50 protocol) and Dialog (Telnet protocol). Proxy objects make full use of inheritance and polymorphism.

The idea behind this is that there is a common abstraction that describes the activities associated with searching these service providers. Common to them is that a search begins with an "Open Session" command. The command could open a Telnet session or be the URL to a web crawler such as Yahoo. Next comes the "Open Database" command that specifies the database or web page (search form) to access for searching. Following this is the "Search" command where the query is posed in the native language of the service. Finally there is the "Quit" command to exit the service. Additional commands include "How Many Hits" and "Get Documents."

Together, these commands constitute the methods for the Library-Service Proxy (LSP) object. The LSP encapsulates the protocol complexities associated with each service. It provides the common interface to library services. Their specificity is resolved at invocation by the parameters that are passed with the methods. The parameters indicate which service is involved so that the desired operation is performed on the appropriate service using the native protocol of the service. For example, after beginning a session with Dialog the method "Search("object technology", title)" invokes an operation to transmit in Dialog's native language the command "select object(w)technology/ti" to find titles containing the phrase object technology.

An example of a protocol that utilizes the LSP object demonstrates how a search process may be implemented based on CORBA (Figure 15). The client creates a query object containing a search string and the intended library service. A local Result Collection object is created that binds the query object to the intended LSP and assigns an object identifier. The Result Collection object interacts with the client program returning the results of the query as they appear. The Result Collection object initiates the search by asynchronously invoking the target LSP which may reside on a remote server. By using asynchronous LSP invocation the client does not need to wait for the completion of the session before doing other tasks.

The LSP conducts the search executing a sequence of method calls that constitute a search session with the associated service. The LSP acts as a CORBA proxy process and is responsible for maintaining a session with the service. CORBA Object Adapters make the necessary protocol translations and invoke the appropriate operations in order to implement the request on the specific library service. Object Adapters also maintain session informa-

FIGURE 15. This is a simple search of Dialog using Stanford University's InfoBus concept of a Library Service Proxy (LSP). The Local Result Collection assigns an identifier (DialogLSP) to the query object and communicates directly with the Dialog LSP. The Dialog LSP translates the query into Dialog's native form and initiates a Telnet session with Dialog. The results are eventually forwarded to the user.

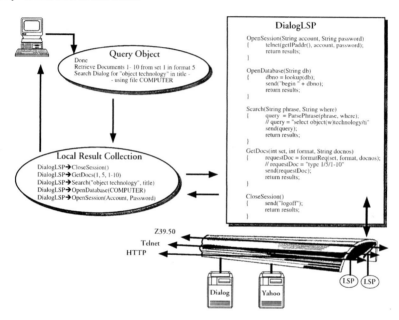

tion, store intermediate results and invoke helper agents, such as "URL-Getters," to facilitate the delivery of documents. Finally, the results are transported back to the Result Collection object where it formats and presents the results to the client.

UMDL PROJECT–UNIVERSITY OF MICHIGAN

The University of Michigan Digital Library Project (UMDL) uses a proprietary architecture to support the federation of loosely-coupled digital library collections and services.[4,18] Initially the project focuses on federating collections in Earth and Space Sciences. Delivery of documents is facilitated by the WWW using the HTTP protocol.

The core of the architecture is the concept of the software agent. An agent is a highly encapsulated module of software representing an element of a collection or service with very specific capabilities. Agents may dynamically team together in order to combine their capabilities to handle more sophisticated tasks such as those that are required to fulfill a complex search request. Collectively, agents provide the underlying infrastructure that give the architecture the properties that characterize object technology.

Agents are autonomous. An agent independently decides to fulfill a request only if it is compatible with the profile of what the agent can do, and the agent is not overloaded with other requests. This type of decentralized control is necessary for scalability. Autonomy is supported by a proprietary communications protocol that agents use to negotiate with each other for resources. This permits the dynamic binding of agents to requests and tasks. Modularity and extensibility are supported since new specialized agents may be added to the system as needed without impacting other agents or disturbing the system. The addition and removal of agents are recorded in a registry.

There are many types of services that are performed. One is the registry service that maintains a directory of agents in the system. The registry contains a description of all available agents, including their characteristics and capabilities. A database is also maintained containing detailed descriptions of each collection.

Selective Dissemination of Information (SDI) is another service performed by a system of agents that offers the automatic delivery of materials to patrons as new resources become available. There are services that provide commerce support to insure that producers are properly compensated for their products. A major service is handling user queries and finding appropriate information sources. This involves the brokering of agents into suitable teams adept in fulfilling the request.

Agents are classified into three groups. There are User Interface Agents (UIA), Collection Interface Agents (CIA) and Mediation Agents (MA). Users Interface Agents mediate user access to the system. They convert queries and other user interactions into a form that can be understood by other agents. UIAs create and maintain user profiles that agents can use to support searching. User profiles are consulted by agents to facilitate the delivery of SDI services. UIAs are also responsible for formatting and presenting search results to users.

The UMDL system defines a collection as a set of documents. The documents may be SGML-based full-text articles, WWW sites, and other multimedia materials. Documents in a collection may reside in a single repository or spanned across multiple databases. Associated with each collection is a Collection Interface Agent. CIAs mediate access to collections. A major role of CIAs is to provide the registry with information regarding the collections. They provide detailed descriptions of the content and structure of each collection. CIAs describe the indexing systems associated with each collection, and how to search them using their native language. This allows UIAs to browse a specific collection directly. CIAs also provide information on how to access the collection. They tell UIAs what protocol to use in order to retrieve specific documents. Some collections are accessed using the HTTP protocol. Others are accessed using Z39.50.

Mediation Agents represent a major class of agents. They manage all the necessary tasks that support the system, such as those tasks that eventually direct a user to a collection based on a specific query or user profile. Mediation Agents communicate only with other agents. Types of MAs include registry agents that manage the registry, and remora agents that provide SDI services. There are MAs responsible for maintaining statistics on various activities. For example, they can determine what the hot topics are on the WWW. The implementation of services, as previously described, involves the execution of multiple tasks and the coordination of many agents. The Task Planner Agent (TPA) is an MA responsible for managing tasks and agents. A special type of TPA is the Query Planner Agent (QPA) that coordinates search services initiated by user queries.

The QPA negotiates with other agents to form a team that can best handle the query. The QPA relies on facilitators, specialized agents adept in the process of negotiation, to help form the team. The QPA consults with registry agents to find appropriate agents to do specific tasks. For example, the registry could direct the QPA to various thesauri agents to help reformulate the query to maximize recall and precision. Index agents are used to communicate with the indexing systems associated with the collections to yield results.

Agents communicate with each other using a proprietary language developed by UMDL called the Conspectus Language. It is a highly structured language that is both syntactically and semantically normalized. The Conspectus Language employs an asynchronous message-exchange mechanism to allow inter-agent communications within a client-server environment. Agents use the "ASK" performative to request information from another agent. The agent responds to the request using the "TELL" performative. Through the standardized exchange of messages, agents learn about the existence and capabilities of other agents. Furthermore, since users, collections, indexing systems and thesauri are represented by a variety of agents circumscribed by their Conspectus Language specifications, an abstracted normalized description of the information space, or metadata, is formed. This provides the necessary interoperability to access information across collections controlled by various search and retrieval methods.

By way of example, a scenario where a user is looking for articles on the El Niño weather phenomena might proceed as follows (Figure 16). The UIA contacts the registry for a TPA that knows about query searching. A QPA is chosen that specializes in subject searches. The QPA consults the registry for agents that can help. The registry indicates that searching full-text databases

FIGURE 16. The UMDL protocol begins with the User Interface Agents (UIA) consulting with a Registry (1) for a Query Planner Agent (QPA). The UIA forwards the query to the QPA (2). It consults the Registry (3) for a team of agents that can facilitate the search. The agents (4) communicate with their respective resources and return a set of results that satisfy the search criteria. The QPA relays this information to the UIAs where they contact the appropriate Collection Interface Agents (CIA). The desired documents are retrieved and sent back to the UIAs (5).

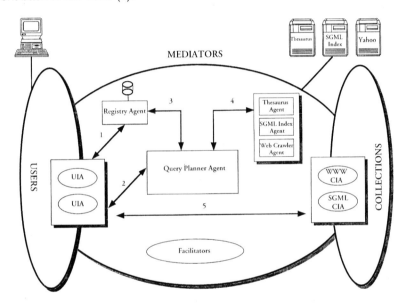

in Earth Science would yield good results. Searching the World Wide Web would also be worthwhile due to the topical nature of the subject. The registry also indicates which thesauri should be consulted.

The QPA coordinates with a facilitator to form a team of agents who are able to execute the various tasks. There are agents who specialize in searching thesauri and reformulating a query using additional terms. There are agents who know how to translate a query using normalized SGML-based regions. The optimized queries are then given to agents representing an SGML-based index and a web crawler such as Yahoo!.

The results to these interrogations are collated based on a specified relevancy algorithm. The results comprise article titles, short descriptions of their contents, and addresses (URLs, for example) of collections that contain the articles. The results are then sent back to the requesting UIA. The UIA may further format the results based on the profile of the user.

Finally, the UIA contacts the CIA of each of the collections chosen by the user. The UIA communicates in the protocol specified by the CIA. In this case, all collections are accessed using the HTTP protocol. The desired articles are delivered to the user.

CONCLUSIONS

So, where is all this leading us? We can say unequivocally, "in the right direction." The DLI Project at the University of Illinois offers an implementation of a full-text information system that provides for searching with a high degree of precision, and retrieval of documents graphically rendered with a high degree of quality and fidelity to the printed version. Successfully utilizing SGML-based materials, the DLI Project has demonstrated that the unique linking capabilities of SGML and the value-added information that can be virtually appended to a document as metadata can ultimately engender a peer-to-peer collaborative work environment envisioned for the next century. The availability of electronic full-text articles will increase as it continues to show to be an efficacious form of publishing.

However, it is only through the ambitious network gateway models proposed by the UMDL Project at the University of Michigan and the InfoBus Project at Stanford University that the grand vision of the digital library can be fully realized. Their models offer the possibility of interoperating truly diverse and heterogeneous collections in a flexible and scalable manner. The DLI system suffers from a lack of these qualities due to its reliance on traditional technologies that statically bind the component databases into a tightly-coupled system and restrict communications to session-oriented connections. Any changes made by a publisher in the structure of its DTD usually result in having to rebuild the databases of all the publishers. Furthermore, as new publishers and links to services are added, the performance of the system deteriorates since the client has to wait for the session manager to complete its dialogue with all of the participating component databases before proceeding. The UMDL and the InfoBus models rely on emerging object-oriented technologies that dynamically bind component databases into a loosely-coupled system and allow for both synchronous and asynchronous communications.

The Stanford InfoBus focuses on protocol interoperability. It defines CORBA-based proxy objects that transparently provide a uniform high-level interface to different services. The DLI system can easily be one of the services that can be represented by a proxy object, and take advantage of the proxy's asynchronous operation. In any case, plugging any service into this virtual information bus will ultimately allow users to focus on their information needs rather than on the specific requirements of the information provider.

Using a plethora of fine-grained modules, UMDL agents focus on identifying appropriate search sources in addition to performing the necessary actions to retrieve results. The DLI system could easily be represented by a host of agents, especially since the granularity of agents corresponds to the granularity of SGML regions. An author agent can lead to an AUTHOR region in an SGML-based document. Ultimately, the UMDL system of agents offers the possibility of creating a federated knowledge-based system that aids users in choosing information sources to search. The UMDL Project is testing a prototype at a local High School with the idea of supporting inquiry-based education using agents as experts in helping students perform research.[1]

There are still many research problems that need to be addressed. The most difficult, of course, is the issue of dealing with heterogeneity. The DLI project has demonstrated that even among collections of relatively homogeneous materials (SGML-based documents from engineering), there are a host of problems associated with schema translation and integration. Adding to the complexity of this issue is the desire to integrate non-text resources (images, for example) and broad categories of information resources from truly disparate disciplines (humanities with science?).

The Digital Imaging Initiative at the University of Illinois is involved in several projects that explore the use of digital imaging and multimedia technology to provide access to non-print collections.[14] The Getty Project will make available over 8,000 digital images from six major US museums and the Library of Congress via the World Wide Web. The key is to make the images searchable. Currently, this is done by associating images with textual metadata. The project has defined a core set of metadata elements to describe the attributes of an image that can be indexed and searched. It is hoped that retrieval across different collections can be standardized by the mapping of these elements to image description. An even more ambitious project is to identify new methods of image retrieval based on colors, shapes and textures within images.

In addressing schema translation and integration, Stanford University's REACH project focuses on semantic heterogeneity among different repositories, and describes a model to integrate their elements into a common structure.[2] Using the concept of a virtual card catalog, schemes from different repositories are treated in a uniform way. Hierarchical relationships among attributes are encoded. For example, an author, composer, artist and reporter are all the same object. A uniform schema will collate them under the same category in the virtual card catalog.

The Interspace Project at the University of Illinois looks at the notion of vocabulary switching to allow conceptual searching across different disciplines.[12] This is motivated by the idea that developments in different disciplines may be relevant to each other. However, the vocabularies used to describe similar concepts prevent users from retrieving information. The project looks at the possibility of searching using concepts rather than words since different words (terms) may represent the same concept in different fields. Concepts are the subjects that are described by terms. For example, the term "El Niño" describes a concept of weather phenomena. Concepts for a given discipline are derived from traditional classification sources. A conceptual space for each discipline is created by evaluating the frequency in which two terms occur together in the same context. Terms are then inventoried under the concepts defined by the discipline's classification system. Terms in one subject area are mapped to similar terms in another. For example, the term "wind tunnel" is used in repositories for bridges and marine drilling. Users can then see how terms are used in different disciplines by the concept spaces they populate. They can also see how similar concepts across disciplines make use of different terms.

The purpose of the Digital Library Projects is not to provide complete solutions but incentives for commercial designers to utilize the various components developed to create their own possibilities. The market is still very immature. There is a paucity of tools available to automate the design and development of federated systems. But the groundwork has been laid, and the direction is clear. Homogeneity cannot be sustained when current trends push applications off large monolithic, centrally-controlled systems. Information providers will continue to own a variety of computer and database systems. They do not want to be locked into any one system. Loosely-coupled federated organizations address these trends by providing location transparency and site autonomy. Based on object-oriented and client-server technologies, scalability, interoperability, extensibility, and rapid development through modularity are supported. The Digital Library Projects have done much to put the market on the road to constructing bridges that will connect the "islands of the archipelago."

AUTHOR NOTE

Robert Ferrer holds an MLS in Library Service from Columbia University, New York and an MCS in Computer Science from the University of Illinois, Champaign-Urbana.

REFERENCES

1. Atkins, Daniel E., William P. Birmingham, Edmund H. Durfee et al. "Toward Inquiry-Based Education Through Interacting Software Agents." *Computer* 29(May 1996): 69-76.
2. Baldonado, Michelle, Q. Wang and Steve B. Cousins. "Addressing Heterogeneity in the Networked Information Environment." *Review of Information Networking* 2(1996): 83-102.

3. Beaver, David. "The Client/Server Revolution." *MacUser* (November, 1991): 191.

4. Birmingham, William P. "An Agent-Based Architecture for Digital Libraries." *D-Lib Magazine* (July 1995). See http://www.cnri.reston.va.us/home/dlib/July95/07birmingham.html

5. Chorafas, Dimitris. *Beyond LANs: Client/Server Computing.* New York: McGraw-Hill, Inc., 1994.

6. Cole, T. W. and W. H. Mischo. "UIUC DLI Testbed: Testbed Database & Client Technologies and Testbed Processing Customization." DLI Spring 1996 Partners Workshop May 2-3, 1996 Grainger Engineering Library: 60-78. Contact Susan Harum, dli@uiuc.edu

7. Kunze, John A. and R. P. C. Rodgers. "Z39.50 in a Nutshell (An Introduction to Z39.50)." *National Library of Medicine* (July 1995). See http://www.informatik.th-darmstadt.de/VS/Infos/Protocol/Z39.50/z39.50-nutshell.html

8. Lewis, Ted G. "Where is Client/Server Software Headed?" *Computer* 28(April 1995): 49-55.

9. Loomis, Mary E. S. *Object Databases: The Essentials.* Reading, MA: Addison-Wesley Publishing Company, 1995.

10. Paepcke, Andreas, Steve B. Cousins, Hector Garcia-Molina et al. "Using Distributed Objects for Digital Library Interoperability." *Computer* 29(May 1996): 61-68.

11. Rao, Bindu R. *C++ and the OOP Paradigm.* New York: McGraw-Hill, Inc., 1993.

12. Schatz, Bruce R. "Information Retrieval in Digital Libraries: Bringing Search to the Net." *Science* 275(January 17, 1997): 327-334.

13. Schatz, Bruce R., Hsinchun Chen, William H. Mischo et al. "Federating Diverse Collections of Scientific Literature." *Computer* 29(May 1996): 28-36.

14. See http://images.grainger.uiuc.edu/ Contact Beth Sandore, sandore@uiuc.edu

15. See http://Walrus.Stanford.EDU/diglib/

16. See http://www.grainger.uiuc.edu/dli/

17. See http://www.si.umich.edu/UMDL/

18. Sheth, Amit P. and James A. Larson. "Federated Database Systems for Managing Distributed, Heterogeneous, and Autonomous Databases." *ACM Computing Surveys* 22(September 1990): 183-236.

19. Thurston, Robert. "CORBA Tutorial." See http://www.cs.umbc.edu/~thurston/cbatop.htm

20. Turner, Fay. "An Overview of the Z39.50 Information Retrieval Standard." UDT Occasional Paper #3(July, 1995). See http://www.nlc-bnc.ca/ifla/VI/5/op/udtop3.htm

21. Yang, Zhonghua and Keith Duddy. "CORBA: A Platform for Distributed Object Computing." *ACM Operating Systems Review* 30(April 1996): 4-31.

Toward Seamlessness with XML

Daniel Chudnov

SUMMARY. Across the Internet, the number and diversity of applications using Extensible Markup Language (XML) are growing rapidly. This growth requires that information service providers take a close look at how the power of XML might be leveraged. Along with Resource Description Framework (RDF), Document Object Model (DOM), and Etensible Style Language (XSL), with XML it is possible to move closer toward seamless integration of information resources and services. After a brief discussion of the relationship between these standards, two short examples demonstrate how new models of integration using XML might arise and take hold in the technologies upon which our community depends. *[Article copies available for a fee from The Haworth Document Delivery Service: 1-800-342-9678. E-mail address: getinfo@haworthpressinc.com]*

KEYWORDS. Extensible Markup Language (XML), Resource Description Framework (RDF), Document Object Model (DOM), Etensible Style Language (XSL), seamless integration, standards

A nascent family of standards is changing the way information content and services are delivered. The Extensible Markup Language (XML), Resource Description Framework (RDF), Document Object Model (DOM), and Extensi-

Daniel Chudnov is IAIMS Assistant and a Librarian at the Cushing/Whitney Medical Library at Yale University in New Haven, CT. Under the IAIMS program, sponsored by the National Library of Medicine, Daniel participates in information integration projects within the Yale medical community and the Yale University Libraries. He is also a co-chair of the Health Level Seven SGML/XML Special Interest Group, charged with creating the standard for the use of SGML/XML in health care. He can be reached at daniel.chudnov@yale.edu.

[Haworth co-indexing entry note]: "Toward Seamlessness with XML." Chudnov, Daniel. Co-published simultaneously in *Science & Technology Libraries* (The Haworth Press, Inc.) Vol. 17, No. 3/4, 1999, pp. 121-130; and: Digital Libraries: Philosophies, Technical Design Considerations, and Example Scenarios (ed: David Stern) The Haworth Press, Inc., 1999, pp. 121-130. Single or multiple copies of this article are available for a fee from The Haworth Document Delivery Service [1-800-342-9678, 9:00 a.m. - 5:00 p.m. (EST). E-mail address: getinfo@haworthpressinc.com].

ble Style Language (XSL) comprise a revolutionary new set of tools for giving users information they need and the ability to integrate that information like never before.[1,2,3,4] Several articles have already appeared in various sources to introduce and explain the formation and intention of these standards from a technical standpoint. Instead of summarizing these new standards in great detail again, in this article examples of how these standards interrelate will serve to demonstrate their growing importance to those responsible for the technical aspects of providing information resources and services.

Foremost among these standards is XML, a restricted subset of SGML optimized for use on the World Wide Web. XML is a standard metalanguage for defining electronic document types and how to mark up documents that match those types. The Architecture Domain of the World Wide Web Consortium has developed XML to solve several of the limitations of HTML with much of the power but only some of the complexity of SGML.[5] For web publishers frustrated by the lack of flexibility in HTML, using XML offers the ability to define new tags or apply stylesheets in a standard, modular fashion. This ability comes with less than the full price of a commitment to SGML, however, because compared to SGML it is much easier to build applications using XML.

That XML fits a vast market need is evidenced by its rapid widespread adoption, heavily publicized even before completion of the final draft specification of XML. Several major initiatives gained substantial industry and vendor support before the end of 1997, including the Channel Definition Format (CDF) for defining how a given set of information content can be delivered across the network, and XML/Electronic Data Interchange (XML/EDI) for defining the syntax of business-to-business messaging.[6] Additionally the immediate proliferation of XML development tools written in a wide variety of programming languages and distributed freely on the internet demonstrates that as intended by design, XML truly is easy to use in building applications, particularly when compared to SGML.[7,8]

For information service providers, the use of XML in standards for aspects of information management related to those addressed by XML is equally significant. RDF is rapidly evolving as a standard XML-based syntax for cataloging and resource discovery based on metadata management. DOM "is a platform- and language-neutral interface that will allow programs and scripts to dynamically access and update the content, structure and style of documents."[3] If browser vendors support DOM widely, web programmers can design web sites that offer richly structured information using XML or HTML knowing that the site will work the same for users with any DOM-compliant browser. For building modular stylesheets, XSL "is meant to make it easier to pour data defined in XML into web page templates," and works by defining rules for how to render XML tags.[13]

How does this alphabet soup of standards fit together? With newly avail-able and lightweight programming environments such as Java and ActiveX, embedding very small programs in web pages to make the web content more interactive is now relatively easy. Those wanting their information to be published in a manner more robust than what HTML allows can quickly build small programs in Java or with Visual Basic that meet their additional needs. Given this ability, these same content providers might find significant economies of scale if their information content were encoded in a consistent manner. With XML, they have a standard for defining and applying their own standard for doing exactly that without much additional processing overhead required by their small programs. These application designers can use XML to define and apply tagsets that describe and structure their information separately from their applications.

Given XML-encoded content, publishers might also use a stylesheet stan-dard such as XSL, which is, like RDF, expressed using XML syntax. To apply a stylesheet to a particular document, the small program doesn't need to grow beyond recognizing which stylesheet to use and applying it appropri-ately, because it can already interpret the stylesheet itself using the XML processing functionality already present. Furthermore, if programmers can build this small program to comply with the DOM specification, they can expect to have to write even less code because they know that DOM-com-pliant web browsers alone will provide much of the processing behavior described here on their own. Finally, if librarians catalogue this information resource using RDF-compliant descriptors, users might be better able to both find that resource and directly access it.

This does not mean that anyone wanting to publish information has to use all or any of these standards. The availability of these standards simply removes several barriers that have long stood in the way of publishers and service providers who want to deliver their information in new ways. With standard and newly easy ways to encode, manipulate, format, and describe their information, providers and vendors can focus their energies on the innovations and special features that make the way they deliver information uniquely suited to their users and clients. To demonstrate, consider the fol-lowing examples:

EXAMPLE ONE:
A SEARCH MARKUP LANGUAGE

Imagine this scenario: A post-doc researcher has been testing new cancer drugs, and frequently reviews the relevant literature for new ideas and to keep up with her cohorts. To stay on top of the literature today, that researcher might depend on a combination of citation management tools and SDI ser-

vices built into a locally available online database. It might also be likely that
to use these tools our researcher must perform a series of transformation steps
between each database and management tool involved in the equation. Additionally, some of the databases involved might not provide such a transformation tool at all, requiring the researcher to separately manage paper.

Certainly paper still works well, and there is no reason to assume that any
new standard will make all of the steps and potential problems inherent in this
scenario go away. Incrementally, however, we might see how these new
standards might improve at least some of these layers of transformation.

Imagine a new kind of environment for managing search results. This
environment might share functionality with both online database interfaces
and citation managers; its user interface might not be terribly novel, but
internally it manages query and result information using XML. Figure 1
demonstrates how this information might be manipulated as XML by the
retrieval application. This overly simple representation of a search and potentially appropriate tags shows several key features of XML.

As shown in Figure 1, XML encoded information depends on tags sur-
rounded by angle brackets such as <search>. These tags can contain a combination of data or more tags, in which case each opening tag must be
followed at the appropriate time by a closing tag, such as </search>. This
construct is defined in SGML, but unlike in SGML, it is impossible to use
tags lacking an actual opening or closing tag instance (such as the HTML
<p> tag, which is often not followed by a closing tag). Alternatively, a tag
might be empty, such as <connector type="AND"/>. The closing slash for
an empty tag is new to XML, but the concept of empty elements is from
SGML. A principal requirement of any XML document is that its tags, empty
or not, nest properly. This expectation of properly nested tags removes much
of the burden of understanding how elements of an encoded document fit
together from the processing application, accounting for a large part of the
decrease in processing overhead in XML compared to SGML.

Why is XML useful in this example? It might not at first seem to offer
much beyond what currently available interfaces provide. Consider the application of XSL stylesheets to Figure 1. To display the results on the screen,
the search environment might apply a stylesheet for onscreen presentation of
results. If the researcher wants to export the results to her citation manager, a
second stylesheet could be used to transform the results into a format appropriate for that tool. Additionally, if the researcher wants to create or
update a web page for others to quickly be able to use her results (she is
known for her good searches), a third stylesheet might be applied which
formats the results as HTML, to be saved as a separate file. For any of these
transformations, the underlying representation of the results remains in
XML–the XSL stylesheets format the XML result data again and again as

FIGURE 1. A Truncated Example of a Search Markup Language Encoded Result Set

```
<search user="Joey_Postdoc" date="07041998">
 <topic>
Weekly check for new research
 </topic>
 <query number="1">
  <query_terms>
   <term_group type="subject">
    <term>cancer</term>
     <operator type="OR"/>
    <term>neoplasms</term>
   </term_group>
   <operator type="AND"/>
   <term_group type="subject">
    <term>drugs</term>
     <operator type="OR"/>
    <term>drug combinations</term>
   </term_group>
   <limit type="reviews"/>
  </query_terms>
  <results>
   <cite number="1">
    <title>Development of new drugs for pancreatic cancers</title>
    <authors>Smith M., Jones F.</authors>
    <journal>JIMA</journal>
    <date>1997 December</date>
    <issue>74(12):2243-9</issue>
    <abstract>...</abstract>
   </cite>
   ...
   ...
   ...
  </results>
 </query>
 <query number="2">
 ...
 </query>
</search>
```

needed, and because these formatting needs are fairly common, the researcher might not even have to generate the stylesheets herself.

Next, consider the flexibility for searching and data manipulation the XML encoding provides. Any piece of information that falls between a set of tags is described in part by that tag. Thus the article entitled "Development of new drugs for pancreatic cancers" is known to be a title. We also know that title is part of a citation that has more information to it (the journal name, authors, etc.), and that citation is one of several in a set of results from a query whose terms we also know, and so on. Knowing these relationships between items of data in a query interface might be useful in several ways. Given that this abbreviated sample result set might be very long and only one of several queries, the researcher might wish to sort all articles by date, or journal name. A more complicated sort function might have the citations ordered by author for each journal title listed, and by year where there are multiple entries by one author.

Finally, consider the result set as a database unto itself. Tools that today allow our researcher to manage references (and perform functions like the sorting described above) might not also store the context in which sets of references were found. A tool that stored the full XML encoded query stream would give the researcher both the citations of interest and the keywords used to find those citations. In effect, the user would over time compile, should she so choose, a derivative database of her own that could itself be queried and reviewed as her research progresses over time. The SDI aspect of regularly performing similar searches might therefore be decoupled from the database itself; a community of users might share expert strategies by referencing the data collected by each other or proscribed by a librarian in this manner, independent of any single database interface.

"Text as Data"

The potential for decoupling search and retrieval applications to better serve users is clearly seen by publishers. At the National Library of Medicine, where the Entrez web-based query engine for retrieval of Medline and sequence data has been actively promoted as an open environment for local development of retrieval clients, XML figures significantly in future plans. According to Brandon Brylawski, Director of the PubMed project, XML will be used for both input and output. "This will permit users to query our databases in any way they wish and receive formatted data in return that they can display as they like, store into their own databases, or compile together with other information. . . Adding XML capability to the engine will permit outside software to get at the details of the data without requiring knowledge of the Entrez engine itself."[9,10] Figure 2 shows a more robust example of how this output from PubMed might look; note the finer granularity of data elements such as the separation of author names (as well as first, middle, and last names).

EXAMPLE TWO:
INTEGRATION OF RESOURCES USING METADATA

The State University Library has decided to implement a metadata approach to cataloguing electronic resources, beginning with online journals.

FIGURE 2. Suggested XML Output from PubMed[10]

```
<ArticleSet>
 <Article>
  <Journal>
   <PublisherName>AAAS</PublisherName>
   <JournalTitle>SCIENCE</JournalTitle>
   <Issn>9731-864X</Issn>
   <Volume>271 suppl. 3</Volume>
   <Issue>5</Issue>
   <PubDate>
      <Year>1996</Year>
      <Month>Mar</Month>
      <Day>3</Day>
   </PubDate>
  </Journal>
  <ArticleTitle>The Elasticity of a Single
   Supercoiled DNA Molecule</ArticleTitle>
  <FirstPage>1835</FirstPage>
  <LastPage>1837</LastPage>
  <Language>EN</Language>
  <AuthorList>
   <Author>
    <FirstName>Kenneth</FirstName>
    <MiddleName>S.</MiddleName>
    <LastName>Strick</LastName>
    <Suffix>Jr.</Suffix>
    <Affiliation>
    Laboratoire de Biophysique de l&rsquo;ADN, Institut
    Pasteur, 25-28 rue du Dr Roux, Paris, 75015 France.
    </Affiliation>
   </Author>
   <Author>
    <FirstName>J.-F.</FirstName>
    <LastName>Allemand</LastName>
    <Affiliation>
     <Institution> Laboratoire de Physique
     Statistique de l&amp;rsquo;ENS, </Institution>
     <StreetAddress>24 rue Lhomond</StreetAddress>
     <City>Paris</City>
     <PostalCode>75015</PostalCode>
     <Country>France</Country>
    </Affiliation>
   </Author>
  </AuthorList>
  <PublicationType>JOURNAL ARTICLE</PublicationType>
```

FIGURE 2 (continued)

```
<Abstract>
Single linear DNA molecules were bound at multiple sites at
one extremity to a treated glass cover slip and at the other
to a magnetic bead. The DNA was therefore torsionally
constrained. A magnetic field was used to rotate the beads
and thus to coil and pull the DNA. The stretching force was
determined by analysis of the Brownian fluctuations of
the bead. Here, the elastic behavior of individual &lgr;
DNA molecules over- and underwound by up to 500 turns was
studied. A sharp transition was discovered from a low to
a high extension state at a force of &sim;0.45 piconewtons
for underwound molecules and at a force of &sim;
3 piconewtons for overwound ones. These transitions,
probably reflecting the formation of alternative structures
in stretched coiled DNA molecules, might be relevant for
DNA transcription and replication.
</Abstract>
<Keywords>
magnetic field;DNA transcription;Elasticity
</Keywords>
</Article>
</ArticleSet>
```

Using a tool based on RDF, every time a new journal or collection of journals becomes available to State U., information about the online resource is added to a database in addition to the library catalog entry. This information might include the extent of the resource available online, the base URL for the resource, and a reference to the query syntax used by the resource to retrieve specific articles (a syntax similar in purpose, if perhaps dissimilar in style, from Entrez, for example) among other data.

Perhaps some of the resources described in this manner are themselves SGML-encoded text databases. A student at State finds a journal article of interest in a citation database that returns XML-encoded results. If a system is in place to connect these three resources–the citation, the online article, and the metadata repository–the student might only need to click on a button next to the citation that reads "check State Library for this title" to get the article. This could work if a go-between application could first pull enough detail about the article into a query for the metadata repository; next, a favorable response from the metadata server would include a base URL and a reference to a system object for building query URLs based on that journal's query syntax; finally, a direct HTTP request from the system object to the online resource could return an XML version (remember, XML is SGML so this transformation might be trivially easy) of the article of interest directly back into the web browser the student has been using all along, where it would be formatted appropriately using a stylesheet and displayed by the DOM-compliant functions built into the browser (see Figure 3).

The slight processing overhead induced by the XML syntax present in several pieces of this example makes it possible for these transactions to occur across several machines over a relatively unnoticeable period of time. XML might in fact become widely used for several lower-level aspects of this sequence, including the object reference syntax itself. One organization doing exactly this is CogniTech Corporation, a health care systems group based in Utah. For a current large project involving maintenance of physician credentialing information, XML is vital for both content- and system-level pieces of the application CogniTech is building.[11] "This project used XML for representing three distinct forms of business domain content," says CogniTech President Dr. Jerome Soller, "the organization of visual components on a page of the user interface; the relationships of the pages within the user interface; and the mapping of the visual components to data object references."[12] A major benefit of this approach, according to Dr. Soller, is that "in

FIGURE 3. Using Metadata to Integrate Resources: A Simple View of the State U. Library Retrieval System

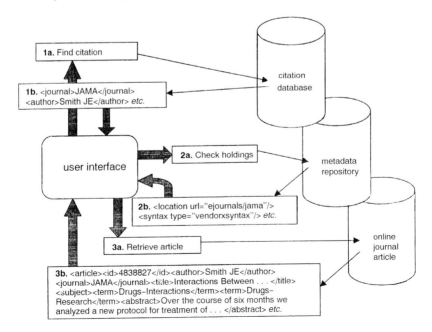

addition to the reduced maintenance of an XML approach, the XML representation is more compact, allowing the physicians to use the system over a modem line to the internet."

CONCLUSION

Ideally this article has described for you a practical view of what these standards will offer. To learn more about how applications built using these standards should be designed, or to follow or participate in the development of the standards themselves, follow the many online references cited below.

The impact of XML on the information industry is already being felt. While the opportunities discussed here for improving the way information is delivered are exciting, the widespread development of numerous resources such as metadata repositories based on XML and related standards is just beginning. Because these standards are designed with ease of use and implementation in mind, however, we should be prepared to set our sights as high as possible. The barriers to realizing better and better information services keep getting smaller.

REFERENCES

1. Bray, T and Paoli J, eds. Extensible Markup Language (XML), online at http://www.w3.org/TR/WD-xml

2. Resource Description Framework (RDF) Model and Syntax, online at *http://www.w3.org/Metadata/RDF/Group/WD-rdf-syntax*

3. Document Object Model, online at *http://www.w3.org/TR/WD-DOM*

4. XSL ref @ W3C

5. Flynn P et al. Frequently Asked Questions about the Extensible Markup Language, Version 1.1, October 1997, online at *http://www.ucc.ie/xml/*

6. XML: Proposed Applications and Industry Initiatives. Online at *http://www.sil.org/SGML/xml.html#applications*

7. XML/XSL Software, online at *http://www.sil.org/SGML/xml.html#xmlSoftware*

8. Matsumura, M. "XML speeds along in standards land," *Javaworld*, February 1998, online at *http://www.javaworld.com/javaworld/jw-02-1998/jw-02-miko.html*

9. PubMed, online at http://www.ncbi.nlm.nih.gov/PubMed

10. Personal communication, December 1997-January 1998.

11. CogniTech Corporation home page, online at http://www.cognitech-ut.com

12. Personal communication, December 1997-January 1998

13. Zelnick, N. "Microsoft Releases First Look at XSL, Launches 3-Tier Plan to Render HTML," *WebWeek*, January 12, 1998, p. 22.

Interface Design Considerations
in Libraries

Steve Mitchell

SUMMARY. The potential of new approaches for information system interface design is truly immense. Interactive, engaging and compelling interfaces and systems for information retrieval and visualization are under development. These will rely on greatly enhanced user options and controls that will fully involve all users at all levels of finding expertise. A major component of these interfaces will be well evolved multi- and hypermedia systems that will better apply traditional, textually presented information while going greatly beyond this to fully emphasize visual metaphor and other "sensorial" modes of understanding to facilitate the information seeking process. This article discusses these developments and associated research in regard to library related public access information systems. It is available on the Web at: http://

Steve Mitchell is Science Reference Librarian at the University of California at Riverside. He is co-founder and co-coordinator of INFOMINE, a pioneering scholarly resources virtual library covering most major academic disciplines (lib-www.ucr.edu). Steve is co-author, with David Bainbridge, of Sustainable Agriculture for California: A Guide to Information (1991, UC ANRPress, Publication 3349, 194 p.).

Pat Flowers (Rivera Library, University of California, Riverside) deserves thanks for her critical reading of the draft of this paper and her many knowledgeable suggestions. Similarly, David Stern (Kline Science Library, Yale University) and Margo Young (Bio-Agricultural Library, University of California, Riverside) deserve thanks for their thoughtful comments. Dr. Candace Schwartz (Graduate School of Library & Information Science, Simmons College) is to be thanked for providing some useful direction in the early going of this article. All opinions and errors found herein remain solely those of the author.

[Haworth co-indexing entry note]: "Interface Design Considerations in Libraries." Mitchell, Steve. Co-published simultaneously in *Science & Technology Libraries* (The Haworth Press, Inc.) Vol. 17, No. 3/4, 1999, pp. 131-181; and: *Digital Libraries: Philosophies, Technical Design Considerations, and Example Scenarios* (ed: David Stern) The Haworth Press, Inc., 1999, pp. 131-181. Single or multiple copies of this article are available for a fee from The Haworth Document Delivery Service [1-800-342-9678, 9:00 a.m. - 5:00 p.m. (EST). E-mail address: getinfo@haworthpressinc.com].

131

libwww.ucr.edu/pubs/stlinfoviz.html *[Article copies available for a fee from The Haworth Document Delivery Service: 1-800-342-9678. E-mail address: getinfo@haworthpressinc.com]*

KEYWORDS. Libraries, interface design, interactive, information retrieval and visualization, enhanced user options and controls, multi-and hypermedia systems, visual metaphor, "sensorial" modes of understanding

INTRODUCTION

Cone trees, information theaters, fisheyes, infocubes, cascades, emotional icons, Benediktine spaces, cityscapes and the general realm of populated information terrains are just some of the linguistic sparklers that greet the librarian researching Web interface design and systems. These signify, at the very least, a whole new generation of significant functions and features for library system interfaces and, just as probably, whole new ways of representing, finding and understanding information. One researcher has characterized what is happening now, in the joining and co-evolution of more powerful and less expensive computing technologies and the development of the Web (the newest electronic mass medium), as an information Big Bang (Young, 3/96). This may not be very far from the truth. One thing is certain though: libraries and related systems are going to be very different, very soon.

The challenge of this article has been to try and determine which ideas, among the rich concepts and terminology found on the InfoBahn in relation to interfaces, we want to explore and which represent the linguistic and conceptual litter that we want to avoid. This challenge of determining not only "what's new" but, more importantly, "what's next" is difficult and my concerns provide just one spin on what's happening.

This research and perspective have been developed in the course of starting a re-design of INFOMINE (http://lib-www.ucr.edu) (Mitchell and Mooney, 3/96; Mitchell, 3/97 and 6/97), a virtual library of links to over 11,000 scholarly resources. Over 5,000 of these concern the life and physical sciences. While very much concerned with understanding some of the new long-range visions in Web related information technology, I am more interested in what is possible or transferable to libraries now and over the next couple of years. Trying to discern viable trends for the Web and library related information and interfaces is a challenge and has been a bit like trying to draw a still life of a basket of live eels: doable but what results may be impressionism. Though relevant to other information retrieval interfaces and systems, the focus is on Web resource finding from the standpoint of virtual libraries and similar finding tools. This is where my experience has been.

A. INTERFACES

The human-computer interface is the means by which information is transferred between ourselves and the computer and vice-versa and includes both the actions involved in such a transference and any influence that one action has upon another–i.e., its consequences either in the real or virtual worlds. You and your computer or terminal, working (or playing) together, are the human-computer interface in the most general sense.

We're concerned here with the processes, dialogues, and actions through which a user employs and interacts with a computer. The human-computer interface is the portal which increasingly mediates most interactions between both librarians and users and the information they require. Think about the change in the format and amount and, therefore, the nature of information over the last fifteen years (but especially within the last three or four years) in a typical academic library environment from overwhelmingly print to multiple electronic formats. Think as well about the changes in finding tools as we move from the print/online catalog and limited numbers of online bibliographic databases to these PLUS the Web with its grand reach, richness of information and corresponding search engines and virtual libraries. These changes mean that the human-computer interface and related issues and concerns are matters in which librarians of all ranks need to seriously school themselves. There are a number of information system environments and research areas with which we need to become comfortable (see Environments to Consider, C1).

Things are changing rapidly. "Visual language researchers and user-interface designers are inventing powerful information visualization methods, while offering smoother integration of technology with task" (Shneiderman, 7/96). Older notions of information retrieval and database management are being pushed aside or augmented by newer notions of information gathering, seeking, or visualization as well as data mining, warehousing or filtering (Ibid.). The standards which undergird the interface environment are evolving rapidly: standards in hardware, display technology, hypermedia and hypertext, markup languages, Web software, data and retrieval. It is difficult to see where it will all end and the probable answer is that it won't. If you haven't already, get comfortable with changing systems' scenery out there among your public terminals (Juliussen 1/97).

New and well designed information systems and interfaces should allow us to better find and more fully use the information they organize and do so in a more timely and effective way than what we are currently using. A good interface actually enhances the quality of our interaction with our systems. Though information overload and anxiety characterize much current information seeking and librarian concern, there is no reason that, with the well designed interfaces which current and probable new tools will allow, our experience shouldn't become more productive, interesting and enjoyable (Shneiderman, 7/96). Still, though, a well-tempered approach is in order as the same author, among many others, cautions that "It will take a decade till sufficient experience, experimentation, and hypothesis testing clarify design issues," (Shneiderman, 1/97c).

No group is better suited than librarians and the library community to play a major role in defining new information systems and interface design processes in the new information environment. To some degree (see the sections on SGML, XML and Z39.50 below) such work has and is occurring. This role should be more evident as the initial Web smoke continues to clear and it becomes more obvious that, while everything is becoming different in relation to format, connectivity, immediacy of communication, interface, etc., everything is still really pretty much the same in terms of content quality concerns and other basic user information seeking and interface needs. This condition is also true for many of the fundamental guidance, organizing and educational roles with which we have long experience. We know the users. Scientific surveys and other instruments, though often contradictory or not adequately reflective of real situations, can be very useful but, really, we do work daily with large numbers of people with real information needs using real information systems. EXPERIENCE is the operative term here and we have as much or more than many of the research communities mentioned below (see Environments to Consider, C1). From this experience, we have learned, as our first covenant, that "Know thy user!" is where it all begins in information system interface design.

B. USERS–DEFINING AND INTERFACING WITH YOUR AUDIENCE

You need to know your audiences. You need to define them and work within their domain of known needs, goals, behaviors, expectations and traditions. As Shneiderman (1/97c) states: "As in any user interface design process, we begin by asking: Who are the users? and What are the tasks? An unproductive answer is that everyone is a user and therefore no analysis is needed. Even when broad communities are anticipated, there are usually implicit assumptions . . ." User studies abound in our profession as well as in those of the Web and hypermedia designer, the graphic designer, the human-computer interaction researcher, and the distance educator. These are our new friends and they give us invaluable outside perspective. Study their work but temper what you find with what you've seen at the reference desk. Interesting related Web sites providing user surveys are available at: QUIS: The Questionnaire for User Interaction Satisfaction (http://www.lap.umd.edu/QUISFolder/quisHome.html) and

The Software Usability Measurement Inventory (http://www.ua.ac.be/MAN/ WP51/t38.html).

Simple concerns, by way of example, include: What are the intended contexts of use (user requirements, needs, goals)? Among the various classes of users, which are the most important? Why are users accessing the site and how frequently will they visit? What experience and expertise do they have (in general information seeking, subject specialized information seeking, libraries, microcomputing, Internet usage)? What types of cultural differences exist among users? What type of information are they looking for? How will they want to use the information–read it on the screen, print it or download it? What type of hardware and software will they use?

Science Academic Audiences–Where They Are Now

Our people are science students and researchers. In many libraries they were the first to recognize the importance of the Web and call our attention to it. We can assume a little about them using the traditional categories of undergraduate and researcher (graduate student/faculty/research and library staff).

Researchers and graduate students generally, as compared to new undergraduates or the public, are familiar with print library usage, traditions, and metaphors in information seeking. They are: Focused and increasingly RE-QUIRE advanced information finding tools and currency and quality in information in order to be competitive (or cooperative) with their peers; Familiar, more or less, with online library systems (searching; displaying; scrolling; indexes; controlled vocabularies; titles, subjects, keywords, and other components of bibliographic records; tables of contents; the Boolean searching system; bibliographic and other databases); Familiar with microcomputer usage at a basic to advanced level, including familiarity with standard microcomputer software and environments (e.g., Windows™, word processors, spreadsheets); Familiar with the Internet through e-mail usage and, especially over the last year or so, most know how to use basic Web browser software and have captured and organized bookmarks but don't perceive themselves as having the time to learn HTML.

The other major group are the undergraduates who have a grasp of basic library usage but are challenged both in learning methodologies in library research in specific areas and in learning the tools and systems relevant to these areas. On the other hand, significant numbers of this group are often surprisingly accomplished in microcomputer usage and/or are relatively open to new information finding techniques and systems beyond the traditional library print and online modes.

Finally, among and between science library user groups, there is, of course, a lowest common denominator of undergraduates that can't read a call number as well as faculty who have never used a word processor. Also, there is an amalgam of researchers, students and library staff that are quite fluent in most information technologies and systems and function as forerunners, testing and clearing paths on which their colleagues and the library will later be skidded forward.

Much of these skill level differences and related design considerations can be viewed as simply a function of frequency of usage. This does mean that ideally we're designing for two or even three distinct user groups. "Knowledge of computers or websites can also influence design, but more important is the distinction between first-time, intermittent and frequent users of a website. First-time users need an overview to understand the range of services and to know what is not available, plus buttons to select actions. Intermittent users need an orderly structure, familiar landmarks, reversibility, and safety during exploration. Frequent users demand shortcuts or macros to speed repeated tasks and extensive services to satisfy their varied needs" (Shneiderman, 1/97c).

Science Academic Audiences–Where They Want to Go/ Where They Could Go

Science researchers often need current information now and they need it in flexible formats. Systems and interfaces need to be easy and efficient to use. These need to be perceived as "time savers." Though traditionally the library and related information systems have been seen as the "other" half of the laboratory or research process, it is laboratory time that is perceived as and often is the far more valuable time meaning that researchers, by and large, desire to economize as much as possible when engaged in information seeking in the library or on library systems.

Major time savings will occur of course via the Web as traditional and non-traditional, library housed and other materials (at a great number of diverse locations) become accessible from the desktop. Furthermore, as most desktop applications are integrated into the Web environment and evolve into the Webtop there will be continued significant gains in time saving. The Webtop means, for example, that as experimental data is being viewed and analyzed with statistics software through a Web site on campus, the researcher can also be examining this week's journal article covering extremely current information on the statistics package being utilized while corresponding with the author, paging through the current version of the manual and/or making notes about all this through numerous WINDOWS/software packages, all of which are activated through a single Web browser on a single machine on the researcher's desk. Researchers will generally in the future (and on some campuses currently) not need to frequent the library but will instead be able to access and immediately utilize much of the information they require where they actually work with it, on their desks or in their labs, at the time of need.

Finally, entirely new forms of information dissemination will accompany all of the above and need to be recognized by librarians. Pre-print bulletin boards (e.g., the High Energy Physics Preprint Bulletin Board–http://xxx. lanl.gov/) and their related, new virtual communities of critics/collaborators already exist (MacColl, 3/96; Harnad, 92). The journal article may become secondary, as a formality in credit taking with an archival-educational (as opposed to a working) role to these pre-print forms. These forms are effective because they function to get the scientific information consumer closer to the point in time in which the information was created. In addition, those consumers can actually, through invited/open critiques during the formative period of the article (this "forum" component being a major feature of the pre-print form), become crucial contributors to the information creation process and make substantial contributions to the final article. Feedback to authors on ideas can be almost immediate. Larger groups, and larger perspectives, can also be involved in these processes. The result again is that significant time is saved.

With so much quantitative change and new efficiencies possible in developing scientific information from the point of idea and data generation to broad dissemination, information technologies will probably have a fundamental influence not only on the nature of scientific information seeking but on the basic, qualitative nature of doing science. Doubling the speed of the dissemination process means that much is now different for our researchers and, through them, for us. Will academic audiences be going beyond the traditional journal article, whether in print or eformat? Probably. What does this mean for libraries and publishers? It is hard to say except to note that there are solid scenarios for many disciplines where our library systems, interfaces and roles, like the journal article or traditional monograph currently, will see major transformations. Academic corporate cultures don't necessarily change fast, however, and the gatekeeper culture in many scientific disciplines is no exception. The result, current events indicate, will probably be very uneven development among different scientific communities. Some disciplines will advance with the technology at a rapid clip and others will not. It is not hard to monitor the development of what will become widespread models; it is only necessary to keep tabs of new information and communication forms as they develop in the more rapidly moving and fairly well-supported disciplines and research areas of physics, medicine, genetics and computer science, among others.

The Librarian Audience

Many librarian communities, until recently, have tended towards some degree of insularity. Our community talks to itself a lot, maybe too much.

Many of us, for instance, "missed" the advent of the Web, lets face it (we're in good company though, considering that Microsoft missed it initially as well . . . and of course most of us were merely waiting for it to "mature" after all). There was even a perception, which has continued, that the Web was not somehow in our best interests (which may have occurred to Microsoft as well). Though I argue throughout this paper that librarians are well suited and will be increasingly required to play major roles in the creation of new types of information systems, mistakes can be made. Many of these mistakes stem from a library-ocentric perception of the role and uses of information together with a strong, undiversified investment in traditional approaches to understanding and organizing primarily print information. Such a view sees the role of the library as the primary societal repository of knowledge, a perception in which users will always be beating a one-way path to our doors. This is being mentioned here because, while this model is in place and still functional, it also can act as a blinder and can get carried forward into system interface design (e.g., virtual or digital libraries that will not let users use information in the way and with the flexibility they would want but, instead, require repeated treks through rigid gateways) and other places where it is neither appropriate nor realistic.

Similarly, we can at times persist in reasserting an old habit of overprojecting ourselves as "Everyuser" and that has increasingly become a mistake when the new technologies are involved. Bringing forward what we know, incautiously and in excess, can be a real problem in that we are no longer on firm ground. While we do in fact generally have a wealth of knowledge about information and related systems and their users to contribute in interface design, we also have much to learn from the research areas of Web and hypermedia usability studies, among many others (see Environments to Consider, C1). Relatedly, continuing education that augments the information technology skills and knowledge of many librarians, on a practical level, remains imperative (Woodward, 4/97).

In most cases, though, we are increasingly designing systems and interfaces which ARE more useful for our user communities because we've taken the time to watch and listen to what other communities involved in information access, design and use are saying and doing: physicists (who brought us the Web) and computer scientists and others exploring the pre-print bulletin board/scientist's virtual communities as a form of scholarly communication; students who, when online, are completely in their native element or, rather, format; geneticists who provide their world wide community with participatory databases; hypermedia and human-computer interface researchers who are developing multi-sensorial means of organizing, accessing and understanding (visualizing) information. We are moving real people (including "papyrocentrist" and "techie" extremes) to our workstations while system design is in process and options remain open and listening to them. In fact, the user is at or becoming the center of the design process (often said, rarely done) because so many unclear and untested options are possible through the new technologies.

User Resistance

It is hard to overestimate the weight of library and research traditions and routines when thinking about user adoption of new systems and interfaces. Tradition, bureaucratic inertia and academic cultures which militate against risk taking can reach a point where they become very debilitating. Still, of course, there are numerous good reasons that systems and interfaces are rejected. People are or perceive themselves to be fully busy handling their current routines to the point that the ability to adopt innovations, even ones designed to specifically replace inefficient older routines, seems overwhelming. Established and efficient work routines can become unbalanced and ineffective in ways that designers often can't anticipate (Chalmers, 7/96a). As, there IS risk in adapting to new systems (Is it truly bug free? Does it interfere with useful routines? Is there adequate support? How long will it be in place before the next better idea replaces it bringing even more lost, "learning curve" time?). Costs, depending on the type of system, can of course be great though increased user capabilities are usually large as well. In addition, established approaches to information finding and organization have worked reasonably well, in fits and starts, for large numbers of people for a long time. Some would respond that we've all contorted ourselves for so long in learning to use existent finding aids and systems (card catalog use begins to be taught in grade school for instance) that we forget that we may be in a contorted position and that our contortions are far from being natural or efficient. Finally, given the long procession of rapidly obsolete software over the last decade, certain types of people have become justifiably nervous when new things are introduced. Fortunately, most have learned to cope and have become adaptable and that is really the major lesson that system educators and implementors need to impart.

User Acceptance

A large contributor to the ability to cope and/or openly accept system changes is the "pull" of good system design and education provided to users by implementors coupled with the "push" provided by researcher peer pressure and competition. How well a system is introduced, the amount of effort that implementors expend, is crucial. In addition, researchers eventually DO develop an awareness and need (through both their own experiences and those of their colleagues at other institutions) for those systems and ideas which really are improvements.

Well designed interfaces exert a proportionally large "pull" factor. The interface is especially crucial because that is what people first experience in using a system. There are systems that sell themselves and there will be systems that in fact are a joy to use and interface design has much to do with this.

C. GENERAL INTERFACE DESIGN:
ENVIRONMENT, TYPES, PHILOSOPHY, AND TECHNOLOGY

"The process of creating anything is roughly the same. The processes of solving problems, responding to audiences, and communicating to others, in any medium, are enough alike to consider identical. . . These issues apply across media and experiences" (Shedroff, 94).

C1. Environments to Consider–Introduction

The following are the more important environments and areas of research (each with its own established traditions and considerable research literature) that offer information which can contribute to better interface design for virtual and digital libraries and other library Web tools. Where we're going with the new information technologies and what we will be doing represent a very big puzzle. There are a lot of pieces with which to contend. To productively anticipate new development, and even to talk about the present, means that you need to be familiar with work that has been done in many if not all of the areas mentioned below. Future good design efforts and efficient system usage will stem from a familiarity with the more salient functions, constraints and coming developments/possibilities in most if not all of these areas. They are all inter-related and borders between these research areas are fluid.

This section briefly lays out many of the different continents which make up the terrain of interface design in a Web environment. They represent some of the new terrain of Library Land. The literature of relevance they represent is large and intermingles in many respects. As you go through this material, you might note that one can't go too far wrong if you introduce yourself to the ideas and concerns involved in the work of Shneiderman (Human-Computer Interaction Laboratory, 1984-1997), Bieber (Full Publication List, 1997), Shedroff, Laurel, Nielsen and their associates, among other individuals, groups and sites represented in the bibliography. These individuals represent the communities of Human-Computer Interface (HCI), hypermedia and graphic design workers. Understanding their issues and concerns in interface development should provide you with a means of better defining and articulating your issues and then triangulating on solutions that will help you meet your own particular application needs.

At the same time you will need to watch: Web related standards development; microcomputer product and service development, specifically among Microsoft, Netscape, Intel and Sun among a handful of other software and hardware manufacturers; and service developments from major telephone, cable and other Internet service provider companies.

While there is much innovative work occurring in libraries, unbeknown to many librarians, much of it stems from and is directly dependent on the research, standards development and/or service areas to be discussed. Increasingly, library system designers come from the communities mentioned or have assimilated their messages. It is time you did as well. To provide yourself with a context for placing Library-identified issues and ideas like acceptance/utility of XML, Z39.50 and/or "metadata" classification schemes (e.g., Dublin Core), it really is important to explore the work of these research communities. As Shedroff (94) states: "To learn each [Web interface design task] well takes time and skill and is more than can be expected of any one person. Therefore, it is important for everyone to learn, at least, an overview of the important issues and techniques of each discipline so that these can be employed correctly in presenting ideas and communicating messages–especially within a team."

All of this also means that optimum skill set combinations for accomplished interface design are expanding as indicated and go beyond traditional approaches to library information system design: "Do not expect that as a developer and HTML programmer you will be capable of creating effective user interface designs. The best of the web combines useful content, competent web mastering, an experienced interface designer and coordinated graphic design" (Miller, nd.) as well as, crucially, thorough knowledge of the application and its users. An underlying problem here is that the ubiquity and ease of publishing on the Web "Provide a unique opportunity for inexperienced information providers to create a new generation of difficult to use systems!" (Bevan, nd.).

Web Environment

There is no better environment for applications that require wide distribution and access. Think of most library user service needs here. The Web is open and it is everywhere (almost) in academia. Many assume that it will be the "major application delivery and interface technology for years to come" (Bieber and Vitali, 1/97). Web browser software as the integrator, or "Webtop," of most major, formerly "Desktop," software applications is the current trend. Web integration of common office and library software, already started with email and document creation functions, mean that librarians need to think of Web-related hypermedia, human-computer interface, and information visualization techniques as what will become common tools for accessing and expressing information in not only the library but in all facets of office and home desktop work. The influences of the Web and/or the need to be workable in that environment, will increasingly be seen in most common software applications. Background sites of interest here include: The World Wide Web Consortium (W3C http://www.w3.org/) and The Web Developer's Virtual Library (http://WWW.Stars.com/).

Web Usability. This area generally concerns user studies and, more generally, human-computer interface studies focused on Web resource usage. As mentioned, things are new enough now that librarian and human-computer interface researchers' assumptions about user behaviors more than ever need to be undergirded by examining real user needs and behaviors. Furthermore, things are still new enough that, regardless of the design community we originate from, most of us are at roughly the same stage and that means we're still pretty close to the ground floor with all of this. Read widely but take it all with a grain of salt. A notable Web site for related background information is Keith Instone's Usable Web: Guide to Web Usability Resources (http://usableweb.com/). Usability studies are occurring via all of the communities and research areas mentioned in this section.

HTML

This of course is the markup language that provides the syntax through which Web information is structured and made usable. Simple to use and easy to learn, it provides for the making of simple structured documents with graphics and provides for collaborative hypertext/hypermedia views of information. Though begun in popular mode with Apple's hypercard, hypermedia/hypertext was successfully launched for most of the world via the advent of the Web. Conversely, the utility and ease of use of hypermedia ensured the Web's success. General sites of interest here include: the newly approved HTML 4.0 Specification (http://www.w3.org/TR/REC-htm140/) and Hypertext Markup Language Resources: The Web Developer's Virtual Library (http://WWW.Stars.com/Authoring/HTML/Resources.html).

HTML Limitations and Development

"World Wide Web authors must cope in a hypermedia environment analogous to second-generation computing languages [i.e., assembler language], building and managing most hypermedia links using simple anchors and single-step navigation" (Bieber et al., 1997). Following this analogy, sophis-

ticated application environments on the World Wide Web will require third-
and fourth-generation hypermedia features. Such features, taken from other
existing non-Web hypermedia environments, might include: typed nodes
and links, link attributes, structure-based query, transclusions, warm and
hot links, private and public links, hypermedia access permissions, computed personalized links, external link databases, link update mechanisms,
overviews, trails, guided tours, backtracking, and history-based navigation
(Ibid.).

Extending HTML

In addition to new hypermedia features mentioned above, there are many
other approaches to extending HTML and Web functionality. One of the most
important for the library community is its evolution, probably via XML
(Extensible Markup Language; see below), towards the features of the more
complex, parental mark-up language, SGML (Standard Generalized Markup
Language; see below). HTML is a document type definition (DTD) or subset
of SGML. SGML is an international standard for describing marked-up text
in an electronic format. HTML, being a single DTD, has the drawback of
being a closed document type: only the existing elements can be used and no
enhancements or extensions can be created unless approved by the appropriate standards committee which is a complex and highly politicized process
(Vitali et al., 97).

Most everyone has an interest in extending the capabilities of HTML.
However, the approval process is difficult given the conflicting needs and
values of various Web communities and commercial entities:

> The current debate on HTML sees two opposing positions as preemi-
> nent. One wants better control over the final appearance (the render-
> ing) of a document. The other advocates better control over the de-
> scription of the structure and role of the parts of the document . . . . The
> first group, lead by graphic designers, would like the standardization
> efforts on HTML to cease and allow ad hoc plentiful extensions to the
> language to cover all visualization needs. The second group, the
> SGML community, would prefer HTML to abstract from the descrip-
> tion of the document's physical appearance, and let style sheets guide
> the final mapping of structural elements to their visual representa-
> tions. Furthermore, commercial software developers often find it irre-
> sistible to improve and detour from the published standard, and seek a
> commercial advantage by extending HTML with new, proprietary tags.
> (Vitali et al., 97)

SGML. Moving towards Standard Generalized Markup Language would
solve certain problems associated with HTML for some communities, includ-

ing ours. It is a widely accepted and influential standard. Its major notable feature is descriptive markup: "An SGML document has its content enriched by embedded tags that describe its parts in terms of their role and meaning, rather than the kind of processing necessary to display them. This allows one to define a generic markup that can be used for any purpose: from display on a wide range of devices (from dumb terminals to highly graphical workstations . . .) to content-based analysis and categorization (useful for large document systems, indexers, search engines, etc.), to processing for information extraction, restructuring, and update. SGML is only interested in the meaningful structuring of the documents, and leaves the task of assigning graphical attributes to document elements to rendering software" (Vitali et al., 97). Other crucial characteristics of SGML include an open set of document types and human-readable representation (Ibid.). An informative general site is The SGML/XML Web Page (http://www.sil.org/sgml/sgml.html) (also see Metadata below).

XML. "The Extensible Markup Language (XML) is an important proposal by the W3C Working Group (the Web standards body) on SGML. XML is a simplified SGML with many of the arcane features removed in order to produce a more usable and understandable language. XML documents thus are still valid SGML documents, which leverages existing software" (Ibid.). Given the support from user communities and major commercial entities it is probable that XML will "take." XML will be very crucial for many library related applications. Useful general sites will be found at: the Extensible Markup Language page (XML) (http://www.sil.org/sgml/xml.html) and Microsoft's Extensible Markup Language page (http://www.microsoft.com/xml/). Interesting papers include those by Microsoft Corporation (6/97), Dougherty (5/97) and Powell (11/97). Also see RDF and Metadata below.

RDF. Resource Description Framework is an open industry standard for describing how metadata for content is defined in Web documents. This metadata is descriptive information about the structure and content of information in a document. RDF emphasizes facilities to enable automated processing of Web resources. RDF metadata can be used in a variety of application areas, for example: in resource discovery to provide better search engine capabilities; in cataloging for describing the content and content relationships available at a particular Web site, page, or digital library; by intelligent software agents to facilitate knowledge sharing and exchange; in content rating; in describing collections of pages that represent a single logical "document"; for describing intellectual property rights of Web pages, and in many others. RDF with digital signatures will be a key to building security/privacy for electronic business transactions, collaboration, and other applications. This standard will also make it easier for users to find what they need while searching and to integrate this information onto their desktop. RDF will be an application of XML. Web resources of note include: Resource Description Framework (RDF)-W3C (http://www.w3.org/Metadata/RDF/) which includes both Frequently Asked Questions about RDF-W3C (http://www.w3.org/Metadata/RDF/FAQ) and Lassila and Swick's Resource Description framework (RDF) Model and Syntax (http://www.w3.org/TR/WD-rdf-syntax-971002/)(see Metadata below).

Proprietary Extensions and Tags. Microsoft and Netscape continue to develop their own proprietary features for commercial advantage as users demand more utility and flexibility in the area of design, among many others. Ultimately this may negatively effect the overall use value of the medium itself in the sense that it means evasion or inhibition in the development of certain standards. Some argue, though, that such "initiative" prepares ways for development that wouldn't otherwise occur and may more quickly meet user/developer expectations and needs.

Displets. "Displets are small Java (see below) modules similar to applets. A properly extended browser would activate them while parsing an HTML document, everytime it encounters pre-declared new tags and would let them handle the display operation for the relevant objects. Declaring both the extensions that will be used in the document and the displet class needed for their display at the beginning of the document, enables any kind of customized extension to the HTML language without loss of generality, while maintaining wide-spread compatibility and stylistic elegance" (Vitali et al., 97).

Web Browser/Viewer Software and Webtops. It is important to keep current with basic browser development. Microsoft's Internet Explorer™ and Netscape's Communicator™ may not always blaze the paths initially followed but in this game it is generally their ball and we play it their way. It is usually in their interests to do the popular thing which may even be or eventually become the right thing. Both companies support XML, for example. General information on browsers can be found at the Microsoft (http://www.microsoft.com/microsoft.htm) and Netscape (http://www.netscape.com/) sites although I normally just follow BrowserWatch (http://browserwatch.internet.com/) or Browser Central: C|net (http://www.cnet.com/Content/Browser/). Note that the term "viewer" is often used as a synonym for "browser" though it also can mean a plugin or software utility that provides extended browser "visual" capabilities.

Specialized and experimental browsers and viewers exist for many focused or unique purposes either by themselves or as adjuncts (viewers) invocable via standard browsers. Elastic Windows (Kandogan and Shneiderman, 4/97; http://www.cs.umd.edu/users/kandogan/papers/uist97/paper.html) and WebTOC (Nation, 1997; http://www.cs.umd.edu/projects/hcil/People/dnation/WebTOC/WebTOC.

html) are examples of new, specialized browsers. COSMO (http:// cosmo.sgi.com/) is just one example of an invocable VRML browser.

It is important to again mention that Web/browser software and desktop/ office software are rapidly co-evolving together resulting in the important concept of the Webtop. It is through browser software and Java (see below) or Java-like capabilities (which provide for real time interactivity) that many standard, standalone desktop applications will soon be integrated and used seamlessly along with typical Web functions. Overall, the advent of the Webtop should mean greatly enhanced productivity, especially for knowledge workers, as Internet and other work routines are efficiently melded together.

Web Browser Adjunct Languages. Sun's Java and Netscape's JavaScript language can solve some interaction problems. Both represent an approach where program execution occurs on the client side (i.e., via a browser on your machine). Java is a simple, robust, object-oriented, platform-independent multi-threaded, dynamic general-purpose programming environment. It is best for creating applications (usually termed applets) (also see displets above) for the Internet, intranets and any other distributed network. When integrated into Web pages, applets allow such things as graphics presentation, real-time interaction with users, live information updating, and instant interaction with servers over the network. Java applets are downloadable from any server. They can run on numerous operating systems and are embedded directly into HTML pages. JavaScript is a scripting language. It improves the looks and friendliness of web sites by adding author-specified user functions (events) to static pages. It allows for client-side intelligence, such as error checking and field validation, in real time. This means again that users can interact with the system in real-time, thus bringing Web interaction more in line with traditional desktop software design. Useful Web resources include: Java/HotJava FAQ Index (http://java.sun.com/faqIndex.html); Java Documentation (http://java.sun.com/docs/index.html); The Java Programming Language: The World-Wide Web Virtual Library (http://acm.org/~ops/java.html); and an article by Jones (3/97), Java and Libraries: Digital and Otherwise.

VRML. The Virtual Reality Modeling Language (VRML) is a standard language for describing interactive 3-D objects and worlds delivered across the Internet. It allows for 3D scenes to be viewed and manipulated over the Internet. With a special VRML browser, the user can connect to an online VRML site, and open a 3D environment to explore. Users can zoom in and out, move around and interact with the virtual environment. The potential here is large and VRML, or its successor(s), is expected to be a major pillar among information visualization techniques of importance to libraries. Don't worry, in most cases egoggles, egloves and eboots, the bane of Lipstick Librarians (http://www.teleport.com/~petlin/liplib/), are not required. General Web sites of value include: On the Net: Virtual Reality Online (http://www.hitl.washington.edu/projects/knowledge_base/onthenet.html); VRML Consortium (http://www.vrml.org/); VRML Repository (http://www.sdsc.edu/vrml/); An Overview of Virtual Reality Modeling Language Version 2.0 (http://vag.vrml.org/VRML2.0/FINAL/Overview.html); and the VR Bibliography (http://www.cms.dmu.ac.uk/~cph/VRbib.html). Articles of interest, among others, include those by Young, 2/96 and 3/96.

Web Utilities. Plugins are utilities that extend the capabilities of browsers. They are helper applications that run within the browser. When a server informs the browser of the type of media it has encountered, the browser sees if the media type is known to it and either displays the object inside the browser window or invokes the helper application to correctly handle the media object. The best known plugins provide for viewing digitized documents and special graphics or hearing audio information. To sample the kinds of things they enable, look at the following general Web site: Plug-In Plaza!: BrowserWatch (http://browserwatch.internet.com/plug-in.html).

Human-Computer Interface (HCI) Studies

This rich research area has a long history. As mentioned previously, HCI involves most aspects of our interactions with computers and is generally concerned with making them sensible if not easy to use for non-specialists. General sites include: HCI Index (http://is.twi.tudelft.nl/hci/); Human-Computer Interaction Resources on the Net (http://www.ida.liu.se/labs/aslab/groups/um/hci/); The HCI Bibliography (http://www.hcibib.org/); and the Human-Computer Interaction Virtual Library (http://usableweb.com/hcivl/). Great work in this area is coming from the Human-Computer Interaction Laboratory (HCIL) at the University of Maryland (http://www.cs.umd.edu/projects/hcil/). HCIL Papers and Technical Reports are available (http://www.cs.umd.edu/projects/hcil/Research/tech-report-list.html).

User Engagement Research. There is a large area of HCI research concerned with "empowering" users by getting them interactively involved at all levels of usage in controlling the processes and outcomes of the systems they use. Interactivity is all about increasing: the amount of control the user has over the tools, pacing, or content; the amount of choice this control offers; and the ability to use the tool or content to be productive. For most users, high levels of engagement with a system result in acceptance and better user (and system) performance. Consult the sites mentioned under HCI above but also look at: UI Index (http://www.vrix.com/uiindex/uiindex.cfm) and User Interaction Design Web (http://www.io.tudelft.nl/uidesign/).

Information Visualization Research. The premise behind information visualization is that the user's own perceptual abilities can be more fully used to understand information. Much more information can often be placed on a single screen using the techniques of information visualization (i.e., images and visual icons) than is possible with text alone. Generally, information visualization seeks to increase speed and effectiveness in finding information and to decrease the mental effort put into each search (Demain, 10/96). Good general sites with numerous examples of relevant projects include: from the HCI community, OLIVE (the On-line Library of Information Visualization Environments) (http://www.otal.umd.edu/Olive/) and, from the library community, The Big Picture(sm): Visual Browsing in Web and non-Web Databases (http://www.public.iastate.edu/~CYBERSTACKS/BigPic.htm). Since much of HCI is concerned with visualization, look at the sites listed under HCI above as well.

Hypermedia/Hypertext Research and Usability Studies. "Hypermedia is concerned with structuring and giving access to an application through its elements' interrelationships" (Bieber and Vitali, 1/97). Hypermedia research pivots on the notion of illuminating direct and indirect multi-directional relationality among concepts and knowledge in multimedia formats including text, images, and audio among others.

Although the Web is for most synonomous with hypermedia, as a hypermedia environment it is quite underdeveloped from the standpoint of hypermedia researchers, some of whom have been working in this area for over two or more decades. There are numerous new and improved hypermedia functions and features which will make their way to the Web and the public, depending on how they survive the gauntlet of the competing commercial interests involved in the process of "standards" development. Articles by Bieber and Vitali (1/97) and Bieber et al. (97) are of interest in this regard.

Just as hypermedia will become more fully developed on the Web through enhanced browser and markup language functionality, it will be more powerfully integrated into standard desktop packages (on or off the Web). The rapidly occurring convergence of the Web with many standard desktop applications, as mentioned, is being augured by the hypermedia they are beginning to share as well as the need for Web distribution of the information these applications help create or contain. Andrews (96) has written an interesting article on these matters.

Desktop and Webtop Software–Graphical User Interface Design

An immense influence, our standard daily application programs and operating systems are the specific tools that have created and structured the microcomputing experiences and, therefore, habits, traditions and expectations of most microcomputer users. Many of us spend much of our time with these and they have formed our GENERAL assumptions about what we increasingly will or should experience when we use a computer or an interface regardless of whether we are using various Web finding tools, library related systems and/or word processors. Interface features learned in using Windows95, Excel or Lotus, for example, will be increasingly expected, for better or worse in, say, Virtual Libraries or Web OPACS. As desktop applications merge into the Web and vice-versa, it will be fascinating to see how both environments inter-pollinate. As Miller (nd.) notes: "Traditional [software] graphical user interface (GUI) design [is] a strong, but incomplete, foundation for good web design. Not all GUI principles apply, but most can help any designer. One can look to OSF/Motif(tm) and Microsoft Windows(tm) style guides for information on foreground and background colors, the organization of menus, on-line help, filtering, and the choice of appropriate GUI objects in addition to multiplatform styleguides which cover the similarities and differences between platforms (Bellcore, 1994). These concepts can be directly applied (with a knowledgeable eye) to web design." The UI Index (http://www.vrix.com/uiindex/uiindex.cfm) is worth a look on this subject.

Distance/Electronic/Online Education and Electronic Classroom Design

Educators have long been interested in the possibilities that these information interaction and distribution technologies represent and, as a result, have created one of the strongest bodies of research on user interaction and the effectiveness of system and interface design. Their concerns are variously bundled under the terms of distance learning or distance education, online learning, hypertext learning and, generally, the electronic classroom. They have long experience with hypermedia applications which they are now exporting to the Web with great speed. A general site to consider viewing is Distance Education Clearinghouse (http://www.uwex.edu/disted/home.html). A very interesting specific project is that of the Teaching Theaters (http://www.inform.umd.edu/TT/).

Information Retrieval/Database Management

Online Textually Focused Information Retrieval in Traditional and Other Finding Tools. "A picture is worth a thousand words" but many of those words may express the user's bewilderment with what the picture is really "saying," i.e., which of the thousand words that come to mind are important? While information visualization will yield great rewards, its downsides, including difficulty in meshing well with the user traditions and imagery (i.e., user visual languages) employed in finding information, leave much room for the efficient if not superior uses, depending on the situation and scale, of text-based finding approaches. The field of text-based retrieval too is experiencing a revolution in increased efficiency since you may have last looked. Very fast machines with very large amounts of memory and storage now make possible, or promise to make possible, intelligent query interfaces that may rebalance the equation in current thinking between the advantages of visualization and textual approaches. Their power should enable more rapid textual interfaces which will better encourage user interaction through immediate response, e.g., in the back and forth process inherent in much Boolean searching. Natural language interfaces, as well, should become more effective as the larger data sets required for them and complex approaches to mapping language become more easily manageable. Of course, the probable outcome of hardware improvement is that both image and text intensive approaches will become even more intertwined as appropriate for the application at hand and that each will inform the other resulting in increasingly rapid mutual development. As a sampler, examine some of the projects occurring at the Center for Intelligent Information Retrieval (CIIR) (http:// cobar.cs.umass.edu/info/ciirbiblo.html). Also, relatedly, see the Library of Congress Experimental Search System (http://lcweb2.loc.gov/resdev/ess/) based in Sovereign Hill's Inquery system (a spinoff of CIIR). Other interesting Web resources include Natural Language as an Interface Style (Long, 5/94) (http:// www.dgp.toronto.edu/people/byron/papers/nli.html); the NIST Spoken Language Processing Group site (http://www.itl.nist.gov/div894/894.01/slp.htm); and the Natural Language Processing Laboratory (http://www.ida. liu.se/labs/ nlplab/). Hildreth (6/97) has written an interesting paper as well on current problems faced by library users in text-based online catalog searching and advocates text-based solutions anchored in better interface design.

Interoperability: Standard Query Translating Interfaces–Z39.50 and Beyond. "There is a growing perception in the Internet community of the need for a standard interface to queryable networked information sources. The horse in this race with which the library community is most familiar is the Z39.50 Information Retrieval Protocol which is a comprehensive standard for information retrieval. It represents a serious investment of resources into the problem of standards based information retrieval. It has made moves toward WWW deployment: Z39.50 extensions to web browsers and web gateways have been developed and Z39.50 URLs have been defined. From a technical viewpoint, Z39.50 meets most of the requirements for an Internet information retrieval standard. It has been designed with flexibility in mind. It has a large and flexible set of query types, and can support the retrieval of non-document resources (although most implementations focus on document-like objects). It also supports stateful information retrieval sessions. However, despite its WWW support and flexibility, Z39.50 does not have broad Internet community support outside the library community which developed it. The perception is that although Z39.50 solves many of the Internet information retrieval problems, it is too large and complex for implementation in widespread commercial applications. Migration from existing systems to Z39.50 can be difficult. Additionally, although Z39.50 guarantees a base level of interoperability, there is a great range of implementable features beyond this base. This means that a sophisticated client that implements some features, and a sophisticated server that supports many other features, may only have minimal, lowest common denominator type interoperability. As a result, the Z39.50 community is now considering paring the standard back to get greater acceptance within the Internet community. This initiative has been called Z39.50 Lite . . . Still, this will take some time which could leave the way open for a less formally developed de facto standard to be deployed ahead of Z-Lite" (Ward, 96). Also see Lynch, (4/97). A general Web site can be found at: Z39.50 page: Z39.50 Maintenance Agency (http://lcweb.loc. gov/z3950/ agency/).

Metadata–Classifying Web Resources. "Metadata is 'information about data'. That is, metadata describes some aspect of data on the Internet. There has been significant activity recently on defining the semantic and technical aspects of metadata for use on the Internet and WWW. A number of metadata sets have been proposed together with the technological framework to support the interchange of metadata. These initiatives will have a dramatic effect on how the Web is indexed and will improve the discovery of resources on the Internet by a significant factor" (Iannella and Waugh, 4/97). Metadata has numerous uses in text as well as image based systems. The usual use we think of in the library community is in classifying documents in textual contexts. A number of examples of familiar approaches, applied to the Web, can be found at: Beyond Bookmarks: Schemes for Organizing the Web (http://www.public.iastate.edu/~CYBERSTACKS/CTW.htm). Also see SGML, XML and RDF (above) as markup languages/descriptive schemes that are metadata focused. Works by Barnard and Ide (7/97), Logan and Pollard (7/97), Dempsey and Heery (3/97) and Arms (2/97) are of interest.

Dublin Core and the Warwick Framework. One of the best known metadata schemes is the Dublin Core. The Dublin Core metadata set is intended to promote and develop the metadata elements required to facilitate the discovery of resources (documents and images) in a networked environment and support interoperability among heterogeneous metadata systems. Among other advantages, when metadata becomes more common (either embedded in documents, such as the META tag in HTML files, or from a separate metadata repository) and indexing services start to concentrate on indexing this information, there should be a marked increase in the effectiveness of Web search engine information retrieval. Related advantages include the searching of fielded data (Iannella and Waugh, 4/97). The Dublin Core working group also recognized that there would be more than just Dublin Core metadata being used on the Internet and that an infrastructure was needed to support any metadata element set. This infrastructure is called the Warwick Framework and is a "container" architecture for aggregating logically, and perhaps physically, distinct packages of metadata (Lagoze et al., 1996). The architecture allows separate administration and access to metadata packages and proposes implementations of the Framework in HTML, MIME, SGML, and distributed objects. The framework is a simple concept, but it has important implications for interoperation, and as the basis for long-lived metadata systems. By factoring complex descriptions into simpler components, interoperation can be addressed at a component level, rather than at an "all or nothing" monolithic level. The framework also allows for lowest-common-denominator descriptions, such as the Dublin Core, to exist beside complex descriptions from specialized communities, such as MARC (Daniel and Lagoze, 12/97; Lagoze et al., 7/96). See the following Web resources for more details: Dublin Core Metadata (http://purl.oclc.org/metadata/dublin_core/) and The Warwick Framework (http://cs-tr.cs.cornell.edu:80/Dienst/UI/2.0/Describe/ncstrl.cornell/TR96-1593).

Automatic Classification of Web Resources. Classification is laborious, takes time and is expensive. The richer and more complex the classifications and the greater the number that are applied to describe the data (i.e., the more metadata that is created) the more costs go up. These costs have always existed in cataloging print materials in libraries but will be much higher in coming innovative textual and information visualization systems and interfaces which often Require large amounts of rich, multi-dimensional, fully-relational data and metadata to properly work at all or to adequately exploit their system advantages over simpler approaches. That is why it is being mentioned here; the lack of truly smart, automated (or VERY streamlined manual) classification systems is or will become the Achilles heel of many library-related information visualization projects. The Dublin Core is really about making such concerns central. One can employ as many or as few Dublin Core fields as wanted. Still, though, most people do have high hopes for the development of smart systems which will be able to take Web site or document information and intelligently classify it and structure the rich data inter-relationships desired. There are a lot of classification projects out there experiencing various, usually minimal, degrees of success. To see some of these go to the site: Project Aristotle: Automated Categorization of Web Resources (http://www.public.iastate.edu/~CYBERSTACKS/Aristotle.htm). In addition, you need to become familiar with the area of research known as data/knowledge/information mining (this is the art of finding new meaning and relationships in old data).

Traditional Graphic Design

Many of the current problems with Web usability stem simply and directly from poor graphic design, style and layout. While many things about the Web really ARE different, generally speaking, tried and true, tested, graphic arts' principles DO apply (Shedroff, 94). Designers of interfaces for information systems usually realize that the electronic medium does not erase centuries of established practice in document design. Though numerous style guides exist, most offer contradictory advice and/or don't employ it in the presentation of their own guides (Ratner, 96). One of the best or at least most frequently cited is Lynch and Horton (97). One thing is for sure, the fields of graphic design, videography, cinematography, typography, illustration and photography can all play a role in interface/site design. If you're a creative person, you need to take some time and understand the principles involved, many of which are simple and straightforward. If you're not a creative person then beg, borrow or steal one. A very interesting and succinct overview of the role of the graphic arts in relation to the Web can be found in Shedroff's article, "Information Interaction Design: A Unified Field Theory of Design." Also see CA Web Resources (http://www.commarts.com/creative/index.html).

C2. Brief Survey of Interface Types: Classifications/Taxonomies and Tools

Classifications–Taxonomies of Interface Types

So what, practically, are we talking about when it comes to both working and prototypical examples of new approaches to, and functions in, interface design? Fortunately, there are a few thorough taxonomies of interface types and design methodologies, replete with examples, that we can draw upon. Among the most interesting, since they address many of the new ideas being expounded by the information visualization and hypermedia communities, are those by Shneiderman and Bieber. Though they come from interface design communities and environments outside the library, their work should be intelligible to us and transfer well.

This section and the one that follows set the table for the remainder of the article. The examples provided show the range of rapidly enlarging design options open to us. Explore them and draw your own conclusions. They range from very specialized to very general applications. Some show signs of the user for the most part having been designed out of the application while a number retain or emphasize a user focus. Here you may see some great ideas heading for collisions with the practical costs of implementing more than just prototypical files. You will also see ideas that just simply aren't "catching" in the commercial software world or which are dependent on a standard being constructed or modified and/or are dependent on a user community coming around to support it (often implying slight to moderate changes in established user practices). Pick your ponies to show or place.

HCIL Taxonomy of Interface Types. The taxonomy by Shneiderman and North and other information visualizers at the University of Maryland's Human-Computer Interaction Lab (HCIL) is one of the most thorough. In this approach information content or data type, as the underlying determinant of interface design, structures the classification scheme. The relevant articles representing this taxonomy are those by Shneiderman (9/97) and North (nd.). Shneiderman's students have also put up a site called OLIVE (On-line Library of Information Visualization Environments) (http://www.otal.umd.edu/Olive/) which represents this typology in depth. Young (3/97) also provides a typology from the information visualization community.

HCIL taxonomy types are:

1-Dimensional: linear data types include textual documents, program source code, and alphabetical lists of names which are all organized in a sequential manner.

2-Dimensional: 2-dimensional planar or map data include geographic maps, floor plans, or newspaper layouts.

3-Dimensional: real-world objects such as molecules, the human body, and buildings have items with volume and some potentially complex relationship with other items.

Temporal: time lines are widely used and vital enough for medical records, project management, or historical presentations to create a data type that is separate from 1-dimensional data. The distinction in temporal data is that items have a start and finish time and that items may overlap.

Multi-dimensional: most relational and statistical databases are conveniently manipulated as multi-dimensional data in which items with n attributes become points in a n-dimensional space.

Tree: hierarchies or tree structures are collections of items with each item having a link to one parentitem (except the root).

Network: sometimes relationships among items cannot be conveniently captured with a tree structure and it is useful to have items linked to an arbitrary number of other items.

Hypermedia Community Taxonomy

Since hypermedia relationships are the basis of Web information, it is instructive to view a typology of relationships as seen from a "relationship management" or hypermedia researcher's point of view. The following typology comes from Bieber and Vitali (1/97):

> *Schema relationships* provide access to information related through an application's design documents or database schemas, such as information about elements that appear in different but related database tables (for example, information in a retail system about a product and about companies that frequently order the product).
>
> *Information relationships* provide access to parameters and descriptive information.
>
> *Occurrence relationships* provide access to all uses and views of a piece of information.
>
> *Process relationships* provide access to logical tasks that users must perform with the application, such as subtasks within a project management system or stages in a workflow management system.
>
> *Statistical relationships* provide access to elements that take place under similar circumstances or elements in which one doesn't occur unless another also occurs.
>
> *Structural relationships* provide access to generic relationships within the constructs of a software package, such as interrelating spreadsheet cells referred to in a formula, database fields referred to in a query, and variables referred to in an equation that occurs in a mathematical modeling system.
>
> *Ad hoc relationships* are declared by users to link anything that they want to connect in some way.

Several different methodologies associated with these hypermedia relationships exist and are elaborated upon in the above article.

Interface Ideas–Piquing Your Appetite with Specific Software, Design Approaches and Projects

For specific projects and techniques, there are a number of general lists from the human-computer interaction community including, among others, the Shneiderman (9/97) and North (nd.) papers, the OLIVE Site mentioned above as well as papers by Fox (nd.) and Young (3/96). Several HCI and other sites provide large indexes of links to related working and/or prototypical projects and tools including: Human-Computer Interaction Virtual Library (http://usableweb.com/hcivl/); Human-Computer Interaction Resources on the Net (http://www.ida.liu.se/labs/aslab/groups/um/hci/); HCI Index (http://is.twi.tudelft.nl/hci/); UI Index (http://www.vrix.com/uiindex/uiindex.cfm); User Interaction Design Web (http://www.io.tudelft.nl/uidesign/); and User Interface Software Tools (http://www.cs.cmu.edu/afs/cs/user/bam/www/toolnames.

html). From the library community, McKiernan and Wasilko (6/97 and 7/97) and Mckiernan (7/97) have provided useful product smorgasbords and webliographies that include projects from the HCI, hypermedia and other design communities to create a library spin on what's useful. Examine their: BigPicture–information visualization related (http://www.public.iastate.edu/ ~CYBERSTACKS/BigPic.htm); Onion Patch–online catalog related (http:// www.public.iastate.edu/~CYBERSTACKS/Onion.htm) and Project Aristotle– automatic classification related (http://www.public.iastate.edu/~CYBERSTACKS/ Aristotle.htm).

Among the many projects that I've found intriguing and that illustrate approaches that are indicative of the kinds of system and interface design functionality that is starting to be possible are the following exemplary projects:

Information Visualization or Hypermedia Oriented:
- *LyberWorld* (http://www-cui.darmstadt.gmd.de/visit/Activities/Lyberworld/) (also see Inquery below);
- *Spire* (http://multimedia.pnl.gov:2080/showcase/?it_content/spire.node);
- *Visage System* (http://www.cs.cmu.edu/Groups/sage/project/visage.html);
- *SiteMap* (http://lislin.gws.uky.edu/Sitemap/Sitemap.html);
- *Spotfire* (http://www.ivee.com/)
- *NASA EOSDIS* (http://www.cs.umd.edu/projects/hcil/Research/1995/dq-for-eosdis.html)

Text Retrieval Oriented:
- *Inquery* (http://ciir.cs.umass.edu/inquerypage.html) and the INQUERY Library of Congress Experimental Catalog (http://lcweb2.loc.gov/resdev/ess/);
- *Verity* (http://www.verity.com/);
- *AskJeeves* (http://www.askjeeves.com/)

D. INTERFACE DESIGN PHILOSOPHY, POSSIBILITIES AND ELEMENTS

D1. General Considerations and Philosophy Information Interaction Design

Brenda Laurel states that interactive media "is not about information, it is about experience." She further believes that "Knowledge is the pay-off of any experience. It is the understanding gained through experiences, whether bad or good. Knowledge is communicated by building compelling interactions with others or with tools so that the patterns and meanings in their information can be learned. Knowledge is fundamentally participatory" (Shedroff, 94).

More than ever before, the new, Web centered interface design tools allow the creation of compelling, user-empowering information finding and exploration tools.

Information Interaction Design Principles

Shedroff's (1994) work, "Information Interaction Design: A Unified Field Theory of Design," represents a good, clear and easily digestible explanation of a general approach to design that is of use in the context of libraries addressing interface design. From the world of the graphic arts, it speaks to the generalist which means many of us working in libraries. With his work as background, many of the specialist approaches to design are more easily understandable. Specifically, Shedrow's work is useful in providing a unified context and design philosophy with which to understand the various environments, techniques, approaches and elements involved in Web and virtual/digital library interface design. Shedroff terms his approach Information Interaction Design and sees it as the intersection of three different disciplines–Information Design, Interaction Design, and Sensorial Design.

Information Design has roots in the publishing and graphic design worlds and addresses the organization and presentation of data. It addresses the transformation of data into valuable, meaningful information. It is something that everyone has always done to some extent but has only recently been identified as a discipline in itself with proven processes.

Interaction Design is "at once both an ancient art and a new technology. Media have always affected the telling of stories and the creation of experiences, but currently new media offer capabilities and opportunities not yet addressed in the history of interaction and performance . . . [This] is also the most critical component to the success of interactive products." More specifically, interactive design is concerned with structuring meaningful, appropriate, timely and empowering interactions which provide the user with a pronounced sense of system engagement and control (see section D3c).

Sensorial Design is simply the employing of all techniques with which we communicate to others, involving all senses. "Visual Design disciplines such as Graphic Design, Videography, Cinematography, Typography, Illustration, and Photography are usually the first to be recognized and employed (right after writing), but just as important are the disciplines that communicate through other senses . . . The disciplines of these sensorial media are worlds unto themselves, with their own histories, traditions, and concerns" (see sections D3a and D3b).

Other General Principles. The following considerations need to be emphasized in interface design and are common themes throughout the literature of the various design communities:

- Use known metaphors, visual or otherwise.
- Use known traditions in information seeking as appropriate.
- Engage the user through appropriate multi-media approaches (i.e., engage more of the user) and the provision of user action, feedback, and control functions.
- Help the user via appropriate help screens and action feedback.
- Provide clarity, consistency and simplicity as appropriate: "The most important goal of effective communication is clarity. Clarity is not the same as simplicity. Often, simple things are clear if the message is intended to be brief and small, but often the message is about a complex relationship that can only be presented with a necessarily large amount of data. This complexity can be made to appear clear by effective organization and presentation and need not be reduced to meaningless "bite-sized" chunks of data, as simplification usually does. Clarity refers to the focus on one particular message or goal at a time, rather than attempting to accomplish too much at once. Simplicity is often responsible for the 'dumbing' of information rather than the illumination of it" (Shedrow, 94). Shneiderman, similarly, sees that "The ideal user interface is as simple as possible, and it makes key features as clear as possible" (1/97b).

D2. Interface Metaphor and Tradition in Design

The usage of appropriate metaphor, whether visual or textual, is everything in system interface design. Appropriate metaphor is all about making the unfamiliar seem familiar, if not useful and even friendly.

Metaphors provide recognizable contexts that make systems intelligible. "Pointing" within a Windows™ application is an example (you're really manipulating cursor position on a monitor via a mouse, not pointing). Metaphor is crucial in interface design because there are often no real world, familiar parallels for things you can do on a computer. Metaphors in interface design play the vital role of generating known "abstract representations which both hide the underlying complexity while offering a simple and recognizable graphical [or textual] representation . . . " (Young, 3/96).

A great concern in this, however, is that the development of a sensible metaphor which will be recognizable by a mass audience is neither easy nor straightforward. Metaphor is the crucial bridge between the user's experience and the system. Only if this bridge extends well into the user's experience will it convey familiarity and ease of use. Young states that the problem of designing useful metaphors "will prove a great hurdle in the acceptance and widespread use of information visualization systems" (Ibid.). Shedroff (94) points out that: "It is important that the context implied is the one intended and that it matches the desired understandings. Too often, metaphors set the wrong context and help create expectations that are not accurate and that cannot be met."

Generally, common threads throughout the literature indicate that, if possible, you want to build on known metaphors, visual or otherwise. "Windows" (indicating a type of graphical user interface) is a metaphor that has "taken" and can be regularly applied at this point. Relatedly, for library and information retrieval systems, it is often appropriate to use the many print and online traditions with which users are familiar as metaphor. It isn't that new metaphors can't be made to work, witness the world wide "WEB," it is just that marketing takes time and therefore costs more to sell, ingrain and ultimately make familiar and useful. Interesting sites dealing generally with metaphor include: Tom Rohrer's Metaphor page (http://metaphor.uoregon.edu/metaphor.htm) and the Conceptual Metaphor Home Page (Lakoff–http://cogsci.berkeley.edu/).

Metaphor and Visualization–More Than Image

Visualization through image utilization relies on good metaphor but metaphor is more than image alone. Good metaphor represents a rich, multimodal whole system usually relying on not only image but image-informing text and action. In the current focus on the importance of image metaphor in visualization, the crucial, often underlying role of text (and conceptualization as distinct from visualization) in metaphor as well as text in image can't be forgotten. After all, metaphor and information visualization, when done most efficiently provide the means to utilize all perceptual and cognitive bases through which understanding is achieved. This whole system approach (where conceptualization and visualization synergistically work together) in interface design utilizes visual perception and understanding, verbal (visual and audio) understanding, cognition, memory and experience simultaneously.

Perhaps because verbal metaphor is so universal (and largely invisible) in our day-to-day experience (we make use of them constantly without being aware of doing so), it has become invisible. Arguments, for example, have "sides" and "weak points," can be right "on target," and can be "shot down." The point, for our purposes, may be that some assume that interface metaphors exist or are important only when icons or graphics are used (Purins, S., nd.)

Another consideration with general metaphors is that, within the general need to actively engage the user, they provide the means for promoting and guiding action.

General, Established and New Metaphor

Expansive metaphors include characteristics which provide the interface builder with the largest degree of user familiarity, richness and expansiveness in metaphoric detail and flexibility. These expansive metaphors, really metaphor systems, are desirable because they provide the most fertile ground or material for the designer.

Established General Metaphors. There are several large-scale metaphors that we're familiar with, the "desktop" being among the most familiar in microcomputing. "Windows," "file" management (cabinets, folders, documents), "my briefcase," "recycle bins," "network neighborhoods" and so on are all associated with the desktop metaphor and probably are quite familiar to most users. Another, as mentioned, is that of computer and data systems as "Library" (again, virtual and digital libraries as well as computer programming libraries). It is noteworthy that the Library metaphor has always been in the public domain while the "desktop" required corporate muscle to become a "reality." Hence, in NEW metaphor creation, unless you have one that is crystal clear, it might be best if you, like G. Gordon Liddy, "follow the bucks" and the lead of the large corporate interests in microcomputing and build on their metaphors. Other metaphors that you'll see on the Web and desktop include: books with chapters, encyclopedia with articles, television with channels, shopping mall with stores and museum with exhibits (Shneiderman, 1/97c).

New General Metaphors. There are many valuable new large-scale metaphors. Examples include:

- *City of Knowledge* with gates, streets, buildings, and landmarks and with the computer as knowledge explorer (Shneiderman, 1/97c).
- *Computer as Theater:* This metaphor is compelling because it unites visualization (all modes), verbal understanding (language) and action. Action is represented in a direct and visible fashion. This wholistic, unified metaphor embodies all elements involved in the rapid evolution of information technology and understanding (Laurel, 1991). The only addition would be the addition of the term "participatory" which does have real parallels in modern theater and brings the audience (the users) into the center of the action or tool.
- *Computer Game or Arcade:* Much of current experience in information visualization and user engagement stems from the computer game. Though probably not directly appropriate to scholarly applications, the game image does provide compelling, action-oriented metaphors that hint at where we should be going.

Internet Highway

Cockpits or Computer Control Panels: " . . . Like cruise-control in auto-mobiles and remote controllers for televisions, [these] are designed to convey the sense of control that users seem to expect. Increasingly, complex pro-cesses are specified by direct-manipulation programing or by graphical specifications of scheduled procedures, style sheets, and templates" (Shneid-erman, 1/97a).

Information Farms

Information Watersheds

User Traditions and Experience with Metaphors and Modes of Information Seeking

Everyone brings to information systems "a diverse space of actions [and experiences]. Some of these are learned from youthful experiences with books or libraries, others are trained skills such as searching for legal prece-dents or scientific articles. These skills are independent of computer imple-mentation, acquired through meaningful learning, demonstrated with exam-ples, and durable in memory" (Shneiderman, 1/97c). These actions and experiences have great meaning in terms of the systems we design and the kinds of assumptions and approaches we take in design. It can be safely said that most individuals in an academic context derive, for better or worse, their information seeking behaviors from library print and online traditions and systems.

Knowing Your Community and Its Information Seeking Objects/Traditions/ Conventions/Metaphors

In many ways, information retrieval related interface design can and has taken advantage of the fact that information seeking behavior and tradition across society is very centered, naturally, on libraries. Again, think of the terms "virtual" library or "digital" library or even the "online" catalog as obvious examples. We're in the interesting position of being able to take much of what we have always done with both our traditional print activities (developed over the last few hundred years) and our traditional online activi-ties (developed over the last two decades) and, often in the form of metaphor, bring them and thus our users forward into the electronic realm more easily than other institutions. The real challenge for us will probably be in knowing which parts of this tradition to leave at the InfoBahn onramp since more than a few will turn out to be untranslatable and/or quite obtuse in our new environment.

Specific Library and Print Format Metaphors for Interface Objects

Thinking about print format invokes page numbers, indexes, tables of contents, chapters, footnotes, bibliographies, generally standardized type font styles and sizes, generally standardized image/chart/table placement and styles, covers, jackets, page turning, bookmarks, position indicators and many other printing practices. Libraries bring with them a tradition of well organized information, searchable systems/catalogs/databases and associated finding techniques (phrase searching, fielded data searching, full-text searching, Boolean searching and basic browsing) as well as user interaction and orientation. Libraries also bring with them doors, collections, shelves, rooms, help desks, meeting places, instructional areas, bulletin boards, study carrels, reference materials and public computing facilities. Libraries are informal and formal centers of communication and campus and civic life. They are meeting places for both work and leisure. Many of these characteristics are demonstrated in virtual library projects such as the Internet Public Library (http://www.ipl.org/), Cyberstacks (http://www.public.iastate.edu/~CYBERSTACKS/), the Michigan Electronic Library (http://mel.lib.mi.us/) and INFOMINE (http://lib-www.ucr.edu/), among many others. It is unproductive to want to discard many of these useful standards and conventions too quickly. This is a rich field to virtualize; a rich, unified metaphor system from which to pull design ideas.

Traditional Modes of Library Related Information Seeking

Online Text Searching. A traditional and crucial mode of finding, online text searching was for a long time overlooked or understressed in Web interface design. Shneiderman (1/97c) states that "The key interface action in locating a relevant website and in searching within a website is string search." Nielsen's user studies (7/97) show that " . . . more than half of all users are search-dominant, about a fifth of the users are link-dominant, and the rest exhibit mixed behavior. The search-dominant users will usually go straight for the search button when they enter a website: they are not interested in looking around the site; they are task-focused and want to find specific information as fast as possible. In contrast, the link-dominant users prefer to follow the links around a site." Most sites that emphasized "link" finding now provide "search" finding capabilities with the reverse also being true.

Standards in Queries. User expectations have been developed in information finding processes. Libraries have generally provided the places and systems through which they have been developed. For example, users have been trained to know that most systems will provide some form of author, title, subject and abstract "fielded" type searching. Some look for keyword searching and/or exact phrase searching. Others have experienced online full-text searching. Many have come to expect the ability to combine or refine searches through Boolean and adjacency operators. Though there are many problems with user ability to employ many of these techniques (Hildreth, 6/97), we need to remember that they actually are successfully applied by substantial numbers of users and that these traditional online searching methods represent the ONLY means of information seeking, realistically or metaphorically, that are truly operational.

The Boolean System and Adjacency Operators. While Boolean operators are not truly natural language (in real as opposed to Boolean English, "and" usually expands options), the Boolean System represents an extremely powerful set of functions in information retrieval on library and other systems and, in fact, is an established online information seeking TRADITION. Despite problems, this tradition is valuable and worth carrying forward. Users have been trained in its use for close to two decades in most universities and colleges. One of its problems is that it is hard to use visualization techniques to adequately represent a finding technique that, at its most powerful, often is a complex, sustained, rapid, back-and-forth PROCESS (human-computer dialogue). This is one of many cases where visual image approaches may not be able to condense useful information and functionality as well as through a text oriented approach. There have been attempts to employ Venn diagrams or, more commonly, "and," "or" and "not" boxes but these are often very clunky in the sense of constraining both complex Boolean expressions and the essential process of Boolean searching itself (again, the search feedback dependent fine tuning that is often essential for this technique) that more than novice users expect. Visual confusion and load time lag in complex queries graphically represented offers a formidable barrier. Still, see the novel and promising Boolean System visualization called "filternflow" (Shneiderman, 7/96).

Browsing. Indexes or shelves for browsing of course represent a long tradition in information seeking, especially for beginners who are confounded by library (or any) bibliographic or online finding tools. Beginners tend to browse while more advanced users tend to search. These two modes have always provided entry into bibliographic collections for the different skill levels found in user groups and have coexisted for over two decades. Of course, browsing really is a valuable technique for all levels of expertise and allows for the making of "distant," serendipitous information finds. The capability for browsing alphabetic indexes of authors, titles, subjects and keywords has been brought forward by numerous sites on the Web. Browsing tables of contents as well as subject lists closely related to a single known item is also possible (INFOMINE: http://lib-www.ucr.edu/). You can also browse "shelve-like" traditional classification schemes (e.g., Cyberstacks: http://www.public.iastate.edu/~CYBERSTACKS/).

Perhaps the best option in serving different levels of finding expertise is to attend to each one separately. That is, retain a to-the-point, unfettered textual interface for Boolean and adjacency searching for non-novices. Simultaneously a graphically enhanced Boolean searching front-end/guide could be available to help introduce novice searchers to this technique. At the same time, traditional, browsable indexes for both the beginning and the advanced user would be present. With the exception of development costs, there is no reason why serving multiple levels of expertise cannot be done.

Academic User Group Traditions. As mentioned, we are designing for a (relatively) library literate group whose metaphors for information seeking are largely already drawn from both print and library online tradition as well as from desktop software. You can assume more about the knowledge and skills academic users bring to the library and information retrieval system, the Internet and the desktop machine. This may allow us to do different things including going beyond lowest common denominator approaches that have to be taken by public libraries and consumer oriented corporate sites. Again, with students and younger faculty, assume a considerable level of microcomputer skills and experience with a large number of interface types as well as a reasonable familiarity with traditional bibliographic organization and online systems. With most faculty and research staff, assume a relatively deep knowledge of traditional bibliographic organization including online searching and Boolean systems and a relatively shallower level of microcomputer and Internet expertise.

D3. Towards Intuitive User Understanding of Interfaces–Appropriate Integration of New and Traditional Information Seeking Methods and Interfaces

Understanding is usually a multi-modal process. It can, among others, involve the intrinsically related acts of sensing, intuiting, viewing, conceptualizing, and/or visualizing. Understanding represents a focused engagement with what is being presented. Beyond the written word, library systems now have new possibilities in structuring and presenting information which better take advantage of these different modes.

D3a. Engaging the User

New approaches to designing interactive, engaging and compelling interfaces and systems for information retrieval and visualization are under development. Greatly enhanced user options and controls which fully involve all users at all levels of finding expertise are at the core of this. A large component of these interfaces will be well evolved multi- and hypermedia systems which will better apply traditional, textually conceptualized information while going greatly beyond this to fully emphasize visual metaphor and other "sensorial" modes of understanding to facilitate the information seeking process.

D3b. Sensorial Design–Using the Senses

"Use some sense!" Current interfaces for most major library systems don't. They are often entirely devoid of multi-media approaches as integral parts of design and system use. The Web, multi-media launch pad that it is, changes all this in a far reaching way. Interfaces which make fuller use of our senses, beginning with the sense of vision, are becoming possible and are being rapidly developed in a number of ways for a number of specific library related applications. It is time for us to come to terms with "Sensorial design." This is a useful concept that includes but goes beyond information visualization while incorporating traditional modes of visualized information (e.g., text that is read). Sensorial design is a component of Shedrow's Information Interaction Design approach (see section D1). Essentially this is an all-encompassing category including any discipline involved with the creation and presentation of media. These include writing (text), graphic design, iconography, map making, calligraphy, typography, illustration, and color theory (graphics), photography, animation, and cinematography (images), sound design, singeing, and music (sound), and other disciplines. Each of these disciplines have deep traditions and well developed procedures. While they differ in many ways, they all do share some common attributes and concerns which include the appropriate use of media, style, technique, media literacy, bandwidth applicable to the technology of the situation, and an understanding of the human senses (Shedrow, 94).

Sensorial Style and Meaning. Implementing an appropriate "style" for multi-media interface design is not easy. Communication and interaction have to be made to intermesh sensibly and smoothly through several media. "Choosing the appropriate attributes and implementing them consistently is imperative to the development of a cohesive experience. . . . All sensorial details must coordinate not only with each other, but with the goals and messages of the project. The more integrated and careful the synthesis of these processes, the more compelling, engaging, and appropriate the experience, and the more successful the communication and interaction" (Shedrow, 94).

Information Visualization–The Eyes Have It

The premise behind information visualization is that the user's perceptual abilities, primarily visual, can be better used to understand information. While the written word is arguably the best way to communicate ideas, text has meaning only after it has been read and deciphered. Although images are also "read" via the user's visual experiences and expectations, text can be a cumbersome method of dealing with large amounts of complex information. "Much more information can be placed on one screen using the techniques of information visualization than is possible with text alone. Information visualization seeks to increase the speed of searches for data and decrease the mental effort put into each search" (Demain, 10/96). It can potentially do so for reasons of physiology: "Overall, the bandwidth of information presentation is potentially higher in the visual domain than for media reaching any of the other senses. Humans have remarkable perceptual abilities that are greatly under-utilized in current designs. Users can scan, recognize, and recall images rapidly, and can detect changes in size, color, shape, movement, or texture. They can point to a single pixel, even in a megapixel display, and can drag one object to another to perform an action. User interfaces have been largely text-oriented, so as visual approaches are explored, appealing new opportunities are emerging" (Shneiderman, 7/96). Shneiderman indicates the depth of this underutilization: "The remarkable human visual perception seems underutilized by today's graphical user interfaces. Seeing 40-60 icons on the screen seems like a modest ambition when the megapixel displays can easily show 4,000-6,000 glyphs and allow rapid user controlled animation on task-relevant animations" (Shneiderman, 1/97a).

Components of Information Visualization. These have been introduced via the information visualization taxonomies presented in section C2 and the examples they contain as well as through the Web sites listed in that section. Generally we are talking about manipulable 2-D and 3-D visual metaphors, imagery and icons. We are also, though this is usually understressed, talking about the creative and precise use of text. Text, image, other media and action techniques work synergistically together to provide higher levels of information understanding through better interface design.

Problems with Visualizing Information

Though this should change, the visualization paradigm has yet to be widely implemented in standard commercial or academic retrieval systems. Much of the problem is in the simple time lag in waiting for visualization approaches and related hardware/software/interface design to become a bit more standardized, available and acceptable to a mass user base. After all, the sheer number and variety of techniques indicate that, even given research traditions in HCI and hypermedia that go back several years, we are still pretty close to the ground floor of the development of this approach to information. The more successful and useful visualization interface designs and approaches have not been identified. More traditional text based modes and command oriented query languages may suffice or be as good (especially given cost concerns) in many practical situations.

Costs of Structuring Visualization. As mentioned under automatic classification of data in section C1, usually, the greater the degree of relationality and the greater the depth of visualization and therefore the greater the number, complexity and richness of data elements, the greater the cost/labor in adding this data and structuring it. The rewards are great but the costs are as well. That is why there is a continuing CRUCIAL concern with automating or at least streamlining these processes with both new types of information (e.g., the automated creation of metadata or intelligent descriptive and/or fielded information about Web sites as they are traversed and ordered by smart agent/spider/indexing programs) and more traditional modes of information (going back and restructuring online bibliographic catalogs). One flavor of this is embodied in the currently popular concept of data or knowledge mining. This area as well requires maturation and moving beyond the realm of high powered research and Fortune 500 outfits. The problem of providing copious amounts of expensive, rich data is a real problem because it is likely that this would be required of databases and information retrieval environments in order to allow full utilization of advanced visualization and information retrieval tools. In other words, some of the advantages offered by these advanced interfaces might be unrealizable without rich data.

The problem of data development costs and, more generally, most library systems development costs have some solutions. Fortunately for libraries: (1) There is trickle down meaning that systems developed for other, e.g., corporate, applications eventually may find use in libraries. (2) Some library applications may never be sufficiently complex, large-scale or counter-intuitive to users to require it. (3) It is a fact of library life that users and therefore librarians usually learn to get by with whatever the level of available functionality. This may not be desirable but it means we can wait as, for example, the first waves of experimental auto classification systems roll by. (4) Through enhanced metadata standards and voluntary participation by authors, a great deal of the richness in metadata we are seeking may be reliably supplied (though this is open to question) by document/site creators. (5) Librarians are increasingly having some success in effectively communicating to campus managers the value and competitive advantages offered by the new technologies and are being better funded for their efforts. (6) Increasing amalgamations of library systems will be occurring that will create the organizational structures necessary to better support costly technology in libraries on increasing scales.

Simplicity and Scale of Application–Text-Based Command Oriented Systems as Appropriate Technology. Simple information, which many of our bibliographic databases represent, can often be most quickly and inexpensively and perhaps best represented by traditional, textual modes. Visualization will excel in large data sets where complex patterns and relationships need to be clear and more intuitively understandable.

Ease of Use. Visualized systems certainly have the potential for easier, more intuitive use but many approaches need time to mature. Many of the existing prototypes are still too complex and need to become more user-friendly. The current and coming generations are rapidly improving but it may still be true that much of what we see now is in fact more confounding, at least for the first critical minutes, than text/command based modes of finding.

Well-Done Design Is Harder in Visualization Approaches. Designing interfaces that fully express the potential of these systems will be a much greater challenge than with text. Moving beyond text and combining more than one medium smoothly is a serious challenge. Designing appropriate icons and images within a system emphasizing a strong user feedback/action mode isn't easy.

Lack of Standard Visual Metaphor and Convention in Structuring 2ID and 3ID Information. There are few universally-recognized methods to structure graphic information in terms of multiple dimensions. After all, graphics, like text, really are essentially "read" (interpreted) and make sense only if they play well to the visual imagery and visual understanding brought to the system by the user. Traditional concerns about text in regard to the problem of mismatch between the user's searching vocabulary and the system's indexing vocabulary are also carried forward in image based systems. Thais is why we have spent a lot of time talking about using appropriate metaphor in this paper: if you are not appealing to the experiences, traditions or "languages" (verbal or visual) of the users, as you find them, little improvement will be forthcoming in new approaches to interface design. Unless users can intuitively understand the meaning of the objects and their relationship in space, any visualization of information is of limited value.

Expertise. All of us, since grade school, have had some experience with static textual design layout–fewer of us are capable of good graphic, hypermedia design. Also, purchasing this expertise is expensive.

System Limitations. There are many systems limitations which need to be improved upon. While none will be serious limitations three or four years into the new millennium, they will be for the next couple of years in the library. Limitations include:

- *Limitations of Field of Vision and Occlusion:* Though the visual medium does offer the potential of concentrating and rapidly disseminating considerably more information than text, the field of view ultimately is limited to your computer display. Images can occlude the view of others behind them. There is only so much visual information that, no matter how well arranged, can be perceived through the surface of the monitor (Demain, 10/96). This is why improvements in monitor technology, at a mass level, are so critical to the development of visualization approaches. Fortunately this area is moving forward rapidly.
- *Bandwidth Limitations:* Graphically intensive interfaces require more bandwidth–although this may not be a problem on a local net, it means many visualization schemes are impractical for general use over the Internet. Comparatively, the speed with which simple ASCII text can be transmitted is very rapid (Demain, 10/96) Fortunately, improvements in Internet transmission capabilities are occurring as will the development of parallel, dedicated "Internets." Internet II, for example, is a net dedicated to academic needs (http://www.internet2.edu/). Moving much of the work to the client side, through special browsers and other means, will also contribute to solving the bandwidth problem or at least make the problem local and subject to your machine's limitations.
- *Costs of Visualization Systems:* What will really push visualization into our screens is ultimately inexpensive, standardized software and hardware. Still, right now, sufficient monitors and fast CPUs are hardly the standard for all. Software is not yet standardized and/or sufficiently well-conceived to counter many of the problems mentioned above. In addition, as mentioned, building the data that these systems would optimize can be expensive.

Other Senses–The Ears Have It

Though previously of use for specialized applications only, auditory output (auditory "icons") is important as part of the multimedia suite of "visualization" and "action" tools. Think of the "dink" sound in Microsoft Windows™ indicating a mistake. An interesting resource to examine in this regard is the Survey of the State of the Art in Human Language Technology (Cole, 1996). The section below, "Specific Actions" (D3c), is of note for information on voice input.

D3c. Interactive Design: Inter-ACTING with Information

The majority of the value of new interface design approaches usually associated with visualization may actually come in the form of new modes and means for user interaction and empowerment. The art and science of providing active, controlled and productive EXPERIENCES and therefore compelling and meaningful interaction between the user and the information system implies what Shedrow (94) calls good Interaction Design. The skills required are involved and, though one can draw heavily from experiences in creating good hypermedia, those with a background in the performing arts tend to excel in this type of design. This should tell us a lot since these people tend to think of creating experiences in such a way as to achieve maximum user involvement within the bounds of getting well-defined information across. They are PROCESS oriented and understand the use of timing, pacing and even, if you will, the dramatic multi-media effects necessary to structure compelling, involving experience for users (Ibid.). In addition, involved users learn fast and tend to use systems well. Though most librarians would shun the computer game analogy, the experience of using most text-based, stolidly under-interactive library interfaces is quite a bit like using a bad, poorly conceived computer game. In fact, our systems are about as compelling as playing bingo and involve about as much of the user's attention. ATMs are generally more advanced. The point here, and I'm not advocating the library as entertainment center, is that part of the problem may be that our users are far from being properly drawn into the finding experience. There may be only so far that you can appropriately go in making library systems compelling but, to turn the table, maybe our users are ineffective for reasons better interactive design can change?

Interactive design addresses the creation of meaningful interactions. Such interactions range over a continuum of active vs. passive experiences. Interactivity is concerned with the "amount of control the user has over the tools, pacing, or content, the amount of choice this control offers, and the ability to use the tool or content to be productive. . . It is important to note that there is no good or bad side of this continuum. The only judgment should be if the level of interactivity is appropriate to the goals of the experience or the messages to be communicated" (Shedrow, 94). In libraries, again think of the give and take of most online catalog Boolean subject searches; there is often a need for well designed "active," process-oriented interactions.

Other spectrums with which to gauge interactivity are: how much control the audience has over the outcome or the rate, sequence, or type of action, and how much feedback exists in the interface. Typically, experiences with high interactivity offer high levels of feedback and, at least, some control. Because there are so many possible outcomes involved in using our systems, providing more user control and involvement, for non-novice users who want it, as touched on above, is important.

Finally, there is the spectrum of productivity and creativity. Experiences that allow one to be creative and produce something are typically more interesting, entertaining, and fulfilling experiences. "Co-creative" technologies assist users in the creation process. "People are naturally creative and are almost always more interested in experiences that allow them to create instead of merely participate. While many situations can create anxiety if people are not accustomed to performing with the tools or techniques, if this anxiety can be lessened, through the careful design of the experience or offered assistance, people express their creativity. This could take the form of recommendations, guidelines, advice, or actually performing operations for users" (Shedrow, 94). Because using our systems could actually be a very creative experience, libraries need to understand and implement co-creative technologies as discussed below.

This leads us to "adaptive experiences," "modifying experiences" and their technologies. Adaptive technologies are those that change the experience based on the behavior of the user/reader/consumer/actor. These can include "agents," modifying behaviors, and "pseudo-intelligence." Agents are processes that can be set to run autonomously, performing specific, unsupervised (or lightly supervised) activities and reporting back when finished. Modifying behaviors are those that change the tools and/or content involved based on the actions or techniques of the user. Some games, for example, do this, providing advanced options as the player becomes more proficient. Other possibilities include content changing to reflect point of view or amount of detail desired. These techniques should have the effect of making a device or person in an experience appear intelligent and in control of the situation (Shedrow, 94). As with co-creative technologies, mentioned above, the understanding and implementation of adaptive and modifying technologies is at the heart of new approaches to interface design.

The User in Control–User Action in Direct Manipulation Interfaces vs. Autonomous Agents

"The wish to create an autonomous agent that knows people's likes and dislikes, makes proper inferences, responds to novel situations, and performs competently with little guidance is strong for some designers" (Shneiderman, 1/97a). Many believe that some type of software agent or artificial intelligence will be able to discern their information needs and respond with appropriate amounts of correctly focused information (the following Web resources are of interest in this regard, see: Hermans' Intelligent Software Agents on the Internet–http://www.firstmonday.dk/issues/issue2_3/index.html; Wood's Agents Info–http://www.cs.bham.ac.uk/~amw/agents/; and/or the Information Filtering Project–http://www.enee.umd.edu/medlab/filter/filter_project.html). While this is certainly a possibility, the timeline of its realization goes well beyond our concerns here. Remember the focus on artificial intelligence (AI) on the reference desk in the mid to late '80s? We are still waiting. Autonomous agents are probably more realizable in the area of classification of information (see section C1) and other areas where the domain of possible actions and outcomes is somewhat more finite than in serious information seeking. Information seeking in libraries and related systems is frequently very complex. A typical thorough user subject search can involve several databases and other finding tools as well as several kinds of searches in each database-all of which build upon one another (e.g., a known item search leads to a subject or pattern search which leads to a citation search and so on). In addition, many successful searches seem to involve some randomness or serendipity which allows the seeker to follow "distant connections" or to intuitively reorder established seeking procedures to meet the specific situation. Software agent developers will be quite challenged to correctly infer such needs and situations. Who knows what the future holds for AI in information seeking but we'd be farther ahead investing in user centered, direct manipulation interfaces.

"Direct manipulation interfaces are seen as more likely candidates to influence advanced user interfaces than adaptive, autonomous, intelligent agents" (Shneiderman, 1/97a). Design improvements in direct manipulation interfaces facilitate more than ever the meshing of the user's skills and experience with the information system. The user is more empowered and more centrally placed than in traditional systems or in systems emphasizing autonomous agents. The user's knowledge is greatly augmented by the interface but the user still runs all essential processes. Users have a strong desire to be able to understand and control the systems they use. "Most users want comprehensible, predictable and controllable interfaces that give them the feeling of accomplishment and responsibility" (Shneiderman, 1/97a). When we're not directing the action we often feel less confident and less involved in what we're doing and that's not good in information seeking.

"An alternative to agents and user models may be to expand the control-panel metaphor. Current control panels are used to set physical parameters, such as the speed of cursor blinking, rate of mouse tracking, or loudness of a speaker, and to establish personal preferences such as time, date formats, placement and format of menus, or color schemes. Some software packages allow users to set parameters such as the speed in games or the usage level. . . . More elaborate control panels exist in style sheets of word processors, specification boxes of query facilities, and scheduling software that carries out processes at regular intervals or when triggered by other processes. Computer control panels, like cruise-control in automobiles and remote controllers for televisions, are designed to convey the sense of control that users seem to expect. Increasingly, complex processes are specified by direct-manipulation programming or by graphical specifications of scheduled procedures, style sheets, and templates" (Shneiderman, 1/97a).

Hybrids of the software agent and direct manipulation scenarios are under development and warrant close attention (Lieberman, 98). For example, the software agent could be invoked in known item searches (seeking permutations of an author's name, for example). Another approach would be for the agent to realize when, for non-novice users, its simple methods were either being unsuccessful, too inflexible or were impeding more suitable advanced techniques. It might then shift modes to a direct manipulation approach. Letizia (http://lieber.www.media.mit.edu/people/lieber/Lieberary/Letizia/Letizia-AAAI/Letizia.html) is an example of a helpful agent concept as an adjunct to a user centered approach.

Physical Interactivity, Specific Actions and Feedback Loops

Physical Interactivity. One should note that this alone may help focus users as they interact with interfaces. We like to use our bodies. Consider that searching is often termed "hunting" for information. All of this is to say that learning often occurs most quickly and thoroughly when reinforced by, accompanying or requiring activity.

Specific Actions (including voice and gesture input). A catalog of all pertinent actions which apply in this context would be too lengthy. However, examples of computer-based information actions include: typing/keying, pointing/clicking, cutting/pasting, the setting of radio and other "buttons," scrolling, choosing options within scroll-down and other forms of menus. Also, of course, the traditional information seeking or refining actions of "reading and writing" are still paramount. Shneiderman (1/97c) developed a brief typology of information actions that distinguishes between finite, specific actions called atomic actions, and aggregates of specific actions called molecular actions. Atomic information actions include: reading for detailed content looking for a fact or date; browsing/scanning reading for general content and patterns; "using" (reading, scanning) lists, sentences, paragraphs; following a reference link. Molecular information actions are composed of atomic actions and include: browsing an almanac table of contents; jumping to a chapter on sports and scanning for skiing topics; locating a scientific term in an alphabetic index and reading articles containing the term; using a keyword to search a catalog to gain a list of candidate book titles; following cross references; scanning a music catalog.

Voice commands are important in specialized systems and should play an increasingly broader role. The next step, continuous-speech voice recognition, promises to make voice input a major element in interface design (see the NIST Spoken Natural Language Processing Group–http://www.itl.nist.gov/div894/894.01/slp.htm as well as Cole, 1996). Inputting information into your system by reading instead of keying is a distinct possibility here for many applications. Useful products are starting to emerge at the popular level, e.g., Naturally Speaking (Dragon Naturally Speaking, 1/98–http://fox. nstn.ca/~aai/dnat.htm).

Very importantly, gesture in the form of hand (real pointing), head, eye or body movement will also become common. These techniques will represent improvements on current mouse-based input actions (Skeptical? Did you think 12 years ago that you would ever be using a mouse?).

Feedback Loops. These are crucial to direct manipulation interfaces and exchange information between the system and the user to inform/guide user action in an individual search or whole session basis. Examples include dynamic queries–as you put in your search term the system begins (from the first letter input) to zero in on the alphabetic location of your term. Microsoft product manual index searching is an example. Query previews wherein an estimate of the number of hits is supplied before or as a search is occurring is a useful feedback loop (you can immediately see the term which is wrecking your search and readjust accordingly–the Silverplatter CD interface, among others, provides this). In a broad sense, the textual Boolean searching process itself often requires a large element of very active, rapid, back and forth feedback to be successful. From a broad perspective, the ability of the system to retain a search history in which individual searches can be refined and re-executed is an important feedback mechanism in itself.

D3d. Verbal Imagery and Clarity in Text–Using the Written Word to Advantage

Visualization should and generally does assume, as a major component, the appropriate, clear use of text and verbal "imagery." For quite some time to come, text and text-based approaches will be the dominant partner as text-based systems evolve into visualized systems. Verbal and visual imaging techniques will co-exist and co-evolve together with each informing the other. As mentioned before, text brings with it major effective user traditions and vast user experience, it can be transmitted rapidly on the Internet, and, in a sense, all people who share the same language and words share in a common information structure. The point isn't to consider one in opposition to the other: verbal and visual approaches will work together to enhance the effectiveness of both in interface design.

Perhaps a larger concern in libraries though is that we still have a long way to go with more efficient and clear usage of text. The effective usage of text will be greatly optimized by the new visualization and action approaches. The result should be more easily achieved precision and, ultimately, clarity in meaning in text application in interface design.

CONCLUSION

It is a cliche but change in library systems and interface design is now a constant. From perspectives ranging from basic computing to network/information standards to graphic arts in electronic environments, we are going through an era marked by great advancement and experimentation. This is increasingly a challenging as well as expensive time during which many of our roles will be redefined as will the role of information, scholarly publishing and libraries in general. There are numerous important opportunities rushing by that will effect libraries for some time to come. If you don't have your oar in the water, it's time you put it in.

REFERENCES

The Alert Box: Current Issues in Web Usability. http://www.useit.com/alertbox/

Andrews, K., 1996, Applying Hypermedia Research to the World Wide Web, Workshop on Hypermedia Research and the World Wide Web, Hypertext '96, Washington. http://www.iicm.edu/apphrweb

Apple Computer, Inc. 1997. Apple Web Design Guide. http://applenet.apple.com/hi/web/web.html

Arms, William Y., et al., 2/97, An Architecture for Information in Digital Libraries, D-Lib Magazine. http://www.dlib.org/dlib/february97/cnri/02arms1.html

AskJeeves. http://www.askjeeves.com/

Benjamin, Ben, 8/96, Elements of Web Design, C|Net. http://www.cnet.com/Content/Builder/Graphics/Design/

Barnard, D.T. and I.D. Ide, 7/97, Text Encoding Initiative: Flexible and Extensible Document Encoding, Journal of the American Society for Information Science 48(7):622-628.

Bevan, N., nd., Usability Issues in Web Site Design, NPL Usability Services, National Physical Laboratory. http://www.npl.co.uk/npl/sections/us/frames/fweb.html

Bieber, Michael et al., 1997, Fourth generation hypermedia: some missing links for the World Wide Web, International Journal of Human-Computer Studies, v. 47 (1). http://ijhcs.open.ac.uk/bieber/bieber-nf.html http://www.hbuk.co.uk/ap/ijhcs/webusability/bieber/bieber.html

Bieber, Michael, 1997, Full Publication List, New Jersey Institute of Technology. http://hertz.njit.edu/~bieber/full-pubs.html

Bieber, Michael and Fabio Vitali, 1/97, Toward Support for Hypermedia on the World Wide Web, v. 30 (1): 62-70. Computer (IEEE). http://www.cs.unibo.it/~fabio/bio/papers/1997/IEEEC97/January/IEEEC0197.html

Browser Central:C|net. http://www.cnet.com/Content/Browser/

BrowserWatch. http://browserwatch.internet.com/

CA Web Resources. http://www.commarts.com/creative/index.html

Card, S., 1996, Visualizing retrieved information: a survey. IEEE Computer Graphics and Application 16 (2): 63-67. http://www.computer.org/pubs/cg&a/report/g20063.htm

Center for Intelligent Information Retrieval. http://cobar.cs.umass.edu/info/ciirbiblo. html

Chalmers, M., 7/96a, Pearls, Swine and Sow's Ears: Interface Research in a Multinational Bank. Proc. British National Conference on Databases, Springer Verlag, LNCS 1094, Edinburgh, pp. 222-229. http://www.ubs.com/cgi-bin/framer.pl?/info/ubilab/publications/e_cha96c.htm (abstract)

Chalmers, M., 7/96b, Interface Design: More Craft than Science?, Proc. 5th Intl.

Workshop on Interfaces for Database Systems, Edinburgh. http://www.ubs.com/cgi-bin/framer.pl?/info/ubilab/publications/e_cha96b.htm (abstract)

Cole, R. A. et al. 1996. Survey of the State of the Art in Human Language Technology, National Science Foundation and Center for Spoken Language Understanding, Oregon Graduate Institute. http://www.cse.ogi.edu/CSLU/HLTsurvey/HLTsurvey.html

Cugini, Johm et al., nd., Interactive 3-D Visualization for Document Retrieval, Visualization and Virtual Reality Group, NIST. http://www.cs.umbc.edu/conferences/cikm/npiv/papers/piatko.html

Cyberstacks. http://www.public.iastate.edu/~CYBERSTACKS/

Daessler, Rolf. 1995. Visualization of Abstract Information. http://banzai.msi.umn.edu/~roelf/tut.html

Daniel, R. jr. and C. Lagoze, 12/97, Extending the Warwick Framework: From Metadata Containers to Active Digital Objects, D-lib Magazine. http://www.dlib.org/dlib/november97/daniel/11daniel.html

de Graf, Hans, HCI Index. http://is.twi.tudelft.nl/hci/

Demaine, Jeff, 10/96, Information Visualization, Network Notes, no. 35, National Library of Canada. http://collection.nlc-bnc.ca/100/201/301/netnotes/netnotes-h/notes35.htm

Dempsey, Lorcan and Rachel Heery. 3/97, A Review of Metadata: A Survey of Current Resource Description Formats Work Package 3 of Telematics for Research project DESIRE. http://www.ukoln.ac.uk/metadata/DESIRE/overview/Distance Education Clearinghouse. http://www.uwex.edu/disted/home.html

Dougherty, Dale, 5/97, The XML Files, Web Review. http://webreview.com/97/05/16/feature/

Shneiderman, Ben, et al., Dynamic query user interfaces for networked information systems: the case of NASA EOSDIS, Human-Computer Interaction Laboratory, University of Maryland. http://www.cs.umd.edu/projects/hcil/Research/1995/dq-for-eosdis.html

Dragon NaturallySpeaking, 1/98, PC/Computing, v11(1):256 (4 pages).

Earnshaw, R. and J. Vince. 1997. The Internet in 3D: Information, Images and Interaction. San Diego, Academic Press, 1997.

Ericsson, Mikeal, nd., Human-Computer Interaction Resources on the Net. http://www.ida.liu.se/labs/aslab/groups/um/hci/

Extensible Markup Language (XML). http://www.sil.org/sgml/xml.html

Fox, David, nd., Graphical Elements for Information Browsing Systems. http://galt.cs.nyu.edu/students/fox/area.html

Gibbs, Simon and Gabor Szentivanyi, nd., Index to Multimedia Information Sources. http://viswiz.gmd.de/MultimediaInfo/

Greene, Stephan et al., Previews and Overviews in Digital Libraries: Designing Surrogates to Support Visual Information Seeking.ftp://ftp.cs.umd.edu/pub/hcil/Reports-Abstracts-Bibliography/3838HTML/3838.html

Grinstein, George and M. O. Ward, 1996, Introduction to Visualization: Vis '96 Tutorial #2, Computer Science Department, Worcester Polytechnic Institute. http://cs.wpi.edu/~matt/courses/cs543/visualize/

Hand, Chris, 10/97, VR Bibliography http://www.cms.dmu.ac.uk/~cph/VRbib.html

Harnad, S., 1992, Interactive Publication: Extending American Physical Society's

Discipline-Specific Model for Electronic Publishing. Serials Review, Special Issue on Economics Models for Electronic Publishing, pp. 58-61. ftp://ftp.princeton. edu/pub/harnad/Harnad/HTML/harnad92.interactivpub.html

Hazen, Mar, 1997, Interfacing the Web, University of Georgia. http://www.fcs.uga. edu/~mhazen/re96/

HCI Index. http://is.twi.tudelft.nl/hci/

The HCI Bibliography. http://www.hcibib.org/

Hermans, Björn, 3/97, Intelligent Software Agents on the Internet, First Monday, Vol.2 No. 3. http://www.firstmonday.dk/issues/issue2_3/index.html

High Energy Physics Preprint Bulletin Board. http://xxx.lanl.gov/

Hildreth, Charles R., 6/97, The Use and Understanding of Keyword Searching in a University Online Catalog, Information Technology and Libraries 16(2):52-62.

Hirsch, Morris and James Allan, nd., A Graphic Interface for User Directed Clustering of Retrieved Documents, Center for Intelligent Information Retrieval, University of Massachusetts at Amherst. http://www.cs.umass.edu/~hirsch/star_query_ paper.html

HTML Watch. http://www.pantos.org/atw/html.html

HTML 4.0 Specification. ttp://www.w3.org/TR/REC-htm140/

Human-Computer Interaction Laboratory, 9/97, WebTOC: A Tool to Visualize and Quantify Web Sites using a Hierarchical Table of Contents Browser, University of Maryland. ftp://ftp.cs.umd.edu/pub/hcil/Demos/WebTOC/handout.html

Human-Computer Interaction Laboratory. http://www.cs.umd.edu/projects/hcil/

Human-Computer Interaction Laboratory, 1984-1997, Papers and Technical Reports, University of Maryland. http://www.cs.umd.edu/projects/hcil/Research/tech-report-list.html

Human-Computer Interaction Resources on the Net. http://www.ida.liu.se/labs/aslab/ groups/um/hci/

Human-Computer Interaction Virtual Library. http://usableweb.com/hcivl/

Human Factors Research Group, nd. The Software Usability Measurement Inventory. University College, Cork. http://www.ua.ac.be/MAN/WP51/t38.html

Human Interface Technology Laboratory, 5/97, On the Net: Virtual Reality Online http://www.hitl.washington.edu/projects/knowledge_base/onthenet.html

Hypertext Markup Language Resources: The Web Developer's Virtual Library. http://WWW.Stars.com/Authoring/HTML/Resources.html

Iannella, R. and A. Waugh, 4/97, Metadata: Enabling the Internet, CAUSE97 Conference, Melbourne. http://www.dstc.edu.au/RDU/reports/CAUSE97/

INFOMINE. http://lib-www.ucr.edu/

Information Filtering Project, University of Maryland. http://www.enee.umd.edu/ medlab/filter/filter_project.html

Inquery. http://ciir.cs.umass.edu/inquerypage.html

Instone, Keith, nd., Usable Web: Guide to Web usability resources (formerly WebHCI). http://usableweb.com/

Instone, Keith, 5/97, Human-Computer Interaction Virtual Library. http://usableweb. com/hcivl/

Internet Public Library. http://www.ipl.org/

Java Documentation. http://java.sun.com/docs/index.html

Java Programming Language: The World-Wide Web Virtual Library. http:// acm.org/ ~ops/java.html

Java/HotJava FAQ Index. http://java.sun.com/faqIndex.html

Jones, Paul, 3/97, Java and Libraries: Digital and Otherwise, D-Lib Magazine. http:// www.dlib.org/dlib/march97/navy/03norris.html

Juliussen, Egil, 1/97, Technology 1997 analysis & forecast: Computers, IEEE Spectrum, v34:49-54.

Kandogan, Eser and Ben Shneiderman, 4/97, Elastic Windows: A Hierarchical Multi-Window World-Wide Web Browser, Human Computer Interaction Laboratory, University of Maryland. http://www.cs.umd.edu/users/kandogan/papers/uist97/paper.html

Keeker, Kevin, 7/97, Improving Web Site Usability and Appeal Guidelines Compiled by MSN Usability Research, Microsoft, Inc. http://www.microsoft.com/workshop/author/plan/IMPROVINGSITEUSA.HTM

Koenemann, J. and N. J. Belkin, 4/96, A Case For Interaction: A Study of Interactive Information Retrieval Behavior and Effectiveness, CHI 96, "Common Ground" Conference on Human Factors in Computing Systems,April 13-18, Vancouver, British Columbia, Canada. http://www.acm.org/sigchi/chi96/proceedings/papers/Koenemann/jk1_txt.htm

Lagoze, Carl, Clifford A. Lynch, and Ron Daniel Jr., 7/96, The Warwick Framework: A Container Architecture for Aggregating Sets of Metadata, Cornell Computer Science Technical Report TR96-1593. http://cs-tr.cs.cornell.edu:80/Dienst/UI/2.0/Describe/ncstrl.cornell/TR96-1593.

Lakoff, George, 3/94, Conceptual Metaphor Home Page, University of California, Berkeley. http://cogsci.berkeley.edu/

Lassila and Swick, Resource Description Framework (RDF) Model and Syntax, W3C. http://www.w3.org/TR/WD-rdf-syntax-971002/

Laurel, Brenda. 1991. Computers As Theater. Addison-Wesley. Reading, MA.

Letizia. http://lieber.www.media.mit.edu/people/lieber/Lieberary/Letizia/Letizia-AAAI/Letizia.html

Library of Congress Experimental Search System. http://lcweb2.loc.gov/resdev/ess

Lieberman, Henry, 1998, Integrating User Interface Agents with Conventional Applications, ACM Conference on Intelligent User Interfaces, San Francisco, January 1998. http://lieber.www.media.mit.edu/people/lieber/Lieberary/Attaching/Attaching/Attaching.html

Lipstick Librarians. http://www.teleport.com/~petlin/liplib/

Logan, Elisabeth and Pollard, Marvin, eds., 7/97, "Special Topic Issue: Structured Information/Standards for Document Architectures," Journal of the American Society for Information Science 48(7).

Long, Byron. 1994. Natural Language as an Interface Style. Dynamic Graphics Project, Department of Computer Science, University of Toronto. http:// www.dgp.toronto.edu/people/byron/papers/nli.html

Luke, Sean, 7/97, SHOE 0.993: Proposed Specification http://www.cs.umd.edu/projects/plus/SHOE/spec.htmlhttp://www.cs.umd.edu/projects/plus/SHOE/index.html

LyberWorld. http://www-cui.darmstadt.gmd.de/visit/Activities/Lyberworld/

Lynch, Clifford A., 4/97, The Z39.50 Information Retrieval Standard: Part I: A

Strategic View of Its Past, Present and Future, D-lib. http://www.dlib.org/dlib/apri197/041ynch.html

Lynch, Patrick J. and Susan Horton, 1997, Yale C/AIM Web Style Guide, Yale University. http://info.med.yale.edu/caim/manual/index.html

MacColl, John, 3/96, E-print Archives Key To Paperless Journals, Ariadne, Issue 2. http://www.ariadne.ac.uk/issue2/ejournals/

McKiernan, Gerry, 11/97, Beyond Bookmarks: Schemes for Organizing the Web, Iowa State University. http://www.public.iastate.edu/~CYBERSTACKS/CTW.htm

McKiernan, Gerry, 7/97, Project Aristotle(sm): Automated Categorization of Web Resources, Iowa State University. http://www.public.iastate.edu/~CYBERSTACKS/Aristotle.htm

McKiernan, Gerry and Peter Wasilko, 7/97, Onion Patch(sm): New Age Public Access Systems, Iowa State University. http://www.public.iastate.edu/~CYBERSTACKS/Onion.htm

McKiernan, Gerry and Peter Wasilko, 6/97, The Big Picture(sm): Visual Browsing in Web and non-Web Databases. Iowa State University. http://www.public.iastate.edu/~CYBERSTACKS/BigPic.htm

Marchionini, Gary. 1995. Information Seeking in Electronic Environments, Cambridge University Press, UK.

Michigan Electronic Library. http://mel.lib.mi.us/

Microsoft Corporation, 6/97, XML White Paper. http://www.microsoft.com/xml/xmlwhite.htm

Microsoft Corporation, nd., Extensible Markup Language (XML). http://www.microsoft.com/xml/

Microsoft Corporation. http://www.microsoft.com/microsoft.htm

Miller, Richard H., nd., "Web Interface Design: Learning from our Past," InterMedia Lab, Bell Communications Research. http://athos.rutgers.edu/~shklar/www4/rmiller/rhmpapr.html

Mitchell, Steve, 6/97, INFOMINE: The First Three Years of a Virtual Library for the Biological, Agricultural and Medical Sciences, Proceedings of the Contributed Papers Session, Biological Sciences Division, Special Libraries Association Annual Conference, Seattle June 11, 1997. http://www.lib.asu.edu/noble/slaproc/mitchell.htm

Mitchell, Steve. 3/97, INFOMINE, Ariadne, issue 8.URL: http://www.ukoln.ac.uk/ariadne/issue8/infomine/

Mitchell, Steve and Margaret Mooney. 3/96, INFOMINE-A Model Web-Based Academic Virtual Library, Information Technology and Libraries, 15 no. 1: 20-25. URL: http://lib-www.ucr.edu/pubs/italmine.html

Myers, Brad, 1997, User Interface Software Tools. Human Computer Interaction Institute, Carnegie Mellon University. http://www.cs.cmu.edu/afs/cs/user/bam/www/toolnames.html

Nation, David A. et al., 1997, Visualizing websites using a hierarchical table of contents browser: WebTOC, Human Computer Interaction Laboratory, University of Maryland. http://www.cs.umd.edu/projects/hcil/People/dnation/WebTOC/WebTOC.html

Natural Language Processing Laboratory (NLPLAB), Department of Computer and Information Science, Linköping University. http://www.ida.liu.se/labs/nlplab/

NASA EOSDIS. http://www.cs.umd.edu/projects/hcil/Research/1995/dq-for-eosdis.html

Netscape Netcenter. http://www.netscape.com/

Nielsen, Jakob, 7/97, Search and You May Find, AlertBox. http://www.useit.com/alertbox/9707b.html

Nielsen, Jakob. 1995. Multimedia and Hypertext: the Internet and beyond. Boston, AP Professional.

Nielsen, Jacob. 1993. Hypertext and hypermedia. Boston, Academic Press, Professional.

Nielsen, Jakob. 1993. Usability engineering. Boston, Academic Press.

NIST Spoken Natural Language Processing Group. http://www.itl.nist.gov/div894/894.01/slp.htm

North, Chris, nd., A Taxonomy of Information Visualization User-Interfaces, Human-Computer Interaction Laboratory, University of Maryland. http://www.cs.umd.edu/~north/infoviz.html

OLIVE: the On-line Library of Information Visualization Environments, Department of Computer Science, University of Maryland. http://www.otal.umd.edu/Olive/

On the Net: Virtual Reality Online. http://www.hitl.washington.edu/projects/knowledge_base/onthenet.html

Overview of Virtual Reality Modeling Language Version 2.0. http://vag.vrml.org/VRML2.0/FINAL/Overview.html

Plug-In Plaza!: BrowserWatch. http://browserwatch.internet.com/plug-in.html

Powell, T. A., 11/97, Extend The Web: An XML Primer, INTERNETWEEK, November 24, 1997, Issue: 691. http://www.techweb.com/se/directlink.cgi?INW19971124S0090

Purins, Simon. nd. THE PSYCHOLOGY OF HUMAN-COMPUTER INTERFACE DESIGN. The University of Westminster. http://www.wmin.ac.uk/~ywhlc/human-computer.html

QUIS: The Questionnaire for User Interaction Satisfaction, Human-Computer Interaction Lab (HCIL), University of Maryland at College Park. http://www.lap.umd.edu/QUISFolder/quisHome.html

Ratner, Julie et al., 1996, Characterization and Assessment of HTML Style Guides, CHI 96 Electronic Proceedings. http://www.acm.org/sigchi/chi96/proceedings/intpost/Ratner/rj_txt.htm

Rohrer, Tim, 9/97, Center for the Cognitive Science of Metaphor Online, Philosophy Department, University of Oregon. http://metaphor.uoregon.edu/metaphor.htm

Rohrer, Tim, in press, Conceptual Blending on the Information Highway: How Metaphorical Inferences Work, International Cognitive Linguistics Conference '95 Proceedings, v. 2. Amsterdam: Johns Benjamin. http://metaphor.uoregon.edu/iclacnf4.htm

The SGML/XML Web Page. http://www.sil.org/sgml/sgml.html

Shedroff, Nathan, 1994, Information Interaction Design: A Unified Field Theory of Design, vivid studios. http://www.vivid.com/form/unified/

Shedroff, Nathan, nd., Interaction and Information Design Resources. http://www.nathan.com/thoughts/resources.html

Shneiderman, Ben. 1998. Designing the User Interface: Strategies for Effective Human-Computer Interaction. 3rd edition, Addison Wesley Longman, Reading, MA.

Shneiderman, Ben, 1/97a, Direct Manipulation for Comprehensible, Predictable and Controllable User Interfaces, University of Maryland.ftp://ftp.cs.umd.edu/pub/hcil/Reports-Abstracts-Bibliography/97-01.html

Shneiderman, Ben et al., 1/97b, Clarifying Search: A User-Interface Framework for Text Searches, D-Lib Magazine. http://www.dlib.org/dlib/january97/retrieval/01shneiderman.html

Shneiderman, Ben, 1/97c, Designing Information-Abundant Websites, International Journal of Human-Computer Studies, v. 47 (1). http://ijhcs.open.ac.uk/shneiderman/shneiderman-nf.htmlhttp://www.hbuk.co.uk/ap/ijhcs/webusability/shneiderman/shneiderman.html http://ijhcs.open.ac.uk/shneiderman/shneiderman.htmlftp://ftp.cs.umd.edu/pub/hcil/Reports-Abstracts-Bibliography/3634html/3634.html

Shneiderman, Ben, 7/96, The eyes have it: A task by data type taxonomy of information visualizations, Proc. IEEE Symposium on Visual Languages '96, IEEE, Los Alamos, CA, pg. 336-343.ftp://ftp.cs.umd.edu/pub/hcil/Reports-Abstracts-Bibliography/3665.txt ftp://ftp.cs.umd.edu/pub/hcil/Reports-Abstracts-Bibliography/96-13html/96-13.html

SiteMap. http://lislin.gws.uky.edu/Sitemap/Sitemap.html

Spire. http://multimedia.pnl.gov:2080/showcase/?it_content/spire.node

Spotfire. http://www.ivee.com/

Teaching Theaters, University of Maryland. http://www.inform.umd.edu/TT/

UI Index. http://www.vrix.com/uiindex/uiindex.cfm

User Interaction Design Web. http://www.io.tudelft.nl/uidesign/

Verity. http://www.verity.com/

Visage System. http://www.cs.cmu.edu/Groups/sage/project/visage.html

Vitali, F. et al., 1997, Extending HTML in a Principled Way with Displets, Computer Networks and ISDN Systems, Vol. 29. http://www.cs.unibo.it/~fabio/bio/papers/1997/WWW97/Displets/PAPER155.html

VR Bibliography. http://www.cms.dmu.ac.uk/~cph/VRbib.html

VRML Consortium. http://www.vrml.org/

VRML Repository. http://www.sdsc.edu/vrml/

Ward, N. et al., 96, Discussion Paper: Networked Information Retrieval Standards, Distributed Systems Technology Centre. http://www.dstc.edu.au/RDU/reports/webir.html

Wood, Andy. Agents Info. http://www.cs.bham.ac.uk/~amw/agents/

Woodward, Jeannette, 4/97, Retraining the Profession, or, Over the Hill at 40, American Libraries, 28(4): 32-34.

Young, Peter, 3/96 (rev. 11/96). Three Dimensional Information Visualization. Computer Science Technical Report, No. 12/96. Department of Computer Science, University of Durham. http://www.dur.ac.uk/~dcs3py/pages/work/documents/lit-survey/IV-Survey/index.html

Young, Peter, 2/96, Virtual Reality Systems, Department of Computer Science, University of Durham. http://www.dur.ac.uk/~dcs3py/pages/work/documents/lit-survey/VR-Survey/index.html

Grainger Engineering Library:
An Object-Enhanced User Interface
for Information Retrieval

Eric H. Johnson

SUMMARY. Telnet and HTML-based information retrieval user interfaces provide searchers with neither the power nor the flexibility required for effectively searching multiple databases. Nor do they exploit the existing power of PCs or make good use of client-server technology as a whole. IODyne is an example of an information retrieval client that views databases and queries as objects which you can combine arbitrarily. It has a commandless, hypertextual user interface incorporating modelessness, direct manipulation, feedback, and object persistence. It uses multiple windows to show multiple views of databases simultaneously, and allows you to arbitrarily juxtapose these views. Besides bibliographic retrieval, IODyne provides navigational tools for subject thesauri, classification systems, keyword-in-context (KWIC) databases, and other term suggestion services, represented as distributed objects which are all integrated into a seamless drag-and-drop environment. Persistent representations of sets of queries and repositories can be saved and shared among IODyne users. IODyne demonstrates that, with recent advances in computer and network hardware, as well as object-oriented development environments, entire information systems can be designed around the needs of users

Eric H. Johnson is Research Programmer for C.A.N.I.S./Community Systems Laboratory (http://www.canis.uiuc.edu/) and a PhD student in the Graduate School of Library and Information Science at the University of Illinois at Urbana-Champaign. His research interests include user interface design for information retrieval systems and indexing structures for bibliographic databases.

[Haworth co-indexing entry note]: "Grainger Engineering Library: An Object-Enchanced User Interface for Information Retrieval." Johnson, Eric H. Co-published simultaneously in *Science & Technology Libraries* (The Haworth Press, Inc.) Vol. 17, No. 3/4, 1999, pp. 183-207; and: *Digital Libraries: Philosophies, Technical Design Considerations, and Example Scenarios* (ed: David Stern) The Haworth Press, Inc., 1999, pp. 183-207. Single or multiple copies of this article are available for a fee from The Haworth Document Delivery Service [1-800-342-9678, 9:00 a.m. - 5:00 p.m. (EST). E-mail address: getinfo@haworthpressinc.com].

rather than the limitations of technology. *[Article copies available for a fee from The Haworth Document Delivery Service: 1-800-342-9678. E-mail address: getinfo@haworthpressinc. com]*

KEYWORDS. Searching multiple databases, client-server technology, IODyne, information retrieval client, hypertextual user interface, modelessness, direct manipulation object persistence, navigational tools, term suggestion, drag-and-drop, object-oriented

THE CURRENT STATE OF AFFAIRS

With the huge amounts of bibliographic data currently accessible over the Internet, using outdated information retrieval technology to search bibliographic databases becomes more and more frustrating. The World Wide Web has popularized the use of full-text indexing and searching coupled with HTML-based user interfaces. Online catalog vendors have in turn migrated much of their software to the Web, allowing anyone with Web access to search bibliographic databases. While this does increase accessibility, in terms of retrieval interaction it does not represent a significant advance over vt100 technology. The current generation of desktop PCs have the memory and computational power, and networks have the bandwidth, to do much more to enhance not only the availability of databases but also the usability of retrieval software. Desktop and laptop computers now support multiple windows and multiple network connections. While web browsers use multiple network connections to quicken the downloading of files needed for a webpage, webpages and forms present information in a static, sequential format. Clicking on a link takes you to a different page, which itself must be downloaded from a server or fetched from the disk cache. The result is a series of static screens, which may look very nice with the use of graphics, but again offer little advantage over older display technologies. The careful use of frames can alleviate this somewhat, but still cannot take full advantage of what multiple windows can offer.

What makes the current state of affairs especially bad is how almost every database available for searching on the Internet has its own user interface for searching. This makes using retrieval technology even more difficult, as no two database interfaces will have the same command syntax or require the same sequence of steps in a retrieval session. Information retrieval itself requires considerable intellectual effort, but the effort required to use the technology built up around it far outweighs even that. Indeed, the frustration that users of information systems encounter is nearly always due to the technology rather than the database itself.

Information retrieval standards such as Z39.50 alleviate this somewhat by standardizing the querying and presentation of results at the gateway level, allowing information retrieval clients to be designed independently of databases and servers. A single Z39.50 client can (in principle) connect to any Z39.50 server, and with the configuration information provided can generate queries of the form required by the server and present the results in a consistent way. This allows for client software that can provide a common way for users to send queries to and view results from multiple servers simultaneously. While this at first may seem like only a minor convenience, it offers huge amounts of leverage to the end-user, as will be explained below.

In this paper I take the position that providing effective access to the thousands of repositories coming online in the near future requires that system designers and end-users alike embrace the idea of object-orientation. A good number of system designers have already done so, supported and encouraged by vendors of object-oriented programming languages and development environments.

Although there are no ironclad rules of user-interface design, the literature (see references at the end of this article) provides a great number of detailed guidelines and examples of well-designed and robust graphical user interfaces (GUIs). All of it applies to user interfaces for information retrieval systems.

It is important to understand that not every GUI-based application succeeds in interacting with the user in an object-oriented way. There are a great number of information retrieval applications now available which have GUI elements like windows, icons, menus, and buttons, but which do not display behavior readily distinguishable from the command-line systems of yore. This is chiefly because the designers of such systems impose what they have learned from the old paradigm onto the new. The result is that buttons on such systems are literal transliterations of commands: clicking on a button to do a subject search, for example, takes you into a mode which imposes the same restrictions on you as did the old command-driven interface from which it was derived, although the screen may look prettier than before. In terms of interactivity, this use of GUIs at best does nothing more than spare you from having to remember the names of commands and their various options. More typically, indiscriminate GUIfication results in a user interface that has a profusion of modes and dialog boxes that obscure the operation of an application rather than clarify it.

USING OBJECTS IN INFORMATION RETRIEVAL: IODYNE AS AN EXAMPLE

To take full advantage of what GUIs have to offer you must abandon the idea of user interfaces having *commands* and *modes* and instead embrace the idea of them having *objects* that have *properties* and display *behavior*. This model is based on how we perceive objects in the physical world; a car, for example, has properties like its color, how many passengers can ride in it, and how many valves the engine has, and behaviors like going forward when you step on the gas pedal and stopping when you step on the brake. In this way we can create user interfaces with styles of interaction that make it possible to visualize data as well as directly manipulate them. IODyne provides an example of object-oriented user interface design. IODyne is an Internet client program which allows you to retrieve information from servers by dynamically using *information objects*. Information objects are abstract representations of bibliographic data, typically titles (or title keywords), author names, subject and classification identifiers, and full-text search terms. At another level, information objects include individual bibliographic records, retrieved sets of bibliographic records, subject thesauri, and classification systems. IODyne has no commands and no modes: instead of typing commands, you directly manipulate information objects. A given information object has the same set of behaviors regardless of what other windows you have open, or what particular action you perform with it.

Because action is central to the use of IODyne, the dialogs for constructing searches do not appear much differently from those in other information retrieval clients. The difference is in how you can use them. If you want you can still use IODyne in a way that mimics the interaction you get with command-line interfaces. This is useful as a first step in understanding the new ways of interaction offered by object-oriented GUIs in general and IODyne in particular. However, as you learn new uses for the information objects before you, you can immediately begin to use them in these new ways, even though you may have created them while thinking in terms of the old paradigm.

IODyne uses object-oriented design techniques throughout. This paper, however, mainly describes the user interface. There are a great many details about the practice of user interface design, as well as object-oriented user interface design in particular, that are far too numerous to cover here. The experience of implementing IODyne, however, has brought a number of "core" principles to light that seem particularly relevant to information retrieval interaction, and these are what I focus on in this paper. The point of this paper, then, is not to show you IODyne specifically, but rather to present it as an example of applying object-oriented user interface design principles to the problem of information retrieval interaction. There are consequently a lot of features of IODyne that I do not cover or else gloss over because, again, the point is to illustrate principles of object-oriented design rather than all the features of a particular application.

The references at the end of this paper contain a list of books and articles that I have found particularly helpful in learning the finer points of user interface design, and can fill in any gaps in what follows.

USING IODYNE

Figure 1 shows the IODyne toolbar. It is purposefully designed to be as small as possible, because unlike retrieval systems that mimic online public access catalogs (OPACs), IODyne is designed to run in a windowed environ-ment, like a Windows95™ PC, and coexist with other applications. The typical user of IODyne, at least for the next few years, is expected to be a researcher working in his or her office who runs IODyne alongside word processors and other applications. The primary use of the PC will be to write papers or do calculations, with information retrieval a secondary though important use. IODyne must therefore be able to sit quietly up in the corner (though it may also be minimized) until called upon.

From the IODyne toolbar you initiate almost everything you do with IODyne. Like most Windows applications, IODyne has File and Edit menus, plus other menus specific to IODyne. It also has buttons, checkboxes, and index card file and trash icons. The latter two are the only metaphors (repre-sentations of real-world objects) in IODyne: you use the index card file to store information objects, and the trash for throwing objects away. Every-thing else in IODyne is idiomatic (it does not represent something in the real world, so you must be shown how to use it), designed with the unique capabilities of object-oriented user interfaces in mind. Although other objects in IODyne, like buttons, appear as they do in other GUI-based applications, and you can use them as buttons, you can also use them in ways that are very un-button like but that extend the use of buttons in powerful ways.

You use the Title, Author, Subject, and Text buttons to initiate searches. You can use them just like regular GUI buttons by clicking on them. If you click on the Title button, for instance, you get a Title Search dialog, as in Figure 2. (A *dialog* is a window where you interact with the program by entering text and/or clicking on buttons.)

FIGURE 1. The IODyne toolbar.

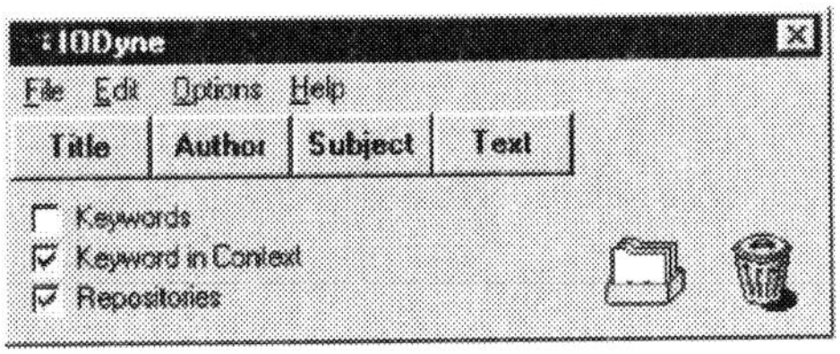

FIGURE 2. The IODyne Total Search dialog. The **Search** button is grayed out because there is no search term entered.

This is a GUI manifestation of a title search command. It looks pretty much like title search dialogs in other retrieval applications, and you can use it that way: type keywords or a phrase from the title you want to search for, select some options, and click on the Search button. This creates a query which IODyne sends to the connected servers.

So far the use of this search dialog looks no different than in other retrieval applications. Notice, however, that it has no Cancel button. This is an indication that the Title Search dialog is *modeless*. A modeless dialog allows you to use other windows while it is active. In contrast, a modal dialog does not allow you to do anything else until you complete what the dialog requires and click either the "OK" or the "Cancel" button. (Think, for example, about how you use a file open dialog. You must either pick a file and click the "OK" button or click the "Cancel" button before you can do anything else in the application. If you try to do anything else while that modal dialog is visible, you get some sort of audible signal that you cannot proceed. In this way it has put the application into a different mode.)

Figure 3 shows the result of a title keyword search. When you form a new query, IODyne transfers the query to a *search document* where it then becomes a persistent information object known as a *query object*. Search documents provide placement for queries as well as the display of query results. The upper part of a search document is a graphical area which provides a place to edit queries, arrange them, and combine them. The lower part displays headline records of search results and provides access to their corresponding full records.

Besides the literal value of the search term, a query object carries other attributes that correspond to the options in the search dialog. These options determine how the search term gets matched to the access points in the database. The specific attribute values are hidden behind the natural-language label on the query object. In Figure 3, the query object has the label "Title stemword," which is the English equivalent of the state of the title search dialog also shown in Figure 3. Any query object on a search document contains a complete representation of the state of the corresponding search dialog, com-

FIGURE 3. IODyne Title Search dialog with the title keyword **networks** entered into it. The **Search** key has been clicked and the search appears on a search document with the results displayed for the connected repositories. The thin black line indicates the result of clicking the Search button.

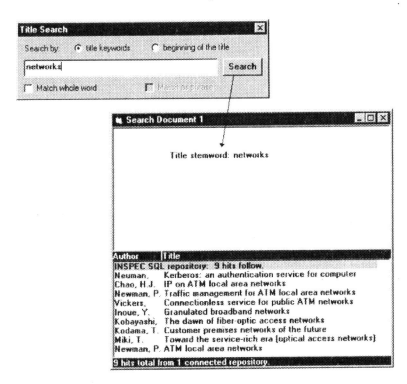

plete with the search term and whatever options you selected when you formed the query. Because of this, you can click on the label portion of a query object to open the search dialog that formed that query object.

Figure 3 also shows that the title search dialog remains on the screen after IODyne has completed the search and displayed the results. This is another indication of modelessness. A modeless dialog remains in view after you use it, and only goes away when you click the close box, the small button in the caption bar in the upper right-hand corner of the dialog that has the "X" in it (this is a standard feature of all windowed operating systems). If the title search dialog was modal, it would disappear when you click on the "Search" button (think again of what happens when you use a modal dialog such as a file open dialog). The title search dialog is therefore available for you to create more title searches.

With any dialog open, you can work elsewhere in IODyne until you want to use that dialog again. Leaving any dialog open does not affect how any other dialog works. You can close any dialog at any time without affecting the operation of any other dialog.

In this way, all dialogs in IODyne are independent. You can have any combination of dialogs open, even multiple occurrences of the same kind of dialog, and arrange them in any way that suits you.

Every object in a search document is clickable. To see the full record corresponding to a headline record, click on the headline record (a single click is sufficient for all hypertext navigation in IODyne) as shown in Figure 4.

Depending on how the repository is configured, a full-record display can contain a number of information objects that are themselves directly manipulable. In IODyne, manipulating an object involves either clicking on it (as in hypertext navigation) or dragging it somewhere and dropping it there. The full record shown in Figure 4 has a number of manipulable objects: the title of the article, the author names, the abstract, the subject identifiers, the text key phrases, and the class codes.

FIGURE 4. On the search document, the headline record for the item **Customer premises networks of the future** has been clicked. In response, IODyne displays the corresponding full record.

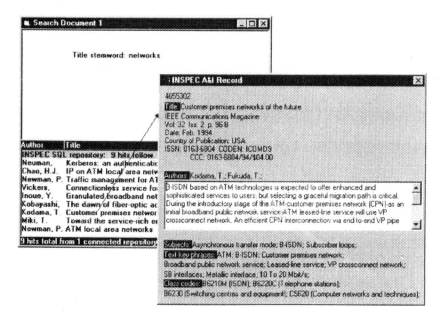

Dragging any one of these (or a selection from the abstract) back to the search document and dropping it there causes the search document to do a search on the connected repositories using that term and a search method (title, author, subject, etc.) appropriate to the object's type. See Figure 5 for an example.

We can now define four principles of object behavior in IODyne.

1. *Modelessness.* In many information retrieval applications, you must go into another mode (such as going back to the "main search menu") before you can do another search, especially if the new search is of a different type. To do a new search in IODyne, you only have to drop an information object (a subject descriptor in this case) onto a search document. You can do this anytime you have a search document displayed, regardless of what other windows you have open, and regardless of which window you drag the object from. This is yet another illustration of modelessness in IODyne.

2. *Direct manipulation.* In most information retrieval applications, you must do everything through either commands or navigation through modal dialogs. Both of these methods separate you from the information you want to manipulate by forcing you to give directions to the system instead of just doing it yourself. In IODyne, you can directly manipulate objects by picking them up in one window and dropping them into another. Different windows impart different behaviors on various objects, which accounts for the different things that objects do in different windows.

3. *Feedback.* When you drag an object in IODyne, you can see immediately that you are dragging it because its outline moves with the mouse pointer (this is the standard indicator for drag-and-drop actions). As you drag an object over a window in IODyne, the window indicates that it can accept the object you are dragging by coming forward; if it will not accept the object you are dragging, it does not come forward. Individual objects in windows can also indicate acceptance of objects dragged over them. When you drop an object onto a window, the window reacts to the dropped object by changing in some way. A search document reacts to a dropped object by showing it in the upper half and showing the results of the search triggered by it in the lower half.

4. *Object persistence.* Search documents provide the basis for object persistence in IODyne. On the search document shown in Figure 5, you can select either query to see its results. You can put any number of queries on a search document and access their results in this way. In other information retrieval applications, you usually cannot recall a result set after you have submitted subsequent queries. Like documents in other applications, IODyne search documents allow you to save and

recall searches for later use and sharing with other IODyne users. IODyne search documents also preserve Boolean combinations of search terms as well as references to the repositories that they were connected to at the time they were saved.

When you drop an information object onto a window, that window imparts behavior onto it. For example, when you drop a subject identifier onto a search document, the search document uses it to do a subject search. So in general, when you drag an object you impart behavior on it by what window you drop it onto. Dragging is a distinct action from clicking: when you drag something, you translate its position to a different place in the same window or implicitly create a copy of it when you drag it to a different window; when you click on something, you do not change its position but rather you merely release the mouse button without having moved the mouse. Objects can

FIGURE 5. Here the INSPEC subject descriptor **asynchronous transfer mode** has been dragged to the search document and dropped there. The search document responds by doing a subject search on the connected repositories and displaying the results.

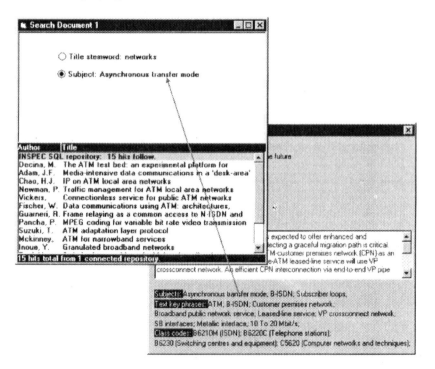

detect the difference between a click and a drag operation, so it stands to reason that you can use these distinct actions to impart different kinds of behavior onto objects.

You can think of dragging an information object in IODyne as equivalent to saying to it, "you go to this window and do what it tells you to do." You can think of clicking on an object in IODyne as equivalent to saying to it "you just do your own thing." In this way you can think of objects in IODyne as having *agency*. You can think of object agency as a fifth principle of object behavior in IODyne: objects react in different ways to different things you do to them. Drag them and they do one kind of thing, click on them and they do another.

If you have used any kind of hypertext application, such as a World Wide Web browser, you have already experienced clicking on HTML links and having them react by taking you to where they point on the Web. As objects, however, HTML links only recognize and react to one kind of action, a click. By taking you to where it points on the Web, an HTML link does its own thing, but that's all it knows how to do. You can't drag an HTML link anywhere else and have it do something useful in a context other than the Web page on which it resides.

Like HTML links, information objects in IODyne always take you to the same place when you click on them. However, each kind of information object takes you to its own kind of space. Subject terms, for example, take you into the appropriate subject thesaurus and show you where they live in it.

In Figure 6 you can see a similar kind of behavior to more conventional hypertext: you click on a link and it takes you somewhere.

The left-hand side of the subject thesaurus display in Figure 6 has use for terms, related terms, and chronological information for the current subject identifier. The right-hand side shows the location of the current subject identifier in a hierarchy. If it resides in more than one hierarchy, you can select which hierarchy to view. The selection box encloses the top term of the hierarchy.

All of the subject identifiers displayed are hypertextual. Clicking on any subject identifier in the thesaurus display makes it the current term, and the display changes to show the other terms in relation to it.

You can drag subject identifiers to other windows in the IODyne retrieval environment, and they do various kinds of things depending on the kind of window you drop them on. Dropping a subject identifier onto a search document initiates a subject search, for example.

The subject thesaurus window itself, as with all windows in IODyne, has object behavior. If you drop an object on it, like a title keyword for example, the thesaurus display will try to find a subject identifier to match the literal value of that object. You can keep one or more thesaurus windows open and

FIGURE 6. Here the INSPEC subject identifier asynchronous transfer mode has been clicked on, opening the INSPEC thesaurus and displaying the thesaurus record for that term.

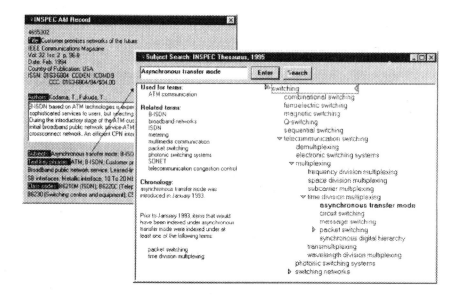

play them off against each other, with other term suggestion windows, and with search documents to find search terms and navigate through bibliographic data, all without using a single command.

USING KEYWORD TOOLS

The previous section illustrated IODyne's basic user interface object behavior. IODyne also has keyword and keyword in context (KWIC) tools that work alongside search dialogs and search documents to help you select search terms.

Figure 7 illustrates the use of the KWIC tool with the thesaurus display. Here, instead of starting with a title keyword search for "networks," as in Figure 3, we start with the INSPEC thesaurus and the keyword "networks" to try locating search terms (in this case subject identifiers) before actually doing a bibliographic search.

The KWIC tool actively responds to what you type in the text entry box of the search dialog. It works the same with all search dialogs. In Figure 7, the KWIC tool shows INSPEC subject identifiers containing the word "net-

FIGURE 7. Keyword in context (KWIC) window alongside the subject search window. The word **networks** has been typed into the subject search window's search term entry field.

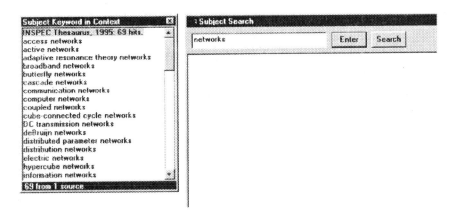

works." The KWIC tool scrolls if the list is longer than the window can accommodate, and, like most windows in IODyne, you can resize it.

After you have typed a complete keyword, when you type more letters the KWIC tool only shows you the phrases containing words that begin with what you have typed. See Figure 8 for an example.

In Figure 8, the KWIC tool only shows INSPEC subject identifiers containing the word networks that also contain words starting with the letter *c*. As you continue to type, the KWIC tool continues to cull the list of terms to match the narrower criteria corresponding to the longer context string.

By clicking on phrases in the KWIC tool you can quickly examine disparate parts of a thesaurus containing subject identifiers that contain common keywords (see Table 9). Because the KWIC window is linked to the search dialog in this way, you can click on phrases as a shortcut to dragging them into the thesaurus window. Dragging still works, but in this situation clicking is faster if you want to send the phrase to the current search dialog.

In sum, the KWIC tool responds to what you type in a search dialog, and the search dialog in turn responds to phrases you click in the KWIC tool.

Dragging terms from the KWIC window allows you drop them wherever you want. This way, instead of only being able to select thesaurus records from the KWIC list of thesaurus terms you can, for example, use them immediately for bibliographic retrieval by dropping them onto a search document.

The KWIC window works the same way for all search dialogs. It is an example of a "floating tool" that you can modelessly switch on when you

FIGURE 8. Continuation of Figure 7. Typing an additional **c** after the word **networks** causes the KWIC window to cull the list of keyword phrases to only those with other words starting with the letter **c**.

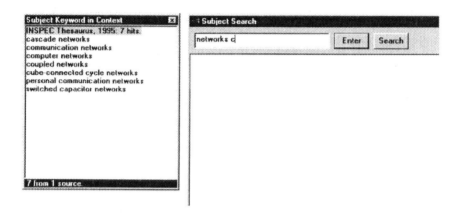

FIGURE 9. The INSPEC thesaurus term **computer networks** has been clicked in the KWIC window. The subject search dialog responds by displaying the thesaurus entry for computer networks.

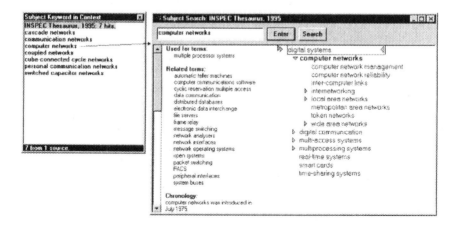

need it and back off when you don't. The keyword window, another such tool, works in a similar way to the KWIC window but is not described in this paper.

GENERALIZED USE OF DIRECT MANIPULATION

Examples from this paper so far illustrate only some of the ways in which you can use direct manipulation to navigate information spaces (e.g., thesauri) and construct search queries. Direct manipulation is central to the use of IODyne, as it is to object-oriented user interfaces in general. As implemented in IODyne, modelessness and feedback, two of the other aspects of object-oriented behavior described above, fully depend on direct manipulation; without the ability to directly move objects among windows, the same functionality would require modal dialogs and context menus, which are difficult and tedious to use, and you would still not have the control you have with drag-and-drop.

Direct manipulation allows for *idiomatic* application of user interface objects which can extend their functionality in powerful ways. In contrast to the *metaphoric* application of a user interface object, which represents it as a "real world" object on the computer screen and attempts to transliterate its mechanical function, idiomatic application extends its use in ways that are only possible on a computer. Like idioms in the realm of natural language, you must learn a user interface idiom before you can use it, but if it is executed well you only have to learn it once.

For example, in IODyne you can use buttons just as you can in other applications: click on a button and a dialog appears, or the application carries out some kind of function. In this case, the button is a metaphor for buttons on such real-world devices as household appliances: it is like a small rectangle of metal or plastic, attached to the inner workings of the device and presenting itself as something that you can push with your finger. When you then push on it makes the device do something. This is such a parsimonious metaphor, and is so easily assimilated by users, that it can be used almost without explanation.

But IODyne also extends the use of buttons just as it extends the use of subject terms and other information objects. Recall from Figure 2 how clicking on the Title button opens the title search dialog with an empty search term entry field. Instead of clicking on the Title button, you can drop an information object, like a subject term for example, onto it. The Title button responds by opening a title search dialog with the literal value of the information object already entered into the search term entry field (see Figure 10).

This use of a button is idiomatic because you have used it in a way made possible only within the context of a graphical user interface. Once demonstrated, it seems like a perfectly natural extension to the metaphoric use of the

FIGURE 10. The subject term internetworking has been dropped on to the Title search button of the IODyne tool bar, "casting" it as a title keyword. The Title button responded by opening the title search dialog with the term **internetworking** entered into it.

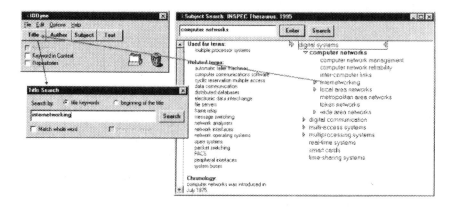

button; clicking on the button opens the dialog with an empty search term entry field, but dropping something on to the button opens the dialog with the content of that thing already entered into the dialog, like dropping a pickle into a jar. You do have to be shown how to do it (although after a fashion you might discover it accidentally), but once you have seen it and then done it you are not likely to forget it. That's an idiom.

You can then edit the search term to suit your search and change any of the available options in the search dialog, exactly as if you had opened the search dialog with an empty search term entry field and typed the search term yourself. Clicking on the Search button then places the query on the topmost search document, exactly as in Figure 3.

The Author, Subject, and Text Search buttons all accept dropped objects the same way as the Title Search button does, and open their respective search dialogs with the content of the dropped object entered into the search term entry field. In this way, you can "cast" a copy of an existing information object as a different search type without having to retype it.

When you click the Search button, IODyne finds a default location on the topmost search document for the resulting query object and places it there. But you can instead drag the Search button to precisely locate a query object on a search document. You can drag query objects around on a search document after you have created them, but with this technique you can create and locate them in one step.

Figure 11 shows two ways to drag buttons in IODyne. The upper example

FIGURE 11. The upper arrow illustrates dragging a Search button from a Search dialog to create and locate a new query object on a search document. The lower arrow illustrates dragging a search method button to create and locate a new query object with an empty search term on a search document.

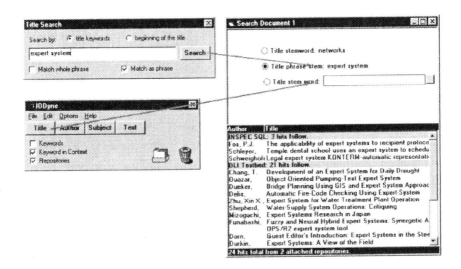

is what was described in the previous paragraph, dragging a search dialog's Search button to locate the new query object. The lower example shows how you can completely bypass the search dialog and drag the button from the IODyne toolbar directly to the search document. This creates a query object with an empty search term directly on the search document. You then type your search term into the temporary text entry field, press the Return key, and IODyne sends the query to the connected repositories.

Once you have created a query on a search document it is not immutable. As mentioned previously, you can drag query objects around on a search document, but you can also change them and delete them. Figure 11 yields a clue about editing search terms directly on a search document. You can edit any existing query object by clicking on the search term and editing it just like you can text in any text field. If you click in the descriptive part of the query object (to the left of the colon), IODyne displays the appropriate search dialog with the appropriate options selected and the search term entered so that you can edit it (see Figure 12).

When you open a search dialog this way, IODyne "attaches" it to the query object still on the search document. When you edit the search term and/or any of the search attributes in the dialog and click the Search button

FIGURE 12. Clicking on a query object opens a search dialog with all appropriate properties set.

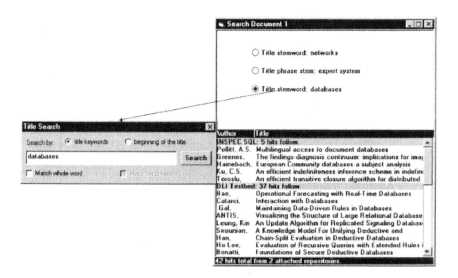

(or press the Return key), IODyne changes that query object. You can also drop the Search button onto some other part of the search document to create a new query object.

Another way to replace query objects is with drop-and-replace. You really can drop an information object anywhere on a search document, including on top of an existing query object. When you drop an information object on top of a query object, IODyne replaces it with a new query object made according to the attributes of the information object.

You can delete query objects altogether by dragging them to the trash, represented by the trash can icon at lower right on the IODyne toolbar.

None of the idiomatic uses of user interface objects described here are new; they are merely an application of user interface techniques that have been in common use since the introduction of the Apple Macintosh ™ in 1984 and more recently with the introduction of Microsoft Windows95 ™. They should, in fact, look familiar to users of any windowed operating system. The only difference comes in the application of them to information retrieval interaction. Here instead of dragging file and folder icons around, you drag information objects around. In both cases, the style of interaction is the same. The differences are in how the objects behave rather than in how you manipulate them.

Although direct manipulation saves a lot of typing and makes for general ease of use, it has an even more important cognitive benefit. In command-based retrieval systems, commands are a symbolic element of interaction that interferes with the symbolic elements of the information you want to retrieve. For example, if while using a command-based OPAC you see the term "asynchronous transfer mode" in a bibliographic record and decide to use it in a subject search, you will have to type at least one command, and in many cases two or three, before the software is in the proper mode for you to type the search term. In recalling the intervening commands you may well forget the term you want to use when you finally get to where you can use it. In IODyne you have no such problem. When you see an information object you want to use, such as a subject term, you drag it to where you want to use it and drop it there. Thus you can retrieve information as quickly as you can identify useful search terms, without having to think about using the technology and in the process derailing your train of thought. In this way, ideally, the retrieval technology seems to disappear, leaving only what seems like pure information objects and spaces.

SIMULTANEOUS MULTIPLE VIEWS

Multiple windows are another aspect of windowed operating system that offer great possibilities for enhancing information retrieval interaction. As illustrated in Figures 3 through 13, IODyne uses multiple windows to allow drag-and-drop interaction between search dialogs, search documents, and term suggestion tools. In IODyne you can open any combination of windows, and arrange them in any way you like, to facilitate your information retrieval task. Many uses of IODyne involve recurring patterns of multiple window use. Recall Figures 7 through 9, where the KWIC window is used to locate terms in the INSPEC Thesaurus. This use of the KWIC window also gives you simultaneous views of an alphabetized keyword list and a thesaurus display. You can use them in any sequence, the KWIC window to navigate the thesaurus by keyword and the subject display to navigate it structurally. You can also open multiple subject displays to show different regions of the same thesaurus or regions from multiple thesauri and classification systems side by side. This use extends to any combination of term suggestion services.

You can also drag information objects from one window to another, creating a series of closely related views of a thesaurus, for example. A convenient way to open a new subject window from a subject identifier in the current subject window, for example, is to drag the subject identifier to the Subject button on the IODyne toolbar, similar to what is illustrated in Figure 10. The exception here is that the subject identifier gets cast as a subject term again, which makes no difference to you: you are merely using this casting mechanism to open another window of the same type with a specific term.

The ways in which you use multiple views is determined by the specific task at hand, and is limited only by your imagination as well as the size of the computer screen. Obviously, the larger the screen, the better it can accommodate multiple windows.

THE DOCUMENT PARADIGM

I have been using the term "search document" throughout this paper to designate the kind of window in which you construct bibliographic searches and view their results. Search documents are documents in every sense of the word–like documents in other applications, you can save them, revise them, and share them with other users. Besides live queries, which IODyne resubmits when you open a search document at a later time, search documents can also store search terms and bibliographic records for use in subsequent searches. A search document also stores references to the repositories connected to it the last time it was saved, and automatically reconnects to those repositories when you reopen it.

In keeping with the multiple view concept, IODyne allows you to open multiple search documents at one time. This allows you to put searches side by side for direct visual comparison, whether you want to compare the same search on different repositories or different searches on the same repository, or whatever. This also allows you to drag-and-drop query objects from one search document to another.

Although IODyne provides new ways to look at and use thesauri and classification systems, search documents provide the center of operation. A key feature of search documents mentioned above but not elaborated on is their ability to connect to and query multiple repositories simultaneously. This allows you to search multiple repositories with a single query. Combined with multiple views, you can use thesauri and other term suggestors with multiple repositories as well, even repositories for which particular term suggestors were not intended.

Figures 11 and 12 show a search document connected (or "attached") to two repositories: "INSPEC SQL" and "DLI Testbed." These have totally different structures, query languages, and protocols, and yet the same query objects access them both. The search document has already been connected to the repositories, and each new query object causes IODyne to query the servers in the forms required by those servers.

You can build queries and attach repositories to search documents in any order. Figure 13 shows a search document with two existing query objects, a title stemword search for "networks" and a subject search for "circuit

FIGURE 13. Dropping a repository onto a search document "attaches" it to the
search document. Any query object selected on the search document forms a
query sent to the repository.

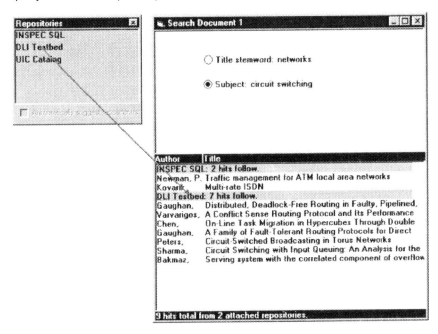

switching." The subject identifier "circuit switching" was obtained from the
INSPEC thesaurus, and retrieved the two records shown under the INSPEC
SQL repository. The INSPEC SQL repository is indexed using the INSPEC
Thesaurus, so it stands to reason that a subject search with an INSPEC
subject identifier would retrieve records from it. The two query objects in
Figure 13 were created with only the INSPEC SQL repository attached. The
DLI Testbed repository is attached to the search document by dragging its
label over from the list of available repositories, and IODyne responds by
connecting to that repository and submitting the selected query to it.

In this way a subject identifier was used to retrieve records from a repository even though that repository was not indexed using the thesaurus. You
can, of course, also drop subject terms from a thesaurus onto a search document that has repositories already attached to it. The outcome is the same.

IODyne manages cached results so that if a query has not been sent to a
repository it can be when the need arises. In Figure 13, when the title stemword query for "networks" is selected again, there will be cached results for
it from the INSPEC SQL repository but not from the DLI Testbed repository.

In this case, IODyne uses the cached results from the INSPEC SQL repository but must submit a query to the DLI Testbed repository. IODyne always caches query results, so subsequent references to that query on that repository can be retrieved from the cache.

The upshot of all this is that on a search document you can create query objects and attach and detach repositories in any order and IODyne will handle all the necessary server query submissions. IODyne maintains the state of each repository along with the results it has cached from each repository, and automatically determines when it can use results from the cache and when it must submit a query to a server. This is one way in which IODyne allows you to think more about your retrieval task and less about the technology you must use to perform it.

Two object-oriented user interface principles illustrated here are *persistent concurrency* and *commutative order of construction*. IODyne displays *persistent concurrency* by always showing results consistent with the current state of an object, and commutative order of construction by allowing you to assemble the components of an object in any order and still have its end behavior the same.

Besides lending persistence to queries by giving them a place to live as objects, the use of search documents prepares the practice of information retrieval for the advent of object-oriented operating systems that support generic document types and the use of software tools within generic documents, rather than applications that only support their own kinds of documents. With this next generation of operating systems, you will create documents directly with the operating system and populate them with text, images, spreadsheet cells, and even live query objects using software tools that all work with the generic document type. In this seamless world of documents and tools, the idea of applications will disappear. Although IODyne is at this point a distinct application, its document type, toolbar and modeless dialogs operate in ways that resemble how documents and software tools will work in object-oriented operating systems within the next few years.

REPRESENTING REPOSITORIES AS OBJECTS

The information retrieval interaction described in this paper requires that the retrieval client have standardized representations of the repositories that it connects to, and that it can use these to decide how to handle user requests that the repository server does not directly support. For example, Figure 13 illustrates a subject search done on the DLI Testbed repository even though the database has no subject identifier fields and is not an INSPEC database. IODyne uses configuration objects to represent each repository it connects to. These must be prepared in advance by a repository administrator and include information about how to connect to, query, and display records from the repository. The current proposal for repository configuration objects (RCOs) used by IODyne requires that they interpret at minimum title, author, subject, and full text searches, corresponding to the standard search methods provided by the IODyne tool bar. If a repository does not support a particular search method, the repository administrator must provide a suitable alternative. Since the DLI Testbed repository, for example, does not support subject searching directly, but does support a variety of full text field searches, its RCO specifies that a subject search be implemented as a phrase search on the article abstract. Each of the 7 records retrieved from the DLI Testbed in Figure 13, then, have the phrase "circuit switching" in the article abstract. Since it is not always clear how these substitutions are made, IODyne also provides ways for you to find out exactly how a search was performed.

The framework that specifies Title, Author, Subject, and Text as standard search methods supports extensions to these methods as well as the definition of new methods by a repository administrator. For example, SGML repositories support various kinds of specific field searches on full text, such as abstract, section title, body text, figure caption, and citation author. The administrator of such a repository can specify each of these as an extension to the Text search method, and IODyne provides the means for selecting these in the Text search dialog.

A repository administrator can also define a new search method. An administrator of an astronomy collection, for example, may want to allow searching by the names of astronomical objects or telescopes, and define new search methods accordingly.

Each RCO creates a proxy that runs as a thread in the IODyne client. As of this writing, gateway software that will run RCOs on remote machines is in the planning stages. This will provide, in effect, a system of distributed repository objects for users of IODyne, with remote machines doing query and result translation.

With digital library collections represented as standardized, distributed RCOs, online collection managers will be able to assemble collections of RCO references and put them online for IODyne users.

With standard representation by RCOs, either locally on your IODyne client or remotely in gateways, repositories may range from simple WAIS-based servers to sophisticated catalog, A&I, or full-text servers that employ all term suggestion services available in IODyne. Multiple simultaneous connectivity combined with multiple views allows you to augment searching on "dumb" servers with term suggestion from "smart" servers in the same subject domain. And despite the large range of server capability, you can use them all in virtually the same way.

CONCLUSION:
USER INTERFACE CENTERED SYSTEM DESIGN

Less than ten years ago, limited RAM and disk memory, bandwidth, and CPU speed meant that system designers had to emphasize performance over ease of use, and users were willing to accept that. Those limitations no longer apply, but many of the systems developed under them will continue to operate well into the next century. This is not so much of a problem as is the way of thinking that remains: while client/server architecture can make older database servers useful under the new paradigm, we still see powerful desktop computers (the "client" end) used as dumb terminals. This is as true for World Wide Web-based interfaces as it is for PCs running vt100 emulators; the "nice-looking" interfaces that you can get with the Web use the extra power of newer PCs to make outmoded forms of information retrieval interaction merely look better, rather than improving their power or usability in any substantive way. IODyne is an example of an information retrieval client that makes full use of the power and capacity of modern desktop PCs, as well as the bandwidth of modern IP networks, to enhance retrieval interaction for the user. Multiple simultaneous connections to servers, the use of windowing to provide multiple views, and the performance necessary to provide adequate responsiveness to the user with such a client have existed for not even the past five years.

Given the advances in hardware that have occurred, the time is now ripe for user interface centered system design. The experience we have had in implementing IODyne bears this out, but it has also indicated that taking such a stance has repercussions for the design of an entire system. While bibliographic databases and servers can operate the same as before, they require gateways such as Z39.50 or the gateway that we briefly described above. While Z39.50 has as a goal standardized bibliographic interoperability, the gateway we have proposed does this while providing additional protocol elements that enhance the user interface by allowing the client to be less stringent in how it forms server queries. This functionality can also be brought within the IODyne client for use with Z39.50 and other kinds of gateways, as well as for older technologies such as WAIS. Term suggestion databases, however, such as keyword and keyword-in-context lists, thesauri, and classification systems, require specially developed offline processing, though they can be delivered via standardized database connectivity tools such as ODBC or even with CGI over an HTTP gateway.

As the World Wide Web gets better at handing distributed objects, it may be possible to run IODyne fully within Web browsers in the coming years. As of this writing, the plan is to reimplement IODyne as a Java application (the current prototype is implemented in Visual Basic). It may be possible, however, to provide certain components in applet form, such as the KWIC tool and the subject navigator for use with Web-based retrieval interfaces.

The long-term goal for object-oriented user interface designers should be to create readily recognizable interaction idioms and user interface objects that are seamlessly combinable in powerful ways. These should work equally well in digital libraries as in any other information systems application. Current visually-based development environments, which allow developers to place controls like buttons and text boxes on forms, provide something like this but at a much lower level than what we need. What finally evolves may be a system that will not have a separate development "mode" at all but will consist of a community of objects and spaces that actively and intelligently communicate with databases and present results of queries as the user manipulates what amounts to a graphical language of objects.

REFERENCES

Apple Computer, Inc. *Macintosh Human Interface Guidelines* in the "Apple Technical Library" series. Reading, Massachusetts: Addison-Wesley Publishing Company, Inc., 1992.

Collins, Dave. *Designing Object-Oriented User Interfaces.* Redwood City, California: Benjamin/Cummings Publishing Company, Inc., 1995.

Cooper, Alan. *About Face: The Essentials of User Interface Design.* Foster City, California: IDG Books Worldwide, Inc., 1995.

Tognazzini, Bruce. *TOG on Interface.* Reading, Massachusetts: Addison-Wesley Publishing Company, Inc., 1992.

Tognazzini, Bruce. *TOG on Software Design.* Reading, Massachusetts: Addison-Wesley Publishing Company, Inc., 1996.

EXAMPLE SCENARIOS

MAGIC:
A Connecticut Collection of Geodata
for the Geo-Scientist

Patrick McGlamery

SUMMARY. This paper discusses MAGIC, the University of Connecticut's Map and Geographic Information Center and its' Web manifestation (http://magic.lib.uconn.edu/). MAGIC is a place, real and virtual, where the user can go to find collections of materials serving the geodata needs at the University of Connecticut. The map collection exceeds 180,000 sheets of maps and includes aerial photography for the state, hydrographic charts and a variety of formats of spatial information. Since 1994, MAGIC has been collecting public domain geodata with the explicit intent of making those data network accessible to its primary client. The MAGIC collections focus on the state of Connecticut and currently number over 14,000 files and stores over 5 gigabytes of compressed data files in a variety of file formats. *[Article copies available for a fee from The Haworth Document Delivery Service: 1-800-342-9678. E-mail address: getinfo@haworthpressinc.com]*

Patrick McGlamery is Map Librarian at the University of Connecticut Libraries Map and Geographic Information Center.

[Haworth co-indexing entry note]: "MAGIC: A Connecticut Collection of Geodata for the Geo-Scientist." McGlamery, Patrick. Co-published simultaneously in *Science & Technology Libraries* (The Haworth Press, Inc.) Vol. 17, No. 3/4, 1999, pp. 209-216; and: *Digital Libraries: Philosophies, Technical Design Considerations, and Example Scenarios* (ed: David Stern) The Haworth Press, Inc., 1999, pp. 209-216. Single or multiple copies of this article are available for a fee from The Haworth Document Delivery Service [1-800-342-9678, 9:00 a.m. - 5:00 p.m. (EST). E-mail address: getinfo@haworthpressinc.com].

KEYWORDS. MAGIC, Map and Geographic Information Center, geodata, University of Connecticut, map collection, aerial photography, spatial information, public domain geodata

One of the givens of our traditional library is that it is a place where the user can go to find material gathered together. That is, that there are collections of material. In libraries these collections follow collection development policies and rules. The Web obfuscates the need for physical collections, but we still need the notion of a collection, albeit a virtual collection.

MAGIC, the University of Connecticut's Map and Geographic Information Center and its' Web manifestation (http://magic.lib.uconn.edu/), is a centralized location, serving the geodata needs at the University of Connecticut. The MAGIC primary user community is the students, faculty and staff of the University of Connecticut, the secondary community is the citizens of the State of Connecticut and tertiary are all of the other users. The map collection exceeds 180,000 sheets of maps and includes aerial photography for the state, hydrographic charts and a variety of formats of spatial information. Since 1994, MAGIC has been collecting public domain geodata with the explicit intent of making those data network accessible to its primary client. The MAGIC collections focus on the state of Connecticut, but the digital collection is almost exclusively Connecticut. Utilizing FTP, HTTP and HTML, MAGIC is a relatively low-tech solution to distributing a deep, rich collection of digital geodata to a sophisticated statewide user community.

The MAGIC geodata collection follows many of the same constraints as its paper counterpart, the MAGIC map collection. That is, it is a developed collection, it is constrained by storage, there is a logical access to the collection and it is managed in a systematic way. Libraries carry the cost of storage in digital libraries as well as conventional ones. In fact, that is a primary role for libraries, and that is not going away. There are comparisons between map cases and harddrives. Both are gray boxes, both are storage units with prescribe capacities and both cost around $700. The difference is that the hard drive is smaller, easier to stack, and much easier to move material into and out of.

The MAGIC geodata collection includes over 14,000 files and stores over 5 gigabytes of compressed data. MAGIC's geodata collection development plan is to collect data in the public domain for Connecticut. These data include cartographic, attribute, raster and other forms of geodata. The data are acquired from federal, state and local data producers. The data are acquired on CD-ROM, tape, disk, and via the Internet. After acquisition, the data are converted to ArcINFO and MapInfo interchange formats (E00 and MIF), and compressed. Metadata are collected when possible. Metadata are data about data. That is, they are text files that describe large numeric databases in a systematic and standard manner. Of course MARC is a form of metadata, but there is a standard for spatial metadata developed by the U.S. Federal Geographic Data Committee. Metadata, the FGDC and the National Spatial Data Infrastructure are described in full on the FGDC site: http://www.fgdc.gov/

The MAGIC data are passive files, that is, there is no processing done on-the-fly at this time. The files are as passive as books on a shelf. ArcINFO and MapInfo are used to process the data. This enables batch processing utilizing student labor, allows the use of a low-end server capable of reasonable I/O and is economical and scaleable.

The contents of the data collection are raster vs. Vector, etc.:

- 1996-1997 Town Profiles (1:24K ConnDED, includes: housing, local gov., education, economics, demographics, age ranges, administration, and quality of life)
- 1996 Election returns for the Presidential, Congressional Districts, State Senate and House Districts (ConnSS, town, vector/attrib. Data, E00 and MIF)
- 1994 Town Road Units (1:24K ConnDOT, town, vector/attrib. data, E00, MIF and DXF)
- 1995 Town Road Units (1:24K ConnDOT, town, vector/attrib. data, E00, MIF and DXF)
- 1970 decennial census data (for town and tracts, by county, tabular data, DBF)
- 1980 decennial census data (USCensus, for town and tracts, by county, tabular data, DBF)
- 1990 decennial census data (USCensus, STF1A & 3A by towns, tracts and block groups, by county, tabular data, DBF)
- 1990 Census (i.e., block group, 1:100K TIGER, county and town, vector data, E00 and MIF)
- 1980 Census (tract only, 1:100K TIGER, county and town, vector/attrib. data, E00 and MIF)
- 1990 Population data (1:100K USCensus, block group and tract by town, vector/attrib., E00 and MIF)
- 1990 Housing data (1:24K USCensus, block group and tract by town, vector/attrib., E00 and MIF)
- Digital Elevation Model (1:24K, USGS, 7.5 min. quad, raster data, DEM)
- Digital Elevation Model (1:250K, USGS, state, raster data, DEM)
- Drainage Basin (1:24K ConnDEP, 7.5 min. quad and town, vector/attrib. data, E00, MIF and DXF)
- Hydrography Subset (1:24K ConnDEP, 7.5 min. quad and town, vector/attrib. data, E00, MIF, DXF)

- Hydrography (1:24K ConnDEP, 7.5 min. quad and town, vector/attrib. data, E00, MIF, DXF)
- Land Use/Land Cover (1:24K ConnDEP, 1990 satellite derived, town, vector/attrib. data, E00, MIF)
- Land Use/Land Cover (1:250K USGS, 1970 satellite derived, state, vector/attrib. data, E00, MIF)
- Roads (1:24K ConnDEP, 7.5 min. quad and town, vector/attrib. data, E00, MIF and DXF)
- Roads (1:250K ConnDEP, state, vector/attrib. data, E00 and MIF)
- Soils (1:24K NCSS, 7.5 min. quad and town, vector/attrib. data, E00, MIF and DXF)
- Soils (1:250K NCSS, state, vector/attrib. data, E00 and MIF)
- Streets with Address Ranges (1:100K TIGER, county and town, vector/attrib. data, E00 and MIF)
- Surficial Material (1:24K ConnDEP, 7.5 min. quad and town, vector/attrib. data, E00, MIF and DXF)
- Quad Boundaries (1:24K ConnDEP, 7.5 min. quad and town, vector/attrib. data, E00, MIF and DXF)
- Town Boundary (1:24K USGS, 7.5 min. quad and town, vector/attrib. data)
- Town Boundary (1:250K ConnDEP, state coverage, vector/attrib/attrib data E00 and MIF)
- National Wetlands Inventory (1:24K FWA, 7.5 min. quad, vector/attrib./attrib. data, E00, MIF, DXF)
- DOQQ (1:24K USGS; 3.25 min. quad orthophotos, raster JPEG data, UTM Proj.)
- DOQQ (1:24K USGS; 3.25 min. quad orthophotos, raster BIL and JPEG data, CT, NAD '27)
- DRG (1:24K USGS; graphics of the 7.5 min. quad, raster geoTIF data, UTM Proj.)
- DRG (1:24K USGS; graphics of the 7.5 min. quad, raster geoTIF data, CT State Plane, NAD '27)

(ConnDED, Connecticut, Department of Economic Development; ConnDEP, Connecticut, Department of Environmental Protection; ConnDOT, Connecticut, Department of Transportation; ConnSS, Connecticut, Secretary of State)

The services available in the Homer Babbidge map library include consultation and reference services. These still work best in a face to face interview, but have moved to an e-mail initiated interview. The library currently offers various input and output options including a scanner for air photos, digitizing tablets and a table (tracing equipment which capture the "tracings" as digital files), a large format copier and a light table. Various output devices are supported as well. A Size E pen plotter prints, albeit very slowly, a 3' by 4' map and a smaller desktop color inkjet printer provides page size output.

This equipment is used infrequently, but intensely. Graduate students who do not have access to a GIS lab facility most often use them. Typically these users camp out in the map library, capture the data they need for their study area and return periodically. There is little training, though detailed "How-to" documentation helps them through the process. Making these specialized devices available in the Library brings a diverse user community together, fostering the map library as an essential part of the campus spatial information community. Much of the equipment is donated.

ACCESS METHODS

Currently the files on MAGIC number over 15,000 and account for over five gigabytes of storage space. This is storing primarily compressed ASCII and raster data. MAGIC uses the Library of Congress Classification System for organizing both its map and geodata collections. Adapting the "G" Schedule to a sub-directory structure, the digital collection exists on multiple storage devices and are knit together using aliases. File naming conventions are carefully followed. The filename is two or three alphas designating subject, followed by three or four numbers designating location, followed by one or two alphas for format. For example, RO074E.ZIP is the file designation for a coverage of roads for the town of Mansfield in ArcINFO format. Utilizing standards enable extensive management automation and assists in use analysis.

Data are stored on four machines: the MAGIC server, two UNIX machines in the Library Systems office, and the Connecticut Department of Transportation server. The NT Server platform provides for enhanced web server management, most importantly to the map librarian as manager, enhanced transaction logs. MAGIC logs go back to May 1994. The early logs mark the FTP access to the collection. Many of these files were lost, a regrettable oversight. In January 1995, MAGIC became an HTTP server and began to collect more sophisticated logs as well as provide an easier interface for the user. In November 1996, bringing up the NT Server maximized the ability to perform transaction log analysis. These logs are studied, mined for user information. The collection has been developed based on the information gathered. For example, while the sophisticated user is interested in the detailed and specific data at a scale of 1:24,000, most of the users are looking for general "state-wide" mapping. Historical maps of Connecticut were scanned and added to the site, and other statewide data will follow. The site is "fine-tuned" to reflect the user's ability to navigate the collection.

Data extraction by variable and/or spatial query is a goal for MAGIC, moving it from a "shelved" collection of compressed digital geodata to a digital library with reference tools. Until MAGIC can expand to offer a "just-in-time" model for data extraction, the clickable table and map that defines MAGIC will be well served with the batch approach. With comprehensive spatial metadata, a foundation can be built to implement levels of extraction for the web-based client. Scientists will be able to extract a specific drainage basin, for example and soil types and wetlands inventories for that basin. In time, access will be to data on the MAGIC server and through the MAGIC metadata index, stored in various servers statewide. The need for standardized "control" language and a centralized authority and database are best coordinated by the library.

MAGIC uses HTML 2.0 served off of a NT Server 3.51. Navigation is by clickable maps and tables. A recently awarded Federal Geographic Data Committee grant will provide file level metadata coverage, opening the site up as a National Spatial Data Infrastructure site. In the future an enhanced topical search engine of the MAGIC site will provide library-like access to the geodata. Even without the metadata or search engine, the site manages a large amount of traffic for a small state.

HISTORICAL PRECEDENTS

MAGIC began collecting digital data in 1987, when 1980 census tracts of Connecticut and 1980 STF1A and STF3A demographic data were purchased and mounted on the University's mainframe. The SAS/Graph program Ptolemy enabled users to generate demographic maps on-demand. Remarkably, the campus users were more interested in the accessibility of the data than they were of Ptolemy's mapping capabilities. Users were more interested in manipulating new data than creating a "one-off" map. In 1990 when the TIGER files were made available, it was clear that the files would be best served by going on a common server. The first MAGIC server was a 486 30Mhz-machine running Novell. Users logged in and accessed TIGER data in TIGER format, as well as ArcINFO compiled and E00, MapInfo for Windows and DOS compiled and MIF and 1970, 1980 and 1990 demographic data with geo-reference code embedded in the file. Then, as now, all preparatory work was done in the map library. The extent of the prep work was based on the needs of the user community. It was, and is, beyond the capability of most users to convert the varieties of data that are used by the geodata community. A major part of the work done in the map library is to transform data to formats readily usable by the client community. This can account for a fair amount of time. About 20 hours a week of a skilled ArcINFO programmer/graduate student was needed in order to populate the MAGIC site with data from various state and federal agencies in the various formats.

The Map and Geographic Information Center is staffed by one full-time professional librarian. The major part of programming support comes from student employees. Managing student employees and complex programs, networked equipment and data steps is difficult. It is also a reality in today's research library. It means devising ingenious two- and three-hour schedules, scheduling access to limited equipment and licensed software, LAN system administration and juggling tasks between workers . . . and follow-up, follow-up, follow-up. In computer terms, it means batching jobs. Devising and running batches is like preparing a Thanksgiving feast for a large extended family; everyone has their own special covered dish and there is only one oven. A clean and efficient batch workflow is one that makes full use of resources, is easily repeatable, comes to closure and cleans up after itself. In MAGIC, some functions that are batched are ArcINFO import, projection and export jobs, MapInfo conversion from ArcINFO, compression, metadata creation and insertion and classification and placement in the directory hierarchy. These jobs can either be performed, or saved, as a backlog, until resources are available.

The alternative to batching is developing an interactive model. The interactive model requires a dedicated machine and program and a trained project supervisor, typically a programmer. It extracts and processes on demand of the user. The interactive model is more of "just-in-time" than the batch. It requires higher levels of resources in terms of knowledge workers and dedicated hardware and software. The Penn State University Libraries, Maps and Data Center (http://www.maproom.psu.edu/) and The Geographic Information Center at the University of Virginia (http://www.lib.virginia.edu/gic/) are good examples of this model.

CONSIDERATIONS

The cost benefits of the two models are fairly straightforward. The interactive model requires a higher level of administrative interest and support, both fiscal and managerial. Both UVa and PSU have Unix computers in the department, acquired for the support of a spatial data program, planned for by the library administration. Administrative support, when it can be obtained, is an important component to project development. MAGIC, however, developed from the bottom up. Though it has had administrative recognition and support, the level of support has not been that of UVa or PSU. This is probably the more typical situation in academic libraries. Batch processing is a "just in case" model that takes advantage of shifts in labor and talent. It is a model of which, through necessity, most libraries can take advantage.

However, it is the "McPherson Industries" auto-generating program that enables the timely re-population of updated web pages. This program, written in Access and Visual Basic reads the 15,000 files into a database, sorts and arranges them, matches the filename to a textual form and writes the web page. With over 500 web pages managing and editing to assure currency is difficult. This in-house program was created to facilitate the sort of batch site MAGIC currently supports. Its function is to automate the operation of a one-person site as much as possible.

MAGIC should be a scaleable model for a digital spatial data collection. (That is, it responds well to the vagaries of less than steady state State Land Grant University funding.) It lacks the sorts of "digital tools" a digital library should provide. MAGIC is based on tried and true practices of library science that focus more on information content than on context or media. Maps have been primary carriers of spatial information. Computing has fostered a GIS technology that enables the user to process geodata for discrete problem solving. The Map and Geographic Information Center at the University of Connecticut Libraries uses computer technology to solve the problems of supplying its user community with the current generation of spatial information . . . geodata. It can be scaled to federate to a national approach. . .with the attention of a skilled librarian. There are other approaches such as the interactive approach of UVa and PSU. Levels of support for an interactive system are higher than the batch approach of MAGIC.

AUTHOR NOTE

Coming to the university in 1980 from the Library of Congress, Mr. McGlamery has developed MAGIC as a spatial data library, extending the metaphor information to include digital spatial data in vector, raster and tabular formats. The MAGIC web site (http://magic.lib.uconn.edu/) is a rich collection of data for the State of Connecticut, including transportation, demographic, hydrographic and soils data. Mr. McGlamery is active in ALA's LITA and Map and Geography Roundtable, and in IFLA. He is a frequent speaker about geodata, Geographic Information System and libraries at national, regional, and international forums.

Patents in the New World

Timothy Lee Wherry

SUMMARY. Historically patent information has been accessed using a manual system in place since the first patent in 1790. As libraries and information in general became automated, patent information lagged behind. Recently there have been attempts to bring patent information into the new world by governmental agencies, private groups, and individuals. This article discusses these successful and not so successful attempts and lists web sites, digital indexes, full text availability, and private sources that contain patent information. *[Article copies available for a fee from The Haworth Document Delivery Service: 1-800-342-9678. E-mail address: getinfo@haworthpressinc.com]*

KEYWORDS. Patent information, automated, web sites, digital indexes, full text

INTRODUCTION

The United States Constitution was the first constitution in the world to include intellectual property rights. The framers of the Constitution were

---

Timothy Lee Wherry is the author of Patent Searching for Librarians and Inventors and is a frequent speaker on the topic of patents. Mr. Wherry has been researching and teaching patent information for over fifteen years and has written numerous articles on the subject. Past positions have included Engineering Librarian positions at Carnegie-Mellon University, Arizona State University and The Phoenix Public Library. Currently he is Assistant Dean of Academic Affairs for Information Services at Penn State Altoona College.

[Haworth co-indexing entry note]: "Patents in the New World." Wherry, Timothy Lee. Co-published simultaneously in *Science & Technology Libraries* (The Haworth Press, Inc.) Vol. 17, No. 3/4, 1999, pp. 217-222; and: *Digital Libraries: Philosophies, Technical Design Considerations, and Example Scenarios* (ed: David Stern) The Haworth Press, Inc., 1999, pp. 217-222. Single or multiple copies of this article are available for a fee from The Haworth Document Delivery Service [1-800-342-9678, 9:00 a.m. - 5:00 p.m. (EST). E-mail address: getinfo@haworthpressinc.com].

aware of the importance of this right to stimulate the economy and offer an incentive for innovation. Thomas Jefferson, the first Patent Commissioner, said that a patent is the engine that drives the economy.[1]

This concept has been very successful. It has been estimated that eighty percent of the wealth of the United States is based directly or indirectly on patents.[2] Currently, approximately five and one half million patents have been granted in the United States since the first patent in 1790.

There are about 70,000 patents issued every year in the United States. The paper copies of these patents are housed in the huge U.S. Patent and Trademark Office public search room in Arlington, Virginia. The patents are kept in the public search room in compartmentalized shelving called "shoes." The term shoe refers to Jefferson's habit of keeping his own patent documentation in old shoe boxes. (Although Jefferson thought that it was unethical for a Patent Commissioner to hold a patent, he did invent several items including a revolving chair.) To fit these "shoes" patents are still issued on odd sized paper–7" × 9". To perform a patent search, check on patent drawings or to research patent information, the traditional activity was to wander through the shoes, select the proper patent classification and sit down with the stack of paper patents and go through them manually.

Until the mid-1980s, the indexing to the patents was done with several paper indexes published by the United States Patent and Trademark Office (PTO). By looking up a keyword in an index, a patent researcher would then be led to possible patent categories or classifications under which patents were organized. Once the classification had been identified, the manual process of actually retrieving the patents began.

AUTOMATING THE PATENT SYSTEM

Although this system has always had its detractors, it worked for nearly two hundred years; however, as the number of patents grew the problem of effectively and efficiently locating any given patent in a paper based system became increasingly difficult. Not only did the inefficiency of a manual system make locating patents difficult for patent attorneys, searchers, and inventors, it caused problems for the patent examiners–those individuals who decided on the novelty of patent applications. Increasingly it became obvious that something had to be done to bring the PTO into the electronic age.

The task of automating a system of millions of patents was not an easy one. The easiest first step was to implement an automated indexing system. The second step was to make the patent document itself available electronically. The problem was that a patent contains both text and images, so any solution was a technology that included both. CD-ROM was the way to go; then the Internet seemed a logical and perfect solution. Some private companies, seeing the problem the huge federal bureaucracy faced by its inability to move quickly, proposed their own solutions. A company in Alexandria, Virginia developed an automated patent indexing system on CD-ROM before the PTO could do more than propose solutions to its problem.[3] But the PTO did not stand still. It developed in the 1980s a system called CASSIS, which retrieved a portion of the text of recent patents. But without retrospective searching and images this system was severely limited and did not progress much beyond its basic structure for many years. Still the PTO is criticized for not moving quickly enough. Recently, out of frustration with the PTO's inability to provide adequate access to patents, IBM loaded two million patents on the Internet to allow its own people, and anybody with an Internet connection, to search patent documents efficiently.[4]

PATENT DEPOSITORIES

One aspect of the patent system that was not based in Washington, DC was the system of Patent and Trademark Depository Libraries (PTDL). This network of primarily academic and public libraries kept a retrospective collection of at least twenty years of patents on microfilm for public use. The advantages were that patents were available in text and image outside Washington, DC and the problem of loss was minimized by storing the patents on microfilm. The problems were that unlike the PTO public search room, patents on film were not arranged by subject groupings (called classifications) but arranged numerically. This made patent searching very difficult because patents in a given groups could be located only by handling dozens of reels of film.

BREAKTHROUGHS IN DIGITAL PATENTS

In 1994, the PTO developed a product they called USAPAT. USAPAT was a CD-ROM product that included text and image of patent documents and is intended to replace the cumbersome microfilm. Three disks are issued each week containing all the patents issued that Tuesday. (Patents are issued on Tuesday of each week). USAPAT and the patent microfilm will run concurrently until 1999 when the film will be discontinued. USAPAT can be found at the eighty PTDLs in the United States.

INTERNATIONAL PATENTS

It should be noted that although the United States has made progress in automating its patents, the situation is quite different in other countries. One positive development is that full text of European patents from Wila Verlag will appear soon on STN, but that is the only major news concerning full text capabilities of international patents. To keep abreast of developments check http://info.cas.org/stnews. Again, the United States is playing a major role in providing access even in regard to international patents. The USPTO maintains the AIDS Patent Database which lists in full text all AIDS related patents issued by the U.S., Japanese and European patent offices. In all other situations, indexes of patents are available for international patents, full text is available by ordering paper copies, but full text online is not a reality for international patents. For a good listing of sources of international patents try http://www.questel.orbit.com/patents/pt-dbs.html

INTERNET RESOURCES

The following are web pages that offer information about patents–everything from Wacky Patents (http://colitz.com/site/wacky.htm) to discussions of intellectual property. There are some sites that are useful for patent searchers.

The U.S. Patent Citation Database

As the name suggests, this is a site that allows one to search patent citations by various means. A citation is not an entire patent, but contains information such as date, inventor, title, and classifications. The site is maintained by The Community of Science and contains patents issued since 1975. The database is fully searchable using Boolean queries. For example, one can search by state, by country, by classification, or search the entire citation database.[5] The URL for this site is http://cos.gdb.org/work/info/patents.htm

The United States Patent and Trademark Office

This is the site maintained by the PTO at http://www.ospto.gov. It is the main web site for information involving the United States Patent and Trademark Office. Included is a citation searching database, copies of patent forms that can be downloaded, information about patent fees, and general news.

Patent Title Searching

Although not an ideal method of searching patents, title searching can be a beneficial preliminary step for an experienced patent searcher by identifying titles that are obviously unrelated. Patents are not grouped into a single subject category (called classes), but are arranged into many categories depending on the components that make up a patent. Because of this, many patents find their way into categories that bear only a remote connection to their main function. For example, a class that contains patents on harnesses for livestock may also contain a patent for a plow. The reason is that the plow attaches to the draft animal in some unique way so is included in this class although the invention is not a harness. Simply by looking at the title, a searcher could eliminate this patent as unrelated to the search at hand. In addition, although patent titles are sometimes vague and give no hint of the nature of the invention, other patent titles are very exact and descriptive and in this way searchers can eliminate patents that by title are sure not to relate to a given search. One site that contains patent titles is maintained by the University of North Carolina at http://sunsite.unc.edu/patents.

IBM

The previously mentioned site loaded by IBM contains two million patents and is retrospective to 1971. You can find this site by pointing your web browser to http://www.ibm.com.

Other Sites

California inventor Paul Heckel who heads up a group called Intellectual Property Creators maintains a site that presents discussion about patents at http://www.heckel.org. Greg Aharonian provides The Internet Patent News Service as a forum for discussion of intellectual property in the digital age. (To subscribe send email to patents@world.std.com.) The discussions about the mundane world of patents can become stimulating. In one posting Aharonian disputed Patent Commissioner Bruce Lehman's claim that full text of patents were not yet online because of a lack of funding.[6]

THE IMPACT OF FULL TEXT

As patents move more and more into full text online access issues arise. Will these changes necessitate new methods in which patent searchers, attorneys and the general public seek patent information? Attorneys used to using various indexes to locate patents will now be suing terminals not only to identify classifications and patent numbers but to actually view the patent. But this may be a minor issue related only to basic training in using automated systems. A bigger issue is that of providing the access in small libraries which may not have the knowledge, funding, manpower or space to provide the hardware and software necessary to access this information. Then the problem of providing access to only a privileged few, such as was the case before the Patent Depository Program gave access to citizens nationwide, again becomes a roadblock to the public the patent system was designed to serve.

CONCULUSION

Although the USPTO has provided an adequate service for inventors and others for over 200 years using a manual system, in the digital age the system no longer meets the needs of those who require patent information. The technology is in place to create patent databases with image and text capabilities, but the USPTO seems to be struggling with funding and bureaucracy in getting this task accomplished. As time goes on other individual and private companies are taking it upon themselves to provide electronic access. A number of services and web locations are now operational to supplement or replace the services of the USPTO.

REFERENCES

1. Wherry, Timothy Lee. Patent Searching for Librarians and Inventors. Chicago: American Library Association, 1995.

2. Ibid., p. 10.

3. Chadwick-Healey Inc. Introducing APS. Alexandria, VA: Opus Publications Inc., 1982.

4. Zuckerman, Lawrence. "Two Million Patent Filings to be Made Available free; Giant IBM database Placed on Internet." The New York Times. Jan 9, 1997, C3.

5. "About the U. S. Patent Citation Database" {1997} Available http:// cos.gdb. org/repos/pat/docs/uspat.html

6. Walsh, Mark. "Patently Amusing." Internet World. 22, (1997):56-60.

Index

[*Note:* Page numbers of index and article titles are in boldface type.]

Digital products, ownership of, in collection development, 33

Digital resource, content of, 29-30

Direct manipulation, generalized use of, 197-201,198f-200f

Displets, 145

Distance Education Clearinghouse, 149

Distance/electronic/online education and electronic classroom design, 149

DLI Testbed, 202-204,203f

Document Object model (DOM), 121

Document Type Definition (DTD), 94

Dublin Core metadata, 151-152

Elastic Windows, 145

Electronic books, in STM library, 36

Electronic journals, in STM library, 35-36

Electronic products, licensing of, internet sites for, 32-33

Electronic resources
  organization of, 36-37
  promotion of, 36-37
  in STM library, categories of, 34-35
    aggregation of articles and other full text, 35
    electronic books, 36
    electronic journals, 35-36
    indexes, 34-35
    reference materials, 36

Environment
  in general interface design, 140-153. *See also* General interface design, in libraries
  web, in general interface design, in libraries, 141-142

Evaluation, usability, of digital libraries, 39-59. *See also* Usability evaluation, of digital libraries

EXPERIENCE, 134

Extensible Markup Language (XML), 144

integration of resources using metadata, 126,128-130,129f

search for markup language, 123-126,125f,127f

"text as data" in, 126,127f-128f

toward seamlessness with, 121-130

Extensible Style Language (XSL), 121-122

Federated Database Management System (FDBMS), 89-91,92f

Federated Database System (FDBS), 89-91,92f
  loosely-coupled, 91
  tightly-coupled, 91,93

Federated databases, 89-91,92f

Federation of Digital Libraries, University of Illinois, interoperability among heterogeneous information systems, 81-119
  client-server architecture, 83-89, 84f-86f,88f,89f
  CORBA, 106,108-110,109f
  federated databases, 89-91,92f
  mainframe architecture, 82-83, 83f
  metadata, 101-103
  normalization, 99-101
  object technology, 103-106,104f, 106f,107f

Ferrer, R., 3-4,81

Fiar use, digital, 13-15

First-generation online searching, 62-66,64f,65f

Fox, D., 155

From Print to Electronic: The Transformation of Scientific Communication, 27

Full text databases, in Selective Dissemination of Information (SDI) profiles, 71-73

General interface design, in libraries, 140-153

evaluation during system
    development, 45-48
future prospects in, 54-55
procedures for, 40-43
taxonomy of, methods, 43-50
    factors in, 40
    studies of, 148
USAPAT, 219
User engagement research, 147
User Interaction Design Web, 155
User Interface Agents (UIA), 113
User Interface Software Tools, 155

Verlag, W., 220
Virtual Reality Modeling Language
    (VRML), 146-147
Vitali, F., 148,155
VRML. *See* Virtual Reality Modeling
    Language

Wasilko, P., 156
Web browser adjunct language, 146
Web browser/viewer software, 145-146
Web environment, in general interface
    design, 141-142
Web usability, in general interface
    design, 142
Web utilities, 147
WebTOC, 145-146
Webtop(s), 145-146
Webtop software, 148-149
Wherry, T.L., 4-5,217
Whitten, N., 49
Wood's Agents Info, 171
World Wide Web, as digital library, 10,
    11f

XML. *See* Extensible Markup
    Language

Young, P., 155,158-159

Z39.50, 87-89,88f,89f